Displaced: The Human Cost of Development and Resettlement, by Olivia Bennett and Christopher McDowell (2012)

Exodus to Shanghai: Stories of Escape from the Third Reich, by Steve Hochstadt (2012)

Oral History in Southeast Asia: Memories and Fragments, edited by Kah Seng Loh, Stephen Dobbs, and Ernest Koh (2013)

Oral History Off the Record: Toward an Ethnography of Practice, edited by Anna Sheftel and Stacey Zembrzycki (2013)

Sharecropper's Troubadour: John L. Handcox, the Southern Tenant Farmers' Union, and the African American Song Tradition, by Michael K. Honey (2013)

Tiananmen Exiles: Voices of the Struggle for Democracy in China, by Rowena Xiaoqing He (2014)

Tiananmen Exiles

Voices of the Struggle for
Democracy in China

Rowena Xiaoqing He

First published in 2014 by
PALGRAVE MACMILLAN®
in the United States—a division of St. Martin's Press LLC,
175 Fifth Avenue, New York, NY 10010.

Where this book is distributed in the UK, Europe and the rest of the world,
this is by Palgrave Macmillan, a division of Macmillan Publishers Limited,
registered in England, company number 785998, of Houndmills,
Basingstoke, Hampshire RG21 6XS.

Palgrave Macmillan is the global academic imprint of the above companies
and has companies and representatives throughout the world.

Palgrave® and Macmillan® are registered trademarks in the United States,
the United Kingdom, Europe and other countries.

ISBN: 978–1–137–43830–0 (hc)
ISBN: 978–1–137–43831–7 (pbk)

Library of Congress Cataloging-in-Publication Data is available from the
Library of Congress.

A catalogue record of the book is available from the British Library.

Design by Newgen Knowledge Works (P) Ltd., Chennai, India.

First edition: April 2014

10 9 8 7 6 5 4 3 2 1

For those who struggle to keep the spirit of 1989 alive

Contents

Foreword

If yesterday was typical, about 1,400 children in Africa died of malaria. It is a preventable, treatable disease, and the young victims lost their lives through no faults of theirs. Why is it that human beings accept a fact like this as an unremarkable daily event, whereas one murder can grab a headline, is an awkward question. And it raises related questions: Why, for example, should Rowena He and the people she interviews in this book worry so much about a single massacre that happened in Beijing twenty-five years ago? No one knows exactly how many lives of democracy advocates were snuffed out by tanks and machine guns on the fateful night of June 3–4, 1989, but the number was almost certainly lower than that of yesterday's deaths due to malaria.

The specter of the "June Fourth massacre" has had remarkable longevity. It not only haunts the memories of people who witnessed the events and of friends and families of the victims, but also persists in the minds of people who stood, and still stand, with the Chinese state. Deng Xiaoping, the man who said "go" for the final assault, has passed away, but people who today are inside or allied with the political regime responsible for the killing remain acutely aware of it. They seldom put their awareness into words; indeed their policy toward the memory of the massacre is one of repression. However, their actions show us that the memory still remains very much with them. They assign plainclothes officers to monitor and control people who have a history of speaking publicly about the massacre. They hire hundreds of thousands of Internet police, one of whose tasks is to expunge any reference to the massacre from websites and email. Each year, on the "sensitive day" of June 4, they send dozens of police, in uniform as well as in civilian clothes, to guard the periphery of Tiananmen Square (the site of the demonstrations that triggered the massacre) in order to prevent "troublemakers" from honoring anybody's memory. Their official rhetoric holds that "the Chinese people have long ago reached their correct historical verdict on the counterrevolutionary riot." The awkwardness of such jargon is sign enough of its artificiality, but the surer evidence that the authorities know their claims are hollow lies in their actions. If they truly believed that "the Chinese people" approved of their killings, they would throw Tiananmen Square open every June 4 and watch the masses swarm in to denounce the counterrevolutionaries. That they do the opposite is eloquent testimony about what they really know.

In short, there are some very good reasons why a massacre twenty-five years ago matters, even if the number killed is smaller than in other disasters. These particular killings had to do with the fate of a nation. They were an important turning point for a society of more than a billion people.

We know from *The Tiananmen Papers* that leaders of the Communist Party of China felt that they were facing an existential threat in the spring of 1989. Major protests in the streets of not only Beijing but nearly every provincial capital in China led Wang Zhen, Li Peng, and others in the ruling circles to conclude that the survival of their regime was at stake.

Western apologists for that regime sometimes use the words "tragedy" or "mistake" in their accounts of the killing, but these words reflect a misconception. The use of lethal force was no accident. It was a choice, the result of calculation, and moreover was, from the regime's point of view—now as well as then—the correct choice. Tiananmen Square could have been cleared using tear gas, water hoses, or wooden batons. (Batons were the tools of choice when Tiananmen Square was cleared of another large demonstration against Maoist extremism, on April 5, 1976. The clubs were efficient in that case, and few if any lives were lost.)

The reason the regime opted for tanks and machine guns in 1989 was that a fearsome display of force could radiate a power well beyond the time and the place of the immediate repression. Democracy demonstrators in thirty provincial cities around the country could be frightened into retreat. This worked. The Chinese people could be put on notice for years to come that "you had better stay within our bounds, or else!" This, too, worked. The fundamental goal was to preserve and extend the rule of the Communist Party of China. This was achieved.

The tactic did cost the regime severely in terms of its public image, however. This point needs some context.In the early 1950s, a large majority of the Chinese people embraced the ideals that Communist language projected in slogans like "serve the people," and these ideals provided the "legitimacy"—to borrow a piece of political-science jargon—for the ruling elite. The disasters of late Maoism took a heavy toll on that legitimacy, but after Mao died in 1976, and through the 1980s, many Chinese remained hopeful that the Party might finally lead their country toward a more reasonable future. (With no real alternative, how else could one hope?) As of 1989, the Party's legitimacy still rested in considerable measure on this kind of enduring hope, but the bullets of June Fourth ended it once and for all. In the words of Yi Danxuan, quoted in this book, "the gunshots actually stripped away the lies and the veils that the government had been wearing." Now Yi saw that the Party's own power had been its priority all along.

The massacre therefore created a puzzle for Deng Xiaoping and the other men at the top. With no more "legitimacy" to be drawn from claims about socialist ideals, where else could they generate it? Within weeks of the killings, Deng declared that what China needed was "education." University students were forced to perform rituals of "confessing" their errant thoughts and denounce the counter revolutionary rioters at Tiananmen. These were superficial exercises that had little real meaning. But Deng's longer-term project of stimulating nationalism and "educating" the Chinese population in the formula *Party = country* turned out to be very effective. In textbooks, museums, and all of the media, "Party" and "country" fused and patriotism meant "loving" the hybrid result. China's hosting of the 2008 Summer Olympics was a "great victory of the Party." Foreign criticism of Beijing was no longer "anti-communist" but now "anti-Chinese." Conflicts with Japan, the United States, and "splittists" in Taiwan and Tibet were exaggerated in order to demonstrate a need for clear lines between hostile adversaries and the beloved Party-country. Memories of the 1937 Nanjing Massacre, in which scores of Chinese were butchered by Japanese troops, were revived (Mao, for reasons relating to his own political power, had suppressed public memory of Nanjing) in order to provide a pool of emotion from which to pump regime support as needed—although this tactic had to be calibrated, since emotions so strong could be volatile.

The success of these and other efforts at "education" allowed the regime to redefine the bases of its legitimacy as nationalism and money making. (Today, the language of socialist idealism survives, but as a veneer only.) Its new self-presentation allows the regime no escape, however, from the reach of the massacre. As if with a will of its own, Tiananmen seems to come back to undermine whatever the regime tries. In 1989 it delivered a *coup de grâce* to the old socialist claims of legitimacy. Now, when legitimacy depends upon the claim that the Party and the people are one, the memory of the massacre—when the Party shot bullets at the people—is perhaps the starkest of possible evidence that the Party and the people are not one.

So the regime still needs to include these memories among kinds of thought that need to be erased from people's minds. It uses both push-and-pull tactics to do this. "Push" includes warnings, threats, and—for the recalcitrant—computer and cell-phone confiscation, as well as passport denial, employment loss, bank-account seizure, and—for the truly stubborn—house arrest or prison. "Pull" includes "invitations to tea" at which one hears smiling reminders that a better life is available to people who stop talking about massacres; advice that it is still not too late to make this kind of adjustment in life; comparisons with others who are materially better off for having made just that decision; offers of food, travel, employment, and other emoluments (grander if one cooperates by reporting on others); and counsel that it is best not to reveal the content of all this friendly tea-talk to anyone else.

The "pull" tactics have been especially effective in the context of the money-making motive and materialism that have pervaded Chinese society in recent times. Material wealth has become the country's overriding public value, and its pursuit, acquisition, and display have come to dominate people's motives. For many people material living standards have risen considerably, and Western analysts have correctly noted how this rise has bolstered the regime's post-1989 legitimacy. The same analysts err, though, when they repeat the Communist Party's claim that it "has lifted hundreds of millions from poverty." What has actually happened since 1989 is more nearly the reverse: it has been the Chinese people, doing hard work at low wages, who have done the heavy lifting—benefitting themselves, to be sure, but in the process catapulting the elite to much more wealth, and a few of them to spectacular opulence.

In outline, here is how the boom in China's economy came about: During the Mao era, the Chinese people were unfree in all aspects of their lives except the most mundane. After Mao's death in 1976, and even more clearly after the massacre in 1989, Deng Xiaoping relented and told the Chinese people, essentially, that they were still under wraps in the areas of politics, religion, and other matters of "thought," but in money making were now free to go all out. So they did—as would anyone when given only one channel for the application of personal energies. They worked hard—at low pay, for long hours, without unions, without workman's compensation laws, without the protections of a free press or independent courts, and without even legal status in the cities where they worked. There were hundreds of millions of them and they worked year after year. Is it strange that they produced enormous wealth? The fine details of the picture are of course more complex than this, but its overall shape is hardly a mystery or a "miracle."

In 1985 Deng Xiaoping began using the phrase "let one part of the population get rich first." That happened, and, not surprisingly, the ones who got rich first were almost always the politically well connected. Access to political power meant better access to resources as well as better positions from which to practice graft, and the wealth of the elite began to skyrocket in the mid-1990s. Income inequality in China grew until it exceeded that of countries in the capitalist West and fell short only of some underdeveloped countries in Africa and South America. In popular oral culture, and later on the Internet, jokes, ditties, and "slippery jingles" (*shunkouliu*) consistently reflected strong resentment of the wealth of the elite as well as of the unjust means by which the wealth was perceived to have been gained. But such views, like any other free discussion of civic values, were not—and today still cannot be—represented in the official media, where references to equality, democracy, constitutionalism, unauthorized religion, and many other topics that are essential to such a discussion are monitored and often banned.

The emphasis on money, in combination with authoritarian limits on open discussion of other values, has led to a poverty in the society's public values. Vaclav Havel wrote about the "post-totalitarian" condition as one in which a pervasive web of official lies comes to constitute a sort of second version of daily life. Echoing Havel, Shen Tong observes, in the pages of this book, that "the reality of living in a police state" is that "you live a huge public lie." Wang Dan, in explaining the behavior of people who, for no real fault of their own, become inured to lies over time, finds that they "lie subconsciously." China's celebration of money making does make it different from Havel's Czechoslovakia, but hardly better. Far from melting the artificiality (as the theories of optimistic Western politicians have held that it would), the money craze in some ways has worsened it.

The new moneyed classes in China behave as if they are groping to figure out how "new moneyed classes" are supposed to behave. During the Mao years, there was a caricature that helped everyone to understand what bourgeois profligacy looked like—food, drink, sex, shiny shoes, spiffy watches, slick cars, and so on, all of them evil. After Mao, in the era of "getting rich is glorious," people have looked for guidelines about how to behave with money, and the bourgeois caricature is ready at hand, but now valued positively, not negatively. Moneyed Chinese cavort in Paris and Bali, where they lead the world in purchases of luxury items like Chanel perfumes and Louis Vuitton handbags. The purpose of buying handbags is not to carry things but to own a genuine branded handbag (not fake, like many back home) and to be able to show others that one does own the straight-from-Paris item. The traveler might buy extra bags to sell at a profit back in China—a smart way to subsidize the original travel to Paris. Re-selling the bags is chic, going to Paris is chic, the bags themselves are chic. But do these chic ones feel solid inside? Or are they are too busy showing, competing, running, while at another level vaguely sensing (afraid to stop for a square look) that they are running on air?

"Materialism" may not be exactly the right word for this new elite subculture, because it need not involve actual material. "Appearance-ism" might be a better term. The final aim of a person's activity is not a bag but the display of a bag. If the display works, the bag was but its vehicle. What counts is the surface. Hope for China is visible in the fact that, as this subculture has spread, so has satire of it. An effusion of oral and online jokes in recent years has focused on fakes: fake milk, fake liquor, fake antiques, fake photos, fake history, fake singing at Olympics ceremonies, and much more—even a fake lion in a zoo (a big dog in disguise). The Chinese fiction writer Yu Hua has quipped that the only thing you can know to be real is a fake fake.

Nearly all the satire, though, is private or, if public, anonymous. Very few people risk principled objection in public. The regime calls this "dissidence," and the costs of dissidence are high. People find it smarter to lie low, perhaps fulminating in private but not rocking any boats in public. Dissidents are viewed, sometimes even by their own families, as somewhat odd, and as poor calculators of their own best interests. Friends and neighbors keep them at a distance—far less from disagreement with their ideas (as the regime likes to claim), than from fear of absorbing their taint. When Wang Dan, as shown in this book, went to visit his father's hometown after he became known as a dissident, people guarded the entrances to their villages to make sure he didn't come near—and would have hidden him, if he did show up.

Some in the populace accept the regime's lies while others only pretend to, but as time passes this distinction becomes less and less important. In either case people's self-interest is protected and they fit into "normal" society. In the end, as Rowena He puts it, China is left with "a generation that cannot even imagine a society whose youth would sacrifice themselves for ideals."

At a deeper level, though, Chinese people (like any people) do not feel secure living in long-term cynicism and unpredictability. The wealthy send their money abroad—and their children, too, for education. In 2013, several surveys and reports showed sharp increases in the plans of whole families, especially among the wealthy, to emigrate, and there is no reason to think that poorer people would not follow this trend if they had the means.

Reasons for wanting to emigrate are several. Cleaner air, economic and educational opportunity, and family traditions that go back many decades (especially among farmers in south China) are all factors. But there are also some deep-seated preferences about society and government that people act upon even if, for obvious reasons, they would rather not articulate them. Does a future in China really hold out the promise of happiness, even for families that have wealth and power? Emigration as political statement has, in fact, an ancient pedigree in China. In the *Mencius*, China's original classic of political philosophy, compiled around 300 BCE, the virtue of kings is measured by the number of people who gravitate to their lands. Tyrants see their populations flow elsewhere. People like Rowena He, who want the best for China—who love it in the true sense, not the Communist "patriotic" sense—wish it would regain a Mencian magnetism.

Noting the key role of Deng Xiaoping's policies following the 1989 massacre, He writes:

> Deng's policies over the years have led to a booming economy, higher average living standards, and a more prominent place for China in the world, but have also engendered enormous wealth inequality, massive corruption, persistent environmental problems, profound popular cynicism and erosion of public trust, massive expenditure on "stability maintenance," and new signs of belligerence accompanying China's international rise.

Words like these have brought her a shower of invective on the Internet from defenders of today's regime. The commenters likely include both the paid and the unpaid varieties, but they are unanimous on one point: they avoid the substance of what she writes, opting instead for personal attack of the most puerile and intellectually vacuous kind. She is "anti-China," "sells her people to buy her future," is "a whore for foreigners,"and so on. I inflate nothing here. In dozens of examples that I have seen, their analysis goes no deeper than this, and indeed few of the phrases are any more lengthy. What the comments actually report is only that the opponents of Rowena He have no answer for her.

We cannot say that the ethical deterioration in China today is due to the 1989 massacre alone. The cynicism generated by the artificiality of official language has its roots in the 1957 Anti-Rightist Movement and in the Great Leap famine years of 1959–62. Mao Zedong, much more than Deng Xiaoping, is responsible for what the Chinese artist Ai Weiwei has called the "psychic disasters deep within us," that cause people "to walk with a quickened pace and to see with lifeless eyes," as if having "nowhere to go, and nowhere to hide." Still, the 1989 massacre does stand out as a turning point. Without it, Deng Xiaoping's formula for the Chinese people of "money, yes; ideas, no"—a policy that laid the foundation for so much of what we see in China today—would not have wrought its effects. The massacre also laid the foundation of fear—a deeply impacted, seldom explicitly mentioned, but highly effective dull dread—on which the pacification of the populace has rested ever since.

How will this end? We do not know, of course. The Communist Party's techniques of control have been effective, and its push to reinvent premodern authoritarianism in a stable twenty-first-century version has considerable momentum. In broad perspective it seems doubtful that the effort can succeed, although the costs of witnessing the aggressive thrust, not only for China but for the world as a whole, could be fearsome indeed.

Mario Vargas Llosa, winner of the 2010 Nobel Prize for Literature, wrote in early 2014:

> It is hard not to feel a great deal of sadness at the backwardness totalitarianism has imposed on China, Russia and Cuba. Any social progress communism may have brought these societies is dwarfed by the civic, cultural and political retardation it caused, and the remaining obstacles standing in the way of these countries taking full advantage of their resources and reaching a modernity that encompasses democratic ideals, the rule of law and liberty. It's clear that the old communist model is dead and buried, but it is taking these societies plenty of time and sacrifice to shake off its ghost.[1]

Vargas Llosa's comments point up an irony that is locked into the structure of China's state-sponsored "patriotism." Ostensibly aimed to bolster the pride of Chinese people everywhere, this "patriotism" asks for adulation of China's authoritarian regime, which it takes as the country's symbol; simultaneously, though, that same regime, by its behavior, is the leading cause of China's loss of face in the eyes of the world. Imagine how much better Chinese people would feel, how much more unburdened and optimistic, if they could turn to the world and offer—together with everything else they have to offer—an open, law-abiding, and democratic modern government.

Rowena He's book is like a network of streams through high mountains. In separate but intersecting stories, it weaves us through some very large questions about China's fate. It follows four people: her three interviewees, each of whom was an important participant in the 1989 events, and herself. The accounts bristle with life-like detail. We see Wang Dan as a little boy, organizing a band of "martial-arts heroes" among his classmates, and miniature Rowena, left cold and frightened one day when another child at her nursery school takes her blue goldfish blanket. The writing rings of authentic Chinese life. Some of the detail has political significance, as when Shen Tong's family chooses to destroy paper evidence of protests not by burning it, which would produce tell-tale smoke, but by flushing it down a toilet tracelessly. But there is plenty of apolitical detail as well: Shen feeds his baby daughter in his New York apartment while his wife prepares breakfast.

He's interviews have an unedited quality. I do not mean by this that the author or her publisher has been remiss in preparing the manuscript. The book is excellently produced. I mean that the author shares with us the original texture of her interview experiences. She explains how she did them, then lets the gaps and the unexpected turns be part of the record. Her interviewees occasionally tell her to back off or even to shut up. On the whole she sympathizes with them, but does not insist that they be heroes. They have flaws and charms, strengths and foibles, fears and courage, all in a jumble. In short they are normal, complex human beings, credibly presented. And why is this noteworthy? In part because it forms such a sharp contrast with the way China's authorities write about the heroes and villains in their political tracts. Rowena He does a literary inversion, an undermining by example, of the smooth officialese, the stick figures, and the finely edited lies of the regime.

When Deng Xiaoping announced after the 1989 massacre that the Chinese people needed "education," and when his government launched a systematic effort to extinguish their political longings and to mold them into "patriotic" subjects focused on nationalism and money, he could have tipped his cap to Bertolt Brecht, who wrote: "The people have lost the confidence of the government; the government has decided to dissolve the people and to appoint another one." Will the post-massacre Deng plan, extended by his successors, continue to work? Will the Chinese people, thirty years from now, remain content with being what the Deng plan has appointed them to be? This might happen and it might not. In any case the stakes are huge, comparable even to the deaths of African children from malaria.

PERRY LINK

Acknowledgments

In my long journey from China to Canada to the United States, I have incurred debts to many people whose support and understanding have made an enormous difference to my intellectual and personal well-being. I have long looked forward to the moment of writing acknowledgment pages: I imagined that I would feel relieved and relaxed, without deadlines, and with ample time to express my gratitude. As it happened, I had only an hour to write the acknowledgment of my dissertation before I had to officially deposit it in order to beat the last deadline of my graduate student life, and I now have two hours to express my gratitude so that this book can come out for the twenty-fifth anniversary of the Tiananmen Massacre, the origin of and reason for this work.

I am deeply grateful to my mentors Victor Falkenheim at the University of Toronto and Roderick MacFarquhar at Harvard. Their invaluable advice and constant support have been indispensable in my intellectual journey. I am grateful to the Harvard community that has provided me a sound and robust academic home. I will never forget the daily China lunch table organized by Merle Goldman and the dinners that she hosted at her house. My sincere appreciation goes to Harvard faculty members and colleagues: Terry Aladjem, Michele Albanese, Bill Alford, Howe Alison, Barry Bloom, Steven Bloomfield, Joseph Chen, Paul Cohen, Rose Cortese, Timothy Colton, Nara Dillon, Nina Duncan, Mark Elliott, Frankie Hoff, David Howell, Wilt Idema, Adi Ignatius, Susan Kashiwa, Tarun Khanna, William Kirby, Linda Kluz, Shigehisa Kuriyama, Lisa Laskin, Isabella Lau, Harry Lewis, Sandra Naddaff, Elizabeth Sampson, Michael Szonyi, David Wang, Eugene Wang, and Marty White. My friends on campus, Guo Rui, Li Jie, Liu Jundai, Qian Ying, Shi Lihong, Wang Lu, and Zhang Ling, kept me strong with their acceptance, empathy, and encouragement. I would also like to thank my students who have taken the Tiananmen seminars with me, for the enthusiasm and hope they brought to our classrooms.

Scholars of different disciplines, especially those in the fields of education and China studies, have supported me at different stages of my academic journey, and innumerable informal discussions with them have improved the book in more ways than I can count. I want to thank Peter Appelbaum, Bill Ayers, Cheng Yinghong, Thomas Cushman, David Flinders, Edward Friedman, Guo Jian, Andre Laliberte, Li Xin, Liang Xi, Perry Link, Pei Minxin, Peter Perdue, Stanley

Rosen, Bruce Uhrmacher, Edward Vickers, Arthur Waldron, Wu Guoguang, Yu Ying-shih, and Zhou Zehao.

I want to thank my community at the University of Toronto: Margaret Brennan, Elizabeth Campbell, Elaine Chan, Bernie Frolic, Stella Lau, Sarfaroz Niyozov, Shelley Peterson, Michelle Pon, Mitsuyo Sakamoto, Candace Schlein, Dennis Thiessen, and Yukwah Tse-Tso. I am especially grateful to Alister Cumming, Carola Conle, James Cummins, and Patrick Diamond, for their guidance, intellectual recognition, and inspirations.

I wish to express appreciation to my manuscript readers who have provided me invaluable comments at different stages of the book's development: Bill Ayers, Andrew Clark, Paul Cohen, Guo Jian, Madeline G. Levine, Steven I. Levine, Perry Link, Paul Mooney, Linda Mowatt, Forest Reinhardt, and Scott Thompson. I learned a great deal from Nancy Hearst's extraordinary editorial work, which improved the manuscript immeasurably. I am grateful to my editor Chris Chappell and his team at Palgrave Macmillan, especially Erin Ivy, Mike Aperauch, and Deepa John, and to indexer Marilyn Flaig. It has been a great pleasure to work with Bruce Stave, co-editor of this oral history series, who was most helpful, responsible, and encouraging. I am also thankful to Linda Shopes, co-editor of the series, and two anonymous referees for their helpful comments at the early stage of the book's development.

My deepest appreciation is to the three Tiananmen student exiles: Wang Dan, Shen Tong, and Yi Danxuan. This study would not have been possible without their participation and support. I would like to thank the Social Sciences and Humanities Research Council of Canada for supporting my research with their fellowships.

I am deeply grateful to friends, associates, and family friends whose support and encouragement have meant a great deal to me. I am grateful to Jeff Barneson, Henry Chau, Chen Shenli, Chen Yiran, Chen Yuguo, Tara Edelschick, Nilgun Gokgur, Huang Yingfeng, Lai Anzhi, Yanwai Lau, Liane Lee, Eric Li, Yanwai Lo, Luo Siling, Kathy Maclean, Ma Waiyan, Anand Mahindra, Charlotte Mason, Anita Ng, Bernard Ng, Rao Yu, Shen Hetao, David Tam, Tao Ye, Alfred Wong, Charlie Wyzanski, Xing Zheng, Michael Xu, Xue Tianhan, Yang Xiao, Zhang Jiangfeng, and Zhou Fengsuo, as well as Aunt May Deng, Uncle Cheung Chor, Uncle To Mantat, Uncle Lau Mankui, and Uncle Luo Fu. I especially want to thank Linda Mowatt and Patrick Zhang, who have been the best of friends for me, and Uncle Luong Vuong, who always encourages me and supports me unconditionally.

Lastly, I would like to thank my family—my parents, my grandmothers, my brother, my aunts and uncles, and my cousins—who never failed to understand with love. I am particularly grateful to my mother, who taught me to love, to trust, and to smile.

Chronology

Year	China	Year	Yi Danxuan	Year	Shen Tong	Year	Wang Dan
May 4, 1919	Student demonstrations in Beijing.						
October 1949	Founding of the People's Republic of China.						
1966–1976	The Cultural Revolution						
1976	Death of Mao Zedong.	*1967*	Born	*1968*	Born	*1969*	Born
1978–1979	Democracy Wall Movement in Beijing.						
1978	Deng Xiaoping re-assumes power.						
April 15, 1989	Death of former Chinese Communist Party (CCP) General Secretary Hu Yaobang ignites student protests.	*1989*	Student at Guangdong University of Business Studies.	*Spring 1989*	Student leader at Peking University.	*Spring 1989*	Student leader at Peking University.
April 18–19, 1989	Xinhuamen incident, police beat up students.						
April 26, 1989	*People's Daily* editorial condemns demonstrations as turmoil.						
May 13, 1989	Hunger strike begins in Tiananmen Square.						
May 19, 1989	CCP General Secretary Zhao Ziyang's last public appearance when he visited students in Tiananmen Square. He is purged, put under house arrest. Dies in 2005.						
May 20, 1989	Martial law is implemented in the urban districts of Beijing.	*May 5, 1989*	Organized mass demonstration in Guangzhou.				
June 3–4, 1989	Tiananmen Massacre.	*May 23, 1989*	Elected vice-president of the Guangzhou Patriotic Student Federation.				
June 9, 1989	Deng Xiaoping praises army for suppressing "counter-revolutionary riot."			*June 10, 1989*	Leaves China for United States.		

June 1989	*Operation Yellowbird* starts helping dissidents escape China.	*July 1989*	Taken into custody; held for 20 months before trial; sentenced to two years in prison.	*Summer 1989*	His father dies in Beijing.	*July 2, 1989*	Arrested; held for almost two years without trial.
August 1989	Independent Federation of Chinese Students and Scholars (IFCSS) established in Chicago.			*1990*	Publishes *Almost a Revolution*.	*1991*	Tried and sentenced to four years in prison.
1990s	Patriotic Education Campaign is carried out in China.					*1993*	Released from prison.
						1995	Re-arrested and detained for 17 months.
						1996	Tried and sentenced to 11 years.
		1992	Leaves China to study at the University of Mississippi.	*1992*	Returns to China, is detained, and then expelled.	*April, 1998*	Released from prison on medical parole and exiled to the United States.
October 1992	Chinese Student Protection Act is signed into law by President George H. W. Bush.						

continued

Year	China	Year	Yi Danxuan	Year	Shen Tong	Year	Wang Dan
		2000s	Remains politically active	2000s	Becomes US citizen. Goes into business in United States, marries, and raises a family.	2001	Receives MA degree from Harvard University.
		2005	Receives MBA from George Washington University.				
August 2008	Beijing Olympics.	2008	Briefly allowed back into China.			2008	Receives PhD degree from Harvard
		2009	Denied entry to China.			2009	Teaches in Taiwan.
				2011	Participates in the Occupy Wall Street movement.		
June 2014	Twenty-fifth anniversary of Tiananmen Massacre.						

SECTION ONE

Introduction

Surviving 1989

In the spring of 1989, millions of people filled the streets all over China demanding political reforms. The nationwide movement, highlighted by the university students' hunger strike in Tiananmen Square in the center of Beijing, ended with the People's Liberation Army opening fire on its own people before the gaze of the entire world. On the night of June 3, amid the approaching gunshots, the unarmed students in Tiananmen Square gathered near the Monument to the People's Heroes and took their oath hand in hand, shoulder to shoulder:[1]

> For the sake of advancing the democratization of our motherland, for the true prosperity of our nation, for our great motherland I pledge to use my own youthful life to protect Tiananmen and to defend the Republic....Heads may be cut off and blood may flow, but the people's Square cannot be lost. We are willing to use our youthful lives to fight down to the last person.[2]

Even today the number of deaths and injuries on that fateful night remains unknown. More than 200,000 soldiers participated in the lethal action.[3] Historian Timothy Brook argues that the military crackdown is a "massacre," noting that "using combat weapons against unarmed citizens was a moral failure."[4] Intellectuals and student leaders were subsequently purged, imprisoned, or exiled. Scores of workers and other citizens simply disappeared. Many others have been struggling with an open wound ever since.

June 4: The Wound of History

Liane

Child, we need you to return to Hong Kong safely. We need you to leave alive to tell the world what our government did to us tonight.

"The boy's body was all mixed up with blood and flesh. He wasn't moving." When Liane described to me the scene of the Tiananmen military crackdown, she had to struggle to steady her emotions:

> A younger boy was shouting hysterically, "I will avenge my brother! I will avenge my brother!"[5] I tried with all my strength to hold him back when he dashed toward the soldiers. He started to cry on my shoulder. He was just a kid, but he cried like an old man in despair. Shortly afterward, he tore himself loose from my arms and ran after an ambulance shouting "Brother! Brother!" Half an hour later, his body was carried right in front of me, covered in blood. I fainted.

When the 1989 Tiananmen Movement erupted, Liane was an undergraduate journalism student in Hong Kong. She and other members of the Hong Kong Federation of Students[6] went to Beijing to support their fellow students' struggles for a better China. She was outside the Museum of the Chinese Revolution in Beijing on the night of June 3, 1989:

> When I regained consciousness, people tried to put me into an ambulance. I told them that I did not need an ambulance. The wounded needed the ambulance more than I did. A second ambulance came, and again I struggled not to get in. A middle-aged female doctor held my hands and spoke to me in English:[7] Child, we need you to return to Hong Kong. We need you to leave alive to tell the world what our government did to us tonight.

The fear that all the blood would be shed in vain was expressed again and again. One Chinese man asked a Canadian reporter on the street: "Does the world know what happened here?"[8]

In 2008, Liane and I both attended a candlelight vigil held at the University of Toronto to commemorate the nineteenth anniversary of the Tiananmen Massacre. "Mommy, where are the brothers and sisters?" Liane's little daughter asked, jumping up and down energetically. "Where are the brothers and sisters?" Liane must have told her child that they had come for the sake of some "brothers and sisters."

When Liane went over to lay a candle and a flower in front of the memorial plaque, her little girl turned to me and asked: "Where are the brothers and sisters? Mummy didn't tell me. Do you know?" I knelt next to her, put aside the white chrysanthemum, and held her little hands, unable to say a single word. I wish I could have been as eloquent as the female doctor who held her mother's hands in 1989. But nineteen years later, we had no knowledge about what happened to those two boys—we didn't even know who they were, or if they had survived.

There is a magazine photograph, published in 1997, of Liane standing in front of a large group of Chinese students welcoming President Jiang Zemin to

Harvard University. "They accused me of lying," Liane told me. A woman yelled at her: "I was in Beijing at that time. No killing ever took place." The crowd was raising red flags and shouting at Liane: "You are a liar!" A man came up to her and said: "You'd better give up. See how isolated you are."[9]

Somehow that image of Liane standing alone in front of the angry crowd reminded me of the iconic photograph of the "Tank Man," who stood in front of a column of tanks in 1989 and instantly became a symbol of the movement. She is alone, but she is powerful.

Tony[10]

In 1989 the people were using their own bodies to block the guns and tanks to protect us students. These people deserve the same rights that other people in the world enjoy. But why do we have to fight with our blood, generation after generation, for a life with dignity?

I first met Tony at a dinner in Toronto, and when the host told him that I was researching June 4 (*liusi*), as Chinese people generally refer to the events of 1989, he looked at me partly with hesitation and partly with disbelief. "I was there too," he responded tersely. Well aware that most Chinese do not feel comfortable discussing June 4 publicly, even when they live outside China, I didn't press him. I left the dinner that evening knowing little about Tony other than that he had been an undergraduate student at Peking University in the eighties and that he had recently immigrated to Canada, where he had just found a job as a reporter for a local Chinese newspaper.

Almost one year later, Tony phoned me. Sounding sad, he told me that he had just read an article that I had written about the Tiananmen Mothers, families of victims of the June 4 Massacre. It reminded him of the part of his life that he didn't want to remember, of wounds that had never really healed. I asked him if I could interview him and he agreed:[11]

In those days, we went to the Square and participated in the hunger strike. Now in retrospect, we were all so young—everyone sitting next to you was as young. We believed that we could use our young lives to shoulder the fate of China. And we have been shouldering this heavy responsibility since 1989. Sometimes when I look at myself now, I realize how I have been tortured by this burden.

It was very hot in Beijing. I was walking along the Avenue of Eternal Peace, and I never could have imagined that the avenue would soon become a *xuelu* (road of blood) .... No one expected that the tanks would really enter the city or that guns would be fired. No one knew that they were planning such a massacre. The Avenue of Eternal Peace was full of people.

All of a sudden I saw a boy being carried by several young people who seemed to be students. They anxiously asked me, "Where is the hospital?" I told them that the Children's Hospital was nearby. Then they said, "Take him to the hospital," and then they quickly left to help the others who had been wounded. It was already dark so I had no idea where the boy was wounded. I stopped a cab and took him to the Children's Hospital. I was holding him in my arms. He didn't move at all. Blood was everywhere.

From the hospital gate to the emergency room, we had to take several turns. But we didn't need to know the way—we simply followed the blood. It was a *xuelu* (path of blood). The room was packed with wounded people, painfully groaning for help. The doctors were too busy to attend to all the patients. I can never get rid of that scene in my life! Let me tell you, never! We had read about the Nationalist Party's (KMT)'s bloody crackdown on the people since we were children.[12] But from the night of June 3, I learned that blood is not just something written about in books! Blood smells really bloody!

The doctor looked at the boy and pronounced him dead. I couldn't believe him. I just couldn't believe it! The boy was lying on the bench, with blood dripping from his body. After a short while, his blood was everywhere under the bench. I held his hands until they became stiff bit by bit. After I left the hospital, I was shouting madly on the street: "They are killing! They are killing our people!"

Tony kept returning to the hospital to see if anyone had come to claim the boy's body. Judging from his sandals and shorts, he must have been a local child whose home was nearby—unlike the college students whose parents, far from Beijing, had no idea that their children were being killed, to say nothing of looking for their bodies. Seven days later, no one had come to claim the body:

I told the doctors: "I brought this kid here. If you can't find his family, please let me make arrangements for his funeral (*banhoushi*)." But in those days, the government was arresting people everywhere. The doctors knew that I was a student. They told me that I had better leave and stay out of trouble. I was begging them, and they begged me in turn. We ended up crying together.

The boy's body, along with many others, was eventually collected by the government. Tony described himself after June 4 as "living like an animal":

We saw friends being punished and persecuted. We could no longer express our feelings and speak our minds. The only thing we could do was to listen to songs like Lo Ta-yu's *Orphan of Asia*[13] and get drunk.

We had had so much patriotic education and hero education when we were growing up. In all those school years, we learned from history and from geography how great our motherland was. Then the reform and open-door policy gave us so much hope. But when I had to face such a cruel reality, I felt abandoned—abandoned by my own country. What else didn't we sacrifice in 1989? I can no longer identify with the regime but it is also not possible for me to disconnect myself from the country and that piece of land.

The younger generation thinks that we are no longer qualified to talk about patriotism now that we have left the country. They think it is hypocritical. Yes, I chose to leave China, but I had no choice. There is no one who can claim to be patriotic if we can't. We sat in Tiananmen Square fasting for days and nights for our country. I later became successful in my career and was respected by others. I had professional satisfaction, but I could never rid myself of the darkness from the early morning of June 4.

When people talk about 1989, they mainly focus on the cruelty of the Chinese government, but rarely talk about our people, and the beauty of humanity they demonstrated. In 1989 the people were using their own bodies to block the guns and tanks to protect us students. These people deserve the same rights that other people in the world enjoy. But why do we have to fight with our blood, generation after generation, for a life with dignity?

I had little contact with Tony through the years, but I could be sure I would see him at each year's candlelight vigil. In 2008, at the same event where I saw Liane and her daughter, I noticed him only toward the end, standing in a quiet corner, alone, staring at the candle he was holding in his hand. I had no idea how long he had been standing there. When he saw me walking toward him, he started to murmur—half to himself and half to me:

I clearly remember what he looked like. No matter how long I need to wait—as long as I am still alive, I would like to find his family. I want to tell them where he died. I want to tell them that when he died, I was with him.

Ma's Family[14]

If I had instead been educated to love money and power, as the current generation does, I don't think I would have participated in the movement. We were educated to love the nation and the people more than anything else, and we did.

In 1989 Ma was a social sciences faculty member in one of the best universities in China. When I met him over a decade later in his crowded apartment in Toronto, he had just gotten off work— collecting garbage in a downtown hotel.

Ma was not unfamiliar with manual labor, even though he looked every inch like a serious intellectual. During the Cultural Revolution, Ma had been assigned to work in a cement factory carrying bricks for ten years, during which time he taught himself five foreign languages as well as political science. Despite his lack of a formal secondary education, his self-study enabled him to pass the national college entrance examinations when they were resumed after the Cultural Revolution. Ma was admitted by a university in Beijing, and upon graduation was promoted to the faculty. Before the 1989 movement Ma had managed to translate and publish at least one million words' worth of encyclopedias and books in varied fields from their original languages.

I first heard about Ma's story from his former students when I myself was a college student in China. Before the students headed to Tiananmen Square to start the hunger strike on May 13, 1989, Ma and a group of young faculty members had invited them to a campus restaurant so that they could have a nice meal before leaving campus. "That was the best meal I ever had, and a meal that I will always remember," one of Ma's students told me. "Everything changed after that." Most students were expecting a hunger strike lasting a day or two, never imagining that it could continue for seven days. Ma supported his students throughout the movement and stayed with them until the moment when the troops entered the Square. During the purge that followed the military crackdown, all participants were pressured to admit that it had been a mistake to participate in the movement and to express support for the government's actions. But Ma simply refused. As a result, he was expelled from the faculty. When Ma's students heard later that he had remarried, they wondered who would have the courage to marry him.

When I first heard that Ma's family had immigrated to Toronto, where I was studying, I wanted to visit them right away. It turned out that Ma himself was still studying in the United States while his wife and their baby son had just moved to the city. Ma's wife, Lin, warmly welcomed me to their new home. I couldn't help staring at Lin when she opened the door, holding her baby son in her other arm. It was this woman who had married Ma when he was jobless, homeless, and penniless. She was so charming and beautiful, though I did notice the signs of time on her face. I later learned that she had worked in restaurants for years while Ma was studying for his doctoral degree in the United States. Life must have been tough with a man like Ma, but they shared a common belief:

> I didn't understand then, and I still don't understand: Why did the soldiers have to open fire? They had other alternatives. The people were unarmed. I saw with my own eyes—the first line of people fell, and then the second line emerged. The people's army was killing the people!

I sat quietly, listening to her. It is said that women are made of water. I think the women of 1989 are made of water and fire.

After receiving his PhD, Ma faced the immediate pressure of supporting his family. He did not have time to look for a job in his field of study. His English, self-taught during the Cultural Revolution, was heavily accented, probably making it difficult for him to find an academic position in North America. His older daughter with Lin was still in China under the care of her grandparents because they couldn't afford to support two children in the West. Ma decided to study for a masters' degree in computer science, hoping that he would get a stable job to support his family. Unfortunately, the IT market collapsed just as Ma completed his degree. His only choice was to find an unskilled job:

> I have to support my family. For me it does not make much difference whether I work as a laborer or as a professor. I was a laborer in a cement factory for ten years. I am just picking up my old job in a different place and at a different time. My dream is to find a job so that I can bring my daughter from China to stay with us.

The authorities had indicated that if Ma were willing to compromise politically, he would be allowed to return to his teaching position, but he refused:

> I cannot openly express my point of view. Truth is not allowed in university classrooms, especially in the field of political science that I teach. I would only end up in trouble—either expelled from the university or imprisoned.

In 2004 I went with Ma's family to a public forum on the fifteenth anniversary of Tiananmen. After watching a video about the Tiananmen victims, Ma bent over and started to cry. He was not a man of tears. But here he was, crying in public, on foreign soil, for the victims of the Tiananmen Massacre:

> I grew up in an era of heroism and idealism. I am a Marxist. Actually many young intellectuals who went to the Square in 1989 were Marxists. We wanted to build a better China. If I had instead been educated to love money and power, as the current generation does, I don't think I would have participated in the movement. We were educated to love the nation and the people more than anything else, and we did.

In the early 1990s, when my friends and I in China secretly gathered to commemorate the June 4 anniversary, we followed the same rituals each year: silence for the dead and candles lighted in their memory. A friend who hosted the gathering, who was Ma's student, always showed us what he kept hidden under his bed—a loudspeaker from the protests and the T-shirt he wore on the night of the massacre. Amid the sadness, I would draw hope from listening to stories about Ma. The student told us: "When we were withdrawing from the Square on June 4, we saw those official banners supporting martial law hanging on a government building. We were so angry. Ma climbed up to the building and tore them down. He was an inspiration for so many of us students when we were forced into silence."

For many years I had told myself that I would not write about Ma unless his situation changed—I didn't want his students to know about his struggles abroad. For those of us who lived through 1989, we all understand the price one has to pay to maintain integrity during dark times when everything is twisted. Still, I long for a time when idealism is not treated as garbage, when those who remain idealistic do not need to collect garbage.

Rowena

When I first told my father that I wanted to join the student protests in 1989, I didn't know what to expect from him as I always had a hard time getting his permission to go out at night. To my surprise, he said yes without hesitation. It was raining hard outside. Mother quickly took out my poncho, which I normally wore when I biked to school on rainy days. She said a raincoat would be better than an umbrella among the crowd. When I was about to go out, my younger brother emerged from the bedroom holding something in his hands that seemed to be important. He spoke to me seriously as if he were an adult: "Get yourself a soft drink if you get thirsty." He carefully put five yuan into my dress pocket. I knew how long it must have taken him to save that money; it was all he had. When I left home, I felt I was leaving with everything that my family most treasured.

On the night of June 3, Father, Mother, and I didn't sleep. The next day, Father resumed smoking, a habit that he had quit over ten years earlier. I went to school wearing a black armband, a traditional Chinese sign of mourning, but was told by my teacher: "If you don't take that off, no one can protect you from now on." I took off the armband reluctantly trying to hold back my tears.

For a short period of time I would argue with my school friends about whether the massacre was just a story that had been "made-up" by the Americans, as we were being told. As the purges and arrests spread across the country, I shut up. Instead, in order to pass the exams, I recited the official version that "our army has won a glorious victory over a counter-revolutionary riot." At the age of seventeen, I learned to lie to survive.

On one occasion, Father's friends gathered in our small living room, with our doors and windows tightly closed. "I almost started to believe that our country at last has hope," Uncle Li, one of Father's close friends, sighed. The room became terribly quiet as he emphasized the word "hope." Uncle Li was a well-known writer and had been persecuted during the various political campaigns launched by the Communist Party. His wife was forced to divorce him, leaving him with his baby son when he was sent to work in the countryside. Members of his generation who had been persecuted under communist rule generally tried to stay away from politics. Still, Uncle Li took to the streets in 1989, protesting side by side with the students. He drank a lot of wine in our home, leaving the bottles, and perhaps hope itself, on the floor, empty.

Fifteen years later, in 2004, I was once again in a small living room packed with people. This time, they were not friends of my father, but people around my age, who identified themselves as members of the Tiananmen Generation. Unlike Liane, Tony, Ma, or me, who chose self-exile from the country, these people were exiles in the most literal sense—they had been banned from returning to their home country: China. Everyone was kneeling on the dusty floor of the studio apartment, preparing materials for the candlelight vigil for the fifteenth anniversary of the Tiananmen Massacre. The task was not that complicated—all we needed to do was to change the number on the banners and the handout materials from fourteen to fifteen. The number had already been changed from 1 to 15, and it has continued to change with each passing year.

Milan Kundera describes the struggle of man against power as the struggle of memory against forgetting.[15] Tiananmen as a forbidden memory did not end in 1989. It has never ended. 1989 was just the beginning of an end.

CHAPTER I

June 4: History and Memory in Exile

At U.S. immigration control, Chicago's O'Hare Airport, October 15, 2006:

"How long have you been abroad?"

"Two hours."

"Why?"

"The Chinese authorities forced me to re-board the same plane that had just taken me to China."

"You must have done something that made them unhappy."

"Do you know about the 1989 Tiananmen Massacre?"

"Of course."

"I have been collecting donations to support the Tiananmen Mothers and to help the Tiananmen orphans to finish their education."

"That's a good thing. Did you plan to visit your family in China?"

"Yes. My mother is 86 years old."

"She must be sad now that she can't see you."

"Yes, I feel sad too."

"Now you're home."

"Yes, this is the only home I can return to."

—Tao Ye[1]

The 1989 Tiananmen Movement, known in Chinese simply as "Liu Si" (June Fourth), was the most serious open conflict between the Communist regime and the Chinese people since the establishment of the People's Republic of China in 1949. On the surface Tiananmen seems to be remote and irrelevant to the reality of the "rising China," but every year on its anniversary, the government clamps down with intense security and meticulous surveillance. Tiananmen Mothers are still prohibited from openly mourning their family members, exiles are still turned away when they try to return home to visit a sick parent or to attend a loved one's funeral, and scholars working on the topic are regularly denied visas. The Beijing regime has been remarkably, if temporarily, successful in enforcing its official account of 1989 within China, justifying the military crackdown as necessary for stability and prosperity and for countering a Western conspiracy to divide and weaken China. June Fourth encapsulates the relationship between history and memory, power and politics, and intellectual freedom and human rights in the Chinese context. Indeed, it is not possible to understand today's China and its relationship with the world without understanding the spring of 1989.

This book is primarily an oral history of three exiled student leaders from the 1989 Tiananmen Movement in China. All three were banned from returning to China because of their roles in the uprising. Tracing the life trajectories of these exiles, from childhood during Mao's Cultural Revolution, adolescence growing up during the reform era, and betrayal and punishment in the aftermath of June 1989, to ongoing struggles in exile, I explore, in their own words, how their idealism was fostered by the very powers that ultimately crushed it, and how such idealism evolved facing the conflicts that historical amnesia, political commitment, ethical action, and personal happiness presented to them in exile. Following the principles of narrative research, I do not pretend to stand apart from what I investigate, but include my own experiences in my efforts to understand others. Narrative researchers have long acknowledged their prior experiences and perspectives, and their presence throughout the research process, as intrinsic and inescapable aspects of their work.[2] I have shared the fate of the exile community, and instead of posing as a distant, "objective" researcher or reporter, I worked closely with participants over years to construct the stories of our lives as members of the Tiananmen Generation. I have tried to make my roles as a researcher and an individual transparent in the text.

The three student leaders—Wang Dan, Shen Tong, and Yi Danxuan—participated fully in this project. I chose them because they were willing to embark on a multi-year journey and they felt comfortable sharing their experiences and perspectives with me. Given that all three had already been expressing their viewpoints openly in media interviews, speeches, and their own publications, I anticipated, before starting the research, that despite the sensitivity of the topic they would not mind my using their real names instead of pseudonyms. And that turned out to be the case.

Wang Dan was an undergraduate student studying history at Peking University in 1989. He became one of the most visible student leaders of the Tiananmen Movement and topped the most-wanted list after the military crackdown. He was arrested in July 1989 and was kept in custody for nearly two years before being sentenced to four years' imprisonment in 1991. He was arrested again in 1995 and sentenced to eleven more years in prison in 1996. In April 1998, he was released early on medical parole and exiled to the United States as part of a deal struck before President Bill Clinton was to attend a summit in China. He has been banned from setting foot in mainland China ever since. He resumed his university studies in 1998 at Harvard University, receiving his masters' degree in East Asian History in 2001 and his Ph.D. in 2008. Wang Dan has been nominated for the Nobel Peace Prize three times. He is currently teaching in Taiwan.

Shen Tong was an undergraduate student studying biology at Peking University in 1989 and he co-chaired the Student Dialogue Delegation to engage the government in dialogue during the movement. He left China for the United States six days after the military crackdown[3] and was named one of *Newsweek*'s People of the Year in 1989. He published his autobiography, *Almost a Revolution,* in 1990. One month after he returned to China in 1992, he was detained for fifty-four days and then expelled from the country. After ten years as an active dissident, he started his own software business. Beginning about a decade ago, he has been allowed to visit Beijing "on the condition that he stays out of Chinese politics."[4] He has been a controversial figure among the Tiananmen student leaders, in part because he has been accused of doing business with the Chinese government, a charge he denies here. In recent years Shen Tong has resumed his political activism. In 2011, after leaving the software company that he had founded, he participated in the Occupy Wall Street movement. He is currently living in New York City.

Yi Danxuan was an undergraduate student studying business management at the Guangdong University of Business Studies in 1989. He was elected vice president of the Guangzhou Patriotic Student Federation, which led over 200,000 students from 40 universities and colleges during the 1989 movement. After the military crackdown, he was detained for twenty months before a trial that sentenced him to two years' imprisonment. Barred from returning to college in China after prison, he came to the United States to resume his undergraduate studies in 1992. After sixteen years of exile, he was allowed to return to China once, just before the 2008 Beijing Olympics. But one year later, in 2009, he was denied entry when he attempted to visit his father, who had been diagnosed with cancer. He was twice elected president of the Independent Federation of Chinese Students and Scholars, the largest organization that had been founded by Chinese students and scholars in the United States immediately after the Tiananmen crackdown. He is currently living in Washington, DC.

Yi Danxuan's participation made a distinctive contribution to this study in two ways. First, the 1989 pro-democracy movement did not take place only in Tiananmen Square or even Beijing, although that was the general perception because of extensive coverage by Western journalists who had come to Beijing to cover Soviet president Mikhail Gorbachev's visit for a Sino-Soviet summit. Many people remain unaware of the massive protests that engulfed cities and towns throughout the country. Danxuan's story sheds light on the experience of student activism in a location far from the Beijing spotlight. Second, not all the exiled students are well known as "leaders." After imprisonment and exile many had a much more difficult time because they have received much less assistance and support than their more famous counterparts. Their stories, too, deserve to be told.

Despite global sympathy for the students after the military crackdown in 1989, attention since then has focused much more on the persecutors, and international perspectives on the student leaders have changed over time. Inside China, the exiles are like ghosts or invisible men. Most people either don't know anything about them, or they believe the official account that these traitors were collaborating with foreign anti-China forces for personal interests, and that had they succeeded in 1989 they would have led the country into "turmoil." Outside of China, memories fade and urgency subsides. Reports of infighting within exile circles, and of the misbehavior of certain individuals, have made it easy to become cynical about the cohort. My collaborative work with the exiled community over the years has convinced me that it is unfair to criticize their efforts because some of the leaders have fallen short of public expectations. Likewise, it is not reasonable to credit one single individual for any accomplishment achieved as a result of the movement's efforts. In this book I try to present the Tiananmen students' experiences from their own perspectives, letting them speak for themselves, while embedding their stories in changing contexts: China prior to 1989 and North America in the years since. I try to understand how their evolving sense of identity and rights were connected with that of an entire generation, and how such values can be cultivated, hindered, or even destroyed. It is not my intention to offer an overall explanation of what happened in 1989, nor is it to generalize from the twists and turns in the experiences of these three exiles. Instead, I present the complexities, confusions, and complications in the lives and thoughts of three young men who distinguished themselves as student leaders of the Tiananmen Movement—and who, at the same time, identify with every one of us as human beings.

Tiananmen in Post-Tiananmen China

A Chinese student once told me that June 4 was a CIA conspiracy. "The student leaders were taken away by U.S. helicopters directly from Tiananmen Square," he said.

"That sounds more like James Bond than the CIA," I responded.

"They were all holding American passports," he added, "Otherwise, how did they all end up in the United States and living luxurious lives?"

In 1989, scenes of the protests and the June 4 massacre captured the attention of hundreds of millions of newspaper readers and TV viewers around the world. However, although the movement was well known outside of China, at least at the time, memory is elusive and unstable, always subject to ferocious editing and even erasure. Within the country itself memory was deliberately manipulated and suppressed. Immediately after the military crackdown, the government carried out mass arrests and purges throughout the country, and then conducted an elaborate campaign through the state-controlled media and education to reestablish its legitimacy. An official version of the events of 1989 was constructed in this way, and massive efforts were undertaken to enshrine this fiction in the national memory. These official narratives have been disputed by various groups of people who struggle to preserve the memory of June 4. Because public opinion pertaining to nationalism and democratization is inseparable from a collective memory (either truthful, selective, or manipulated) of the nation's most immediate past, the memory of Tiananmen has become a highly contested field.

Tiananmen in Retrospect

The immediate trigger for the Tiananmen uprising was the sudden death of former Party General Secretary Hu Yaobang on April 15, 1989. Hu, who had been responsible for reversing cases of unjustified persecution following the Mao years, had been a proponent of reform with a good public image. People had been outraged that Deng Xiaoping, the leader of the Chinese Communist Party, had removed Hu as Party General Secretary in January 1987 for not being sufficiently tough during the Anti-Bourgeois Liberalization Campaign[5] and for not taking tough measures against the 1986–87 student protests. Because in the aftermath of Hu's downfall reform programs had been cut back on all fronts, students saw an opportunity to push for change by commemorating Hu.[6] Historically, in China mourning the death of a leader was not only legitimate but even officially organized.[7]

The movement rapidly spread throughout the country. Students, demonstrating in large numbers, called for government accountability and transparency, anti-corruption measures, freedom of the press, and freedom of speech. On April 26, the first official judgment on the movement was printed in the lead editorial of the Party's newspaper, the *People's Daily*, designating the student demonstrations as "premeditated and organized turmoil with anti-Party and anti-socialist motives":

> Flaunting the banner of democracy, they undermined democracy and the legal system. Their purpose was to sow dissension among the people, plunge the whole country into chaos, and sabotage stability and unity. This is a planned conspiracy.[8]

The students were outraged by the government's refusal to regard any of their requests as legitimate. The editorial, now known as the "April 26 Editorial," sparked a demonstration with over one million participants in Beijing on April

27. On May 13, two days prior to the highly publicized state visit by Soviet leader Mikhail Gorbachev, students launched a hunger strike in Tiananmen Square:

> In this bright, sunny month of May, we are on a hunger strike. In the finest moment of our youth, we must leave behind everything beautiful about life, no matter how unwilling we are!...Even though our shoulders are still soft and tender, even though death seems to us too weighty, when history demands it, we have no choice but to die...
>
> Farewell mothers and, farewell fathers! Please, forgive me, if your child who cannot be loyal [to the country] and [meet the demands of] filial manner at the same time! Farewell, people! Please allow us to use this means, however reluctantly, to demonstrate our loyalty....The vows written with our lives will brighten the skies of the Republic![9]

According to official estimates, between May 13 and May 24, thirty-two hospitals in Beijing treated 9,158 student hunger strikers, of whom 8,205 required hospitalization.[10] Ultimately, the Party leadership took the decision to employ force to suppress the movement, declaring martial law in the urban districts of Beijing to take effect on May 20. The movement ended with the June 4 military crackdown.

Aftermath—Arrest and Purge

After the military suppression, the state security system relentlessly identified and intimidated those suspected of participating in the movement. Student leaders, together with intellectuals who were considered the "Black Hands" behind the movement,[11] were routinely imprisoned, followed by a "verdict first, trial second" process.[12] Workers were punished more severely than students and intellectuals: at least ten workers in Beijing were summarily tried and executed within ten days after their arrests, and eight are still serving life sentences.[13] University students were forced to attend "political study" sessions each week, to confess to the number of times they had joined demonstrations, to inform on friends, and to study the speeches of Deng Xiaoping.[14]

The General Secretary of the Chinese Communist Party, Zhao Ziyang, who had been in favor of a soft approach to the student demonstrations and who had opposed the imposition of martial law, was purged and placed under house arrest to spend the final fifteen years of his life. Zhao had been a leading figure in the implementation of market reforms in China. While he was still alive, the CCP managed to mute his voice and keep him out of the public eye. But in 2009, four years after his death, he spoke to the world through about thirty audiotapes that he secretly recorded in 1999 and 2000 and that were smuggled out of the country. Based on the transcripts of the tapes, in 2009 *Prisoner of the State: The*

Secret Journal of Premier Zhao Ziyang was published in both English and Chinese to coincide with the twentieth anniversary of Tiananmen. Unsurprisingly, the book has been banned in China.

A widespread purge of media personnel began immediately after the crackdown. Propaganda officers of the People's Liberation Army (PLA) took control of all the major media in Beijing. Although many editors attempted to protect their journalists, high-level decisions were soon taken to remove these editors so that the purge could proceed more smoothly.[15] Two anchors for China Central Television (CCTV), the primary state television station, were removed from their positions because they had dressed in black clothing and had appeared sad while reporting on the army's successful crackdown on the counter-revolutionary riot. Wu Xiaoyong, deputy director of the English-language service of Radio Beijing[16] and son of Wu Xueqian, China's former foreign minister and vice premier, was placed under house arrest because of the following statement that had been broadcast internationally on the night of the massacre:

> This is Radio Beijing. Please remember June the third, 1989. The most tragic event happened in the Chinese capital, Beijing.
>
> Thousands of people, most of them innocent civilians, were killed by fully armed soldiers when they forced their way into the city. Among the killed are our colleagues at Radio Beijing.
>
> The soldiers were riding on armored vehicles and used machine guns against thousands of local residents and students who tried to block their way. When the army convoys made a breakthrough, soldiers continued to spray their bullets indiscriminately at crowds in the street.
>
> Eyewitnesses say some armored vehicles even crushed foot soldiers who hesitated in front of the resisting civilians.
>
> The Radio Beijing English Department deeply mourns those who died in the tragic incident and appeals to all its listeners to join our protest for the gross violation of human rights and the most barbarous suppression of the people.
>
> Because of this abnormal situation here in Beijing, there is no other news we could bring you. We sincerely ask for your understanding and thank you for joining us at this most tragic moment.[17]

Along with many reporters, both the editor-in-chief and the director of the *People's Daily*, the official mouthpiece of the Chinese Communist Party, were dismissed from their posts because of their sympathetic attitude toward the students during the movement. In Shanghai, the *World Economic Herald (Shijie jingji daobao)*, one of the country's most liberal weekly newspapers during the 1980s, was banned from publishing at the end of April. After June 4, editor-in-chief, Qin Benli, was placed under house arrest and four members of the editorial board were detained for between one and twenty months. The paper was officially closed down in April 1990.[18] In March 1991, two days before Qin's death, the head of the Propaganda Department of the Shanghai Municipal Party Committee, announced that Qin had been expelled from the Party.

"Rumors and the Truth"

Chinese authorities blamed "foreign forces" for the Tiananmen protests. An editorial titled "Rumours and the Truth" was published in the *Beijing Review*, China's only national news magazine in English, accusing Western media of spreading rumors and attempting to undermine China's efforts to restore order:

> The true story of the "Tiananmen Incident," which itself had been invented jointly by the media of some Western countries, Hong Kong and Taiwan, and particularly by the Voice of America (VOA), has come out since the riot in Beijing was quelled in June....However, the media have not told their readers, listeners or audience the true story. They are afraid that once the public has learned the truth, people will make their own judgements, and the accusations that China "suppressed the democratic movement" and "trampled on human rights" will be shown to be groundless.[19]

In another issue of *Beijing Review*, an article claimed that "the Chinese government's just action in resolutely quelling the riot in Beijing has been supported by people in all walks of life."[20] Just one week before the crackdown, the cover story of the same magazine had read: "Hunger Strike Shakes the Nation," indicating support for the students.[21]

The official "true story" appeared in a different editorial in *Beijing Review*:

> The plotters and organizers of the counter-revolutionary rebellion are mainly a handful of people who have for a long time obstinately advocated bourgeois liberalization, opposed Party leadership and socialism and harboured political schemes, who have collaborated with hostile overseas forces and who have provided illegal organizations with the top secrets of the Party and state....Taking advantage of students' patriotic feelings...this handful of people with evil motives stirred up trouble.[22]

The regime charged that students were poisoned by "bourgeois liberalization"—shorthand for a universal value system. The official position of universal values was articulated in an article in the *Guangming Daily* newspaper:

> What are human rights? As understood by Western scholars, they are the innate rights of human beings, or the basic rights and freedoms enjoyed by a person as a human...These rights are innate, permanent, universal, and nontransferable. They cannot be taken away....

In the context of Marxism [however], such an interpretation of human rights is unscientific, incorrect, contrived, biased, and idealistically metaphysical...Human rights, like democracy and freedom, are concrete and class-oriented.[23]

On June 9, 1989, Deng Xiaoping, chairman of the Chinese Communist Party Central Military Commission, received the ranking commanders of the martial law enforcement troops and congratulated them for a job well done. In the same month, Deng granted the "Guardians of the Republic" (*Gongheguo weishi*) award to ten soldiers who had enforced martial law. Three months later, a book titled *The Most Beloved Men in the New Era: A List of the Heroes of the Beijing Martial Law Enforcement Troops* was published.[24]

Students of all ages, including undergraduate and graduate students at universities and colleges, were called upon to learn from these national role models. Thousands of members of the official Communist Party youth group, The Young Pioneers, assembled in Tiananmen Square to show that China's revolutionary youth had taken back the Square from the student demonstrators. At the Monument to the People's Heroes where college students had taken the oath "to use their youthful life" to defend their motherland on June 4, the youngsters now pledged to remember the soldiers who had enforced martial law:

> Beloved revolutionary martyrs, may you rest in peace!
> The Young Pioneers will remember you!
> The people will remember you!
> The motherland will remember you!
> Let our brilliant red scarves serve as our pledge.
> We love the Chinese Communist Party!
> We love the socialist motherland!
> We love the People's Liberation Army!
> We will carry on the cause of Communism![25]

Resistance and Truth: The Tiananmen Mothers

The fear created by the massacre is best illustrated in a story told by Professor Cui Weiping, Chinese translator of Vaclav Havel's work. After the twenty-eight-year-old son of one family was killed, the boyfriend of his sister broke up with her. When she later began a relationship with another boy, he too abandoned her after learning of her family's past. She and her mother decided that she would never again mention her brother to anyone she planned to date. She is now married with a daughter, but her husband still has no idea about the death or even the existence of his brother-in-law.[26]

While the Beijing regime set in motion the state machinery to erase or distort any memory of June 4, the Tiananmen Mothers group, represented by Professor

Ding Zilin, has been fighting a war of memory against forgetting. Ding's seventeen-year-old son, Jiang Jielian, was shot and killed during the massacre. Over the years, despite escalating government repression, including police surveillance and dismissal from her job, Ding has spearheaded a campaign to collect information about the victims. Her book, *In Search of the Victims of June 4*, published in Hong Kong in 2005, documented any information she could find about the victims, for instance Xiao Bo, a Peking University lecturer who had been killed on his twenty-seventh birthday, leaving twin infant sons.[27] The list of the victims is arranged not alphabetically but by the date when information about a victim came to light. For example, according to Ding's account, the authorities told Xiao Bo's wife to remain silent about her husband's death—otherwise they would not allow her to remain in their campus housing. The young mother felt that she could not afford to be homeless with her babies, so she remained invisible until Ding reached her in 1993 and added her husband's name as number 008 on the list.[28]

Ding's work has truly been a mission impossible, with no end in sight—the total of sixteen names that she had collected by 1993 had grown to 202 by 2013, and it is still far from complete. The true number is buried under years of cover-up, deception, suppression, and repression. In 2011, China's state-sponsored English-language newspaper *China Daily* published a story headlined "Tiananmen Massacre a Myth." Citing the release of the WikiLeaks diplomatic cables[29] that indicated that there had been no bloodshed in the Square itself, the article claimed:

> Tiananmen remains the classic example of the shallowness and bias in most Western media reporting, and of governmental black information operations seeking to control those media. China is too important to be a victim of this nonsense.[30]

While there is nothing extraordinary here—this has been the official version from the start—the state-sponsored myth is poignantly challenged by Ding's list of victims, which includes individuals such as Cheng Renxing, a twenty-five-year-old graduate of the People's University of China who was shot and killed by the flagpole in Tiananmen Square as, together with other students, he was withdrawing from the Square in the early morning of June 4.[31] Cheng's father, a farmer from Hubei province, was devastated and died in 1995. Cheng's mother tried to hang herself at home but was saved by her ten-year-old grandson, who used his little body to hold up his grandmother for an hour until adults came to rescue her.

But whether people were killed in the Square itself is not the central question. Maps created based on information provided by the Tiananmen Mothers, pinpointing the locations of the documented killings and the hospitals where the victims died, show that state violence was widespread throughout central Beijing.[32]

Since its establishment, the Tiananmen Mothers have been demanding the right to peacefully mourn their loved ones in public, an end to the persecution of victims' families, the release of all those imprisoned for their roles in the 1989 protests, and a full public accounting of the military crackdown. In 2006, the group called for "truth and reconciliation." But so far the regime has turned a deaf ear to their requests. In 2013, in a public statement the Tiananmen Mothers lamented that "hope fades as despair draws near."[33]

In 2012, a Tiananmen father Ya Weilin hanged himself in an empty Beijing parking lot several days before the Tiananmen anniversary. He was marking, as he had in one way or another for the last twenty-three years, the death of his son at the hands of the Chinese government and the People's Liberation Army on the night of June 3, 1989. After twenty-three years of waiting, twenty-three years of petitioning and questioning, twenty-three years of searching for justice, this seventy-three-year-old father made his final dramatic statement without ever seeing justice done for his son and for the Tiananmen Massacre.

In a 2004 video testimony, Ya appeared sad but determined. He and his wife had asked the Chinese government for answers to questions that any parent would want to know: "Why did you use real guns and bullets on your people? Even if you kill a chicken, or a lamb, you should apologize and compensate, right? Such a big China, such a big Chinese Communist Party, you killed my son, but you didn't even say sorry. Are we citizens not allowed to say a single word?"[34] Ya's son is number 131 on Ding's list of victims. Before this young man became a number, he had a name: Ya Aiguo. In Chinese, Ai means "to love" and guo means "country," so the name Aiguo means "Patriotism." The student protesters of 1989 called their movement a "Patriotic Democracy Movement," thus indicating they had no intention of overthrowing the government. But since the night that Ya Aiguo and the others were killed, the word *aiguo* has taken on an entirely new meaning.

Distorted Patriotism

Haunted by the relationship between the military crackdown and the legitimacy of the Party, the post-Tiananmen leadership launched a vigorous campaign on all fronts, appealing to "patriotism" to restore the regime's authority. The regime learned from its experience in 1989 that locking the school gates would not be sufficient to prevent the students from leaving their campuses to join the demonstrations—they learned that they must effectively lock the students' minds so that even when the gates are open, dissent would not recur. Thus, Chinese education in the post-Tiananmen period has shifted from a Marxist-socialist orientation to a nationalist-patriotic focus. Schools at all levels, from kindergarten to university, turned their classrooms into forums for patriotic education.[35] Top Party organs promulgated various related policy documents,[36] including the well-publicized "Guidelines for Patriotic Education" drafted by the Propaganda Department of the Chinese Communist Party's Central Committee in 1994. As a result, textbooks on politics and history were significantly revised[37] to put greater emphasis on China's historical victimhood at the hands of the West and Japan. In one moral education textbook, a lesson titled "Let's Choose Determination" tells the story of a lazy student who is reading a book on the Opium War when he is "struck by a sentence: 'Not studying leads to backwardness, and backwardness leads to getting beaten.'" He then resolves "to study hard in order to become a dignified and strong Chinese person who will never submit to foreign bullying." Another lesson, titled "Be a Self-Confident Chinese Person," relates the experience of a well-known scientist, Dong Dizhou, who had studied in Belgium. According to the lesson, Dong had been humiliated by a Western student who claimed that China was poor because the Chinese were "stupid." Dong responded, "I can't allow you to insult my compatriots and my motherland!" He then challenged the Western student to a competition to see who would first receive his PhD degree. Needless to say, Dong emerged the winner.[38] A study of patriotic education in a Chinese middle school found that teachers believed that patriotic students should

> uphold national dignity, as did those students participating in an international academic competition who refused their gold medals because the flag of the Republic of China [Taiwan] was displayed, or those students who protested at a foreign teacher's display of a map showing Tibet as an independent country.[39]

State history propaganda engages in selective remembering and forgetting, focusing on carefully chosen glories, traumas, and humiliations from China's past.[40] In 2006, Yuan Weishi, a history professor at Zhongshan University, published an article in *Freezing Point* (*Bingdian*), a liberal four-page weekly supplement to the *China Youth Daily*, pointing out that Chinese textbooks teach an incomplete history that fosters blind nationalism and closed-minded antiforeign sentiment. He described the younger generation as "sheep raised on wolf milk." Two weeks after Yuan's article appeared, *Freezing Point* was temporarily suspended by the Propaganda Department of the Communist Party, and two editors were reassigned to other positions.

The Patriotic Education Campaign, extending well beyond school classrooms, intersects with popular discourse through film, television, the print media, patriotic education sites (such as museums and memorials), patriotic theme parks, and "red tours." Nationalism became increasingly evident in popular discourse during the late 1990s, especially in demonstrations against Japan and the United States and books such as *China Can Say No* (1996) and *Behind*

Demonizing China (1997), all of which portrayed the West in general, and the United States and Japan in particular, as inveterately hostile to China. The language in these books was often vulgar, but it was effective in arousing nationalistic sentiments among the populace.

Upon learning of the September 11 attacks in the United States, Monica, a Canadian teacher who was teaching English at a high school east of Beijing in 2001, was caught off guard by her Chinese students' reactions:

> The first bell rings and I begin moving slowly toward my grade eleven classroom in a daze. What will I say to my students? Do they even know? Will I be the first bearer of this terrible news? As I stand facing my students, gripping the lectern to steady myself, I take a deep breath and begin with a simple question, "Have you heard the world news this morning?" I wait for a response. What happens next is shocking, unpredictable, and completely unfathomable. My beautiful Chinese students whom I hold so dear begin, in unison, to applaud. I am speechless, horrified, reeling. We fall into the grip of a tension-filled moment. I am silent. The students are silent. Finally, I ask, in a tone that I hope conveys incomprehension, rather than judgmental rebuke, "Why are you clapping?"[41]

The post-Tiananmen Generation, which has grown up learning a state-approved history in an environment of intensifying nationalism, tends to make no distinction between the regime and the nation. They defend the Beijing government as if they are defending China itself, and consider those critical of the regime to be national traitors. Before the 2008 Beijing Olympics, the world witnessed the global emergence of "China defenders," with thousands of overseas Chinese students raising red flags, protesting an alleged Western media "smear campaign" against China," and cursing the Dalai Lama. In April of that year, a female Chinese student at Duke University, Grace Wang, found herself deluged with obscene messages and threats from hundreds of other Chinese students, simply because she had ventured to mediate between rival groups of Chinese students and Tibetan exiles. She had become a "traitor" in online forums overnight.[42] Chinese students began what they called the "Human Flesh Search Engine" to ascertain her personal information; they then posted online her Chinese name, ID number, and contact details, as well as directions to her parents' apartment in Qingdao, China. A pot of human waste was duly emptied outside her parents' door, and they fled for their safety.

In the same year, a letter signed by "a group of overseas Chinese students" was addressed to the Tiananmen Mothers, calling them criminals who had raised their children to become running dogs of the United States. There is something profound and revealing about a rising China that is so afraid of these elderly "running dogs" and their dead relatives. Surveillance cameras were installed in graveyards near the tomb of Yuan Li, a graduate student who had been killed in

1989. When Yuan's father died in 2011, some Tiananmen Mothers were banned from attending the ninety-four-year-old's memorial.

The Landscape of Exile: "Gaining the Sky but Losing the Earth" (*dedao tiankong, shiqu dadi*)

Many of China's best-known writers and intellectuals, as well as its prominent student leaders, fled the country after the June 4 crackdown. This latter-day Chinese diaspora went mainly to North America and Europe. A group of Hong Kong citizens played important roles in helping these dissidents to escape from China. At the time of the massacre, an underground railroad known as Operation Yellowbird (*Huangque xingdong*) helped some 133 of China's leading dissident students and intellectuals escape to the West, despite the intense surveillance by the Chinese secret police.[43] Details of the operation remained secret until 1991 because the principals feared that any publicity would compromise possible future missions or expose those involved to arrest or persecution; Operation Yellowbird was revealed to the public after one escape mission went badly wrong and the Chinese secret police obtained extensive knowledge about its operations.[44] Regardless, many believe that the successful "Great Escape" by dissidents indicated silent resistance and cooperation from both army and civilians in 1989. Otherwise, escape from China under tightened military control would have been nearly impossible.

In the early 1990s, many Tiananmen exiles found a haven at Princeton University, the same school that had sheltered political exiles from Nazi Germany in the 1930s. Alumnus John Eliot, who happened to be visiting the renowned Princeton professor Yu Ying-shih on the night of June 4, 1989, was outraged by the military crackdown[45] and donated $1 million to set up a program called the China Initiative. With the support of Professor Yu and Professor Perry Link, an eminent scholar of Chinese history and culture, the China Initiative provided a home for intellectuals, former government officials, and student leaders who had fled China after Tiananmen to continue their struggle for a better China.

The Chinese government, having realized that it could achieve more by exiling the dissidents than by holding them in prison, voluntarily released some of them and forced them out of the country.[46] The exiles describe their life in the diaspora as "gaining the sky but losing the earth": they can now enjoy the freedom and rights they longed for, but they are cut off from the land where they fought for these values. Meanwhile, with the machinery of the state in full force, the Chinese Communist Party has successfully demonized and marginalized those in exile. As the scholar Geremie Barmé has written:

> Prominent intellectuals and students had, by the very fact of their exile, suffered a serious blow to their credibility. This was particularly so, since it was widely perceived on the mainland that many of the key agitators of 1989 had sought

refuge with former imperialist powers (that is, France, England, and the United States) and the KMT government in Taiwan. The mainland authorities were well aware of the jealous reaction of its people to reports of dissidents living off the fat of the land overseas, and the official media took delight in portraying them all as traitors to the nation…

Knowing full well that rabid attacks on the exiles would only elicit sympathy for their cause, the Chinese government by and large responded to the activities of the dissidents by ignoring them.[47]

The exile community has grown over the years as more new members have fled the country. Among them is Lu Decheng, one of the three men who threw eggs and paint at the giant portrait of Mao Zedong overlooking Tiananmen Square in 1989. After serving nine years in prison, in 2004 Lu fled across mountains and through jungles, first to Burma and then to Thailand. After spending a year in a Thai prison, in 2006 he was eventually accepted as a political refugee by Canada.[48] Lu's two collaborators, Yu Dongyue and Yu Zhijian, were granted political asylum in the United States in 2009, twenty years after Tiananmen. They had also fled through Thailand. Yu Dongyue had been a twenty-one-year-old fine arts editor in 1989. After seventeen years of imprisonment and years of torture and solitary confinement, he could no longer recognize his family members when he was released from prison in 2006.[49] Former Tiananmen student Fang Zheng also joined his exiled peers in 2009. Fang had been a college student at Beijing Sports College in 1989. He was run over by a tank, which crushed both his legs, as he was peacefully withdrawing from Tiananmen Square with fellow students. He was told by the authorities to say that he had been run over by a car, not a tank; when he refused to lie, he was denied his graduation certificate and bachelor's degree.[50] After surviving twenty years of harassment and surveillance, with the help of the Tiananmen students, Fang started his life in exile.

Older members in exile, such as Fang Lizhi, Liu Binyan, Wang Ruowang, and Ge Yang—leading liberal intellectuals in the 1980s—all died in exile. Others, like Su Xiaokang and Guo Luoji, were banned from returning home to visit their dying mothers or even to attend their funerals. The circumstances faced by the younger generation has varied as time goes by. Wuer Kaixi was second on the government's most-wanted list in 1989; a Uyghur student studying at Beijing Normal University in 1989, he has never been allowed to return to China, and his parents are not allowed to leave China to visit him. Now resident in Taiwan, Wuer has repeatedly tried to turn himself in to the Chinese authorities, in Macau in 2009, in Tokyo in 2010, in 2011 in Washington DC, and in 2013 in Hong Kong, in order to return to China, even if under arrest, but the authorities have consistently refused to take him.

Various organizations and NGOs were established overseas in response to the 1989 movement. Among them, the Independent Federation of Chinese Students and Scholars (IFCSS, *Quanmei xuezilian),* has been among the most influential.

Motivated by outrage at the senseless killings, the IFCSS was established in July 1989. More than 200 universities sent a total of over 1,000 delegates to Chicago to attend the first IFCSS congress held at the University of Illinois at Chicago.[51] The organization successfully lobbied the U.S. Congress to pass the "Chinese Students Protection Act" in 1992. As a result, 80,000 Chinese in the United States were granted "June 4 Green Cards" so that they could remain in the United States and be free from political persecution back in China. Although the IFCSS was initially influential among the Chinese in the United States, in recent years its membership has decreased dramatically as many who have arrived more recently do not want to have anything to do with these "traitors."

Even though the IFCSS helped 80,000 Chinese gain legal immigrant status in the United States, many of its council members chose not to apply for U.S. citizenship. Most of them have been denied entry to China because of their humanitarian aid to families of the Tiananmen victims. Unlike the Tiananmen exiles who were in China during the uprising, most members of the IFCSS were Chinese graduate students and scholars, studying or conducting research in the United States in 1989. They were banned from returning to China because of their support for the victims of the massacre. Tao Ye, whose account appears at the beginning of this chapter, is one of many examples. Tao was a low-profile IFCSS member who had been collecting donations to help June 4 orphans to finish their high school and college educations. He kept his Chinese citizenship during twenty years of residence in the United States. In October 2006, when Tao tried to enter China with his Chinese passport, he was forced to re-board the same plane that had just taken him to China and return to the United States. He tried to reason with the authorities but was told that he was "unwelcome" and that he was "shamelessly delaying a flight of 300 passengers." For helping the mothers whose children had been killed in 1989, Tao himself was deprived of the right to go home to visit his own mother. In January 2012, another IFCSS member, Ge Xun, was kidnapped, beaten up, and interrogated in Beijing while he was on his way to visit Professor Ding Zilin, the representative of the Tiananmen Mothers.[52] Ge Xun had come to the United States in the eighties and had later become an American citizen. He was returning to China to attend his mother's funeral. But, holding a bouquet of flowers, just as he arrived at the entrance of Professor Ding's apartment building, he was spirited away by the State Security agents. His requests to call his family or the U.S. embassy were denied, and he was eventually taken to the Beijing airport and deported to the United States.

Sociologist Richard Madsen compares the Tiananmen protests to a drama "with an unexpected, incorrect ending" because good did not triumph over evil.[53] The unfolding stories in the post-Tiananmen era are, in many ways, a continuing tragedy because the victims are no longer considered victims and the perpetrators no longer perpetrators. Rather, the latter have become the winners against the backdrop of a "rising China."

Researching the Taboo

Conducting research on politically sensitive subjects is always a challenging and sometimes nerve-wracking endeavor.[54] The advent of globalization has intensified this situation, as national governments are now even better able to exert their influence internationally. China presents particular difficulties in this regard: first, the government rarely makes it clear where it draws the "line" for its own political expediency, and second, because the government's confidence has been inflated as the country has emerged as a global economic power. I have personally experienced the conflicts between scholarly research and political pressure compounded by fear. Even though I am based in a democratic and liberal social environment, as a Chinese-born researcher, I am not immune from the political power of the country under investigation. Such political intrusions into contemporary China studies (both inside and outside of China) are indicative of the complicated relationship between power and discourse and between the government and intellectuals in the post-Tiananmen era.

Tiananmen has been a politically taboo subject banned from academic and popular realms during the past quarter century. As researchers Daniel Curran and Sandra Cook pointed out several years after Tiananmen:

> The greatest challenge confronting social scientists in post-Tiananmen China has less to do with research design or the quality and quantity of data than with the skills of reading political signals sent by the CCP government....One cannot simply publish findings because it could mean the end of another academic career or the punishment of respondents.[55]

At the initial stage of this project, neither I nor the exiled students explicitly used the word "fear." Growing up in China with admiration for those heroic revolutionary figures who had sacrificed everything, including their lives, for the nation and a higher cause, we were used to equating fear with cowardice. Instead, I used the word "worry." When I encountered authors who used pseudonyms or veiled the identities of people in their studies, I felt worried. For example, the editors of the book *Cries for Democracy: Writings and Speeches from the 1989 Chinese Democracy Movement* wrote under the Chinese pseudonyms of Han Minzhu and Hua Sheng, meaning "democracy for China" and "Voice of China" respectively. As editors of a book that is frequently cited, they explained their decision in this way:

> With a brutal military assault and a ruthless repression, the Chinese Communist Party once again has demonstrated that it finds it far easier to eliminate its critics than to face their criticisms. We the editors, who cannot at this time reveal our identities, know that our tears and angers will not bring back those who cried for democracy. Yet, we do not despair for China.[56]

In another book, *The Long March to the Fourth of June*, the author, using the name Li Xiaojun, articulates explicitly the reasons for hiding his/her identity:

> I publish this book under a pseudonym. This is because I have to be cautious not only for my own and my family's sake, but for that of my colleagues and friends, especially those who have helped me with information and access to records. Accordingly I cannot say who I am or what my work is, nor am I free to explain my access to the information upon which the following is based. In present-day China it is not possible to write and publish a book like this without consequences: I have written it because I wish China to become otherwise.[57]

While some choose to express their perspectives but hide their personal identities, others suppress their point of view when they have to reveal who they are. I was once excited to find in my department library a thesis entitled *The Children of Tiananmen*. However, the Tiananmen Movement is mentioned only once in the whole thesis, in a five-line footnote.[58] I could tell how hard the author, as a student from mainland China, tried to hide, and at the same time, how much she would have liked to express what she was not saying.

I find myself in a similar situation. Friends and former classmates in China have often asked me, "What on earth have you been studying for your degree all these years?" Most of the time I have either dodged their questions or responded with vague answers. In their eyes, I have done nothing since leaving China except attending graduate school. As a human being, I would have liked to have had recognition for my efforts instead of letting people believe that I wasn't able to articulate clearly what I had been doing or that I wasn't particularly passionate about my work. But fear outweighed vanity.

Other scholars such as Andrew Nathan of Columbia University and Perry Link of Princeton University[59] have both been banned from going to China because of their works on Tiananmen. While studying the Tiananmen exiles, I found myself being exiled from academic activities in China: no conference presentations, publications, or professional opportunities. Political scientist Edward Friedman has flatly said that "studying China is dangerous":

> A narrow concentration of professional power over funding, invitations to second channel talks in China, and conference monies is heightened by the policies of the CCP. It denies visas to critically-minded international academics...No one who works on China wishes to be excluded from visiting the PRC and from doing research there as have scholars Perry Link and Andrew Nathan...As a result, certain discourses are muted while others, friendlier to certain CCP policies, are almost hegemonic.[60]

My concerns went beyond professional development. Whereas a Western scholar can choose a different area of study if denied entry into China, I cannot change my family members or the fact that I was born and grew up there. There is a hidden line that I cannot cross. I don't know where the line is, and that's precisely the root of my fears. Behind that line is my family, my home, and my past. In 2009, Gao Wenqian, author of *Zhou Enlai: The Last Perfect Revolutionary*, shared a personal story at a memorial event for the twentieth anniversary of Tiananmen. Gao had been a former official biographer of China's political leaders. During the purge after 1989 he was dismissed from his position and in 1993 he left China for the United States While abroad, he tried not to upset the authorities so as to retain his right to return to China to visit his elderly mother. When his mother knew that she was dying, she said to her son in relief: "At last, you can publish your book. They can no longer hold you back."[61]

My research journey paralleled a period when China was experiencing economic prosperity and a resurgent populist nationalism. Starting as early as 2003, I had been challenged and attacked by Chinese students on different occasions, including at academic conferences. In 2003 at a comparative education conference, one young student interrupted my presentation. She asserted that China had made much progress and that I should stop "revealing the dark side of the past." I saw her again after the session. She was walking with her peers. She must have told them about my work and they stared at me. It was frightening—and not just because they were so angry at me.

On another occasion, at a conference on oral history, a young Chinese student accused me of lying about historical facts. She continued to speak with confidence to convince the audience of her version of history. Nothing in her story was new to me. I had had to recite those lines too—lies to me—to pass my exams in 1989. Obviously she accepted them as the truth.

Against Amnesia: Narrative as Quest

This oral history project draws not only on in-depth interviews and group discussions, but also, and more broadly, on my collaborative experience with the exiled Chinese student community over many years. I have drawn on the publications of the three exiles as well as existing published materials about them, and on my own published Chinese articles and interview reports. My interviews with Wang Dan and Danxuan were conducted in Chinese so that we could feel more relaxed about expressing ourselves and so that we could communicate most effectively. My interviews with Shen Tong were conducted in both English and Chinese; he switched languages depending on the topic we were discussing. In addition to the individual interviews, I organized two group discussions to deepen the treatment of issues that emerged during the individual interviews. I held the first of these discussions with Shen Tong and Danxuan, and the second one with Wang Dan and Danxuan. In addition to these formal exchanges, over the years I have had numerous opportunities to observe and understand my participants as we have collaborated on projects, participated in events together, and held informal conversations in person or on the phone.

Oral history focuses on the reconstruction of a life and on the preservation of individuals' own words and perspectives in an authentic way. In the individual profile, each participant plays a dominant role as the narrator of his own life story. I have tried to give voice to the exile, so that they could describe how things were then and how things are now; and I have tried to show how each voice had changed with the passage of time. Each profile was crafted to stand independently so that readers, whether they have previously studied China or not, can pick up one chapter and read it without having to look for contextual information.

Oral history draws its power from the spontaneity of oral narratives, which reveals "a virtually unedited and sometimes unprocessed view of personal meaning and judgement that is not altered by the usual limitations of written language."[62] As a bilingual and bicultural researcher, I wanted to capture the original flavor of our language. Instead of undertaking "pure" translations, I have tried to incorporate our Chinese voices into the text without losing the flow of English discourse. This process of translation was further complicated by identity negotiation. The fact that Shen Tong was sometimes comfortable expressing himself in English, while Danxuan and Wang Dan were not at all, was a telling reflection of their struggles with identity in exile. Even when rewritten with the most accurate equivalent English words, the meaning we wanted to convey could still get lost in translation. When I have found it difficult to find a suitable English equivalent, I have included transliterated Chinese *pinyin* in parentheses.

In the oral history profiles and group discussions contained in Section Two of this book ("Triumph and Trauma"), I have sought to explore the exiled students' fights to achieve a moral victory even while they struggled to survive an ongoing personal trauma. As the trauma scholar Bernhard Gliesen has written, "The sovereign hero can survive only in the memory of past triumphs—any living hero would risk being questioned by the challenges of everyday life and by the inevitable blurring of the boundaries between the sacred and the profane."[63] All three participants sought both an "ordinary life" and an ethically "good life" in the traditional Aristotelian sense.[64] While crafting these profiles, I have tried to focus on the new perspectives and information I have derived from the interviews, while at the same time drawing on other materials where appropriate. Readers who are not aware of the existing materials will get a general idea of the related experiences of the participants, while researchers who have studied the relevant literature will find fresh, firsthand perspectives.

Narrative methods of scholarship have risen in prominence in recent years, offering opportunities to connect the lives and stories of individuals to our understanding of larger human and social phenomena. While nobody had warned me about the potential danger of intellectualization—of splitting feeling from thought—in the early stages of my research, I felt uneasy about the fact that behind my clearly defined research questions and straightforward presentations, there would be voices that remained unheard and struggles that remained unrevealed. When I first encountered the narrative approach, I felt that I had found a home. In narrative studies, life stories are considered the "very precondition for knowing" because it is through an "understanding of the self" that we come to an understanding of others.[65] Narrative researchers do not focus exclusively on the primary subject matter of a study. They also go beyond to tell the stories of the research process, "behind the scenes." Narrative accounts throughout the research process aim to foster reflection and to prompt further stories, or to stimulate "resonance through metaphorical connections rather than through strictly logical ones."[66]

This oral history project is grounded in three narrative methods, namely, *life history, narrative inquiry,* and *arts-based inquiry. Life history* is "the story we tell about our life" and the "life story located within historical contexts."[67] Life history work not only creates histories of lives, but also relates those lives to broader historical circumstances.[68] *Narrative inquiry* is a process "involving mutual storytelling and restorying" among the researcher and the participants.[69] *Arts-based inquiry* infuses into scholarly works elements, processes, and forms from the arts, including metaphors, literary writing, singular subjective voices, the use of narrative tension and suspense in the text, and attempts to capture the narrative flow of individual thoughts.[70]

The "incomplete" and contextualizing nature of oral history is especially relevant to this project. Just as the lives of these exiles have evolved with time, so has China, and so has the rest of the world. As time goes by, the images of the exiles have shifted from heroes, or victims, to losers, or traitors. These three men were ready to make sacrifices to enact change in 1989, but the impact of the changing contexts and historical forces on their lives in exile spun out of their control. All three narrative methods work together to illuminate how the exiles' experiences, together with the continually unfolding circumstances of their lives, have influenced their identities and beliefs, which consequently have shaped their decisions and actions in exile.

Who Am I as a Researcher?

When I started my graduate journey, I knew nothing about academia and was uncertain about my future. But I was hopeful. As a young woman who had come all the way alone from China just two years earlier, I was happy to be able to attend graduate school at the University of Toronto. Professors and fellow students started to ask me questions: "What brought you to Canada?" and "What do you want to do for your research?" In those days, I wasn't good at explaining why I had immigrated to Canada and I didn't consider myself an "exile." It didn't occur to me that these two past-future questions were closely related to each other and would have a lot to do with my evolving intellectual perspective in the years to come. I had never thought that scholarship could relate directly to one's life, that it could be a fundamentally autobiographical act.[71] It took me many years to realize that I seemed fated to choose exile as a topic, and to choose a topic while in exile.

I took my first class on narrative methods in 2001 and became addicted to reading narrative studies, most of which started with the author's autobiography. In this scholarly tradition, the subjectivity of the researcher is considered a virtue:

> My subjectivity is the basis for the story that I am able to tell. It is a strength on which I build. It makes me who I am as a person and as a researcher, equipping me with the perspectives and insights that shape all that I do as researcher, from the selection of topic clear through to the emphases I make in my writing. Seen as virtuous, subjectivity is something to capitalize on rather than to exorcise.[72]

I was given the opportunity to write my own memoir in the six narrative courses I took in the following years. The advice we were given was to write without analyzing what or how we were doing and why we were doing it. So although I had written in diaries since 1989, I did not refer to any of them. Instead, I drew on my memories and family stories. I found the process liberating, although I struggled with how much I should reveal about myself and whether I should touch upon painful episodes that I didn't want to remember. As it turned out, the process was healing as well—writing became a kind of therapy.

After some intensive writing, the open-ended and experiential process became messy. Thoughts, feelings, and fragments needed to be understood and woven together. I compare it to the unfolding of a traditional Chinese water-and-ink painting. When you first unfold the picture, you will only see pieces of water and ink here and there. It is hard to tell where the sky is, which part is water, which is cloud, which is stone, and which are the bushes. Not until you unfold the entire picture will you discover the artistic meaning. As Patricia Hampls puts it:

> Memoir is the intersection of narration and reflection, of storytelling and essay writing. It can present its story and reflect and consider the meaning of the story. It is a peculiarly open form, inviting broken and incomplete images, half-collected fragments—all the mass (and mess) of detail. It offers to shape this confusion—and in shaping, of course it necessarily creates a work of art.[73]

I have included the earliest part of my autobiographical writings in Chapter Two, titled *Seeds of Fire*. As the title indicates, I seek there to trace the forces that ground the lenses through which I have done my research. Together with the contextualized life histories of the three Tiananmen student leader exiles, I present an autobiographical narrative of my own experience. I have intentionally kept the original flavor of the writings so that readers will understand what initially led me to the topic. Readers will notice that I do not always provide precise information regarding times and places. I myself did not notice these omissions until much later. I believe I wrote in this manner because of a subconscious fear, when I started writing, of openness, of exposure to scrutiny, of shame. Besides, I remember in images, not in a strict chronological sequence. In this autobiographical chapter, I have provided information about the times and places in the endnotes.

The narratives included in the memoir chapter focus on *the personal*. But somehow *the personal* provides a background closely connected to *the social, the political*, and *the historical*. In the early stages of my life, I did not wonder how my life had been influenced by social or political contexts: things happened as they happened. Without opportunities to see and know the world beyond China during my childhood and adolescence, I had no idea there could be alternative ways of being and of living. Now in retrospect, of course, I realize that there was nothing natural or inevitable about my traumatic separations from my parents: it was the Chinese Communist Party (CCP) that decided that children should be taken away from parents and be sent to the mountains and villages; and it was also the CCP that decided parents should be taken away from their children to be reeducated elsewhere. The personal suffering we had to endure was the consequence of social and political pathologies inflicted on China by the CCP regime.

Tensions and Challenges

Tensions emerged throughout my research process because of the personal nature of the narrative method and the political sensitivity of the project. However, it is precisely the personal exploration that has enabled me to trace the roots of these tensions and to make them transparent to my readers. In this way, the tensions that emerged during the inquiry process have become themes in my inquiry. They are no longer merely abstract questions at the methodological level, but have become part of the actual subject matter.

Another challenge that I have faced has to do with the interdisciplinary nature of this study. Information that may be unnecessary for readers in one field is essential to those who have less knowledge about a given subject. As the author, I have faced the challenge of walking along a tightrope woven from various disciplinary strands to balance various conceptual and theoretical considerations for different readers. Methodologically speaking, I have consciously attempted to attend to different audiences—including those who are familiar with narrative methods and those who are not. The former group may wonder why I defend the approach so forcefully while the latter group may still have a wide range of questions and require more information. But I believe that questions raised about narrative approaches are more questions of perspective than of understanding. In other words, it is not that we do not understand narratives—it is just that we have been trained to conduct research in certain ways and have certain expectations of what research should be like. For me, the best methodology is the one that fits my research needs.

Narrative scholar Carola Conle urges narrative study readers to

> Let yourself be carried by the flow of stories; live with ambivalence for a while, until in the end wholes come into view—although philosophers of hermeneutics will tell us that those wholes are always already constantly in view in the selection of the details, they simply get readjusted as the details become better understood.[74]

I would like to tell my readers the same. Be prepared for a reading experience similar to the experience of doing a jigsaw puzzle. Through the narrative of my story and those of my participants, I hope to invite readers to enter our inner worlds for a more empathetic understanding of our experiences, and to stimulate ongoing and deeper dialogues.

The purpose of this research is not to answer questions such as "how much," "how often," or "so what." The significance of a study does not necessarily lie in filling a hole in the knowledge base. For me, moral purpose is as important as intellectual purpose, and "Ultimately, the research must stand for something."[75] Good research is too often conceived as a methodological question rather than as an ethical one. The educational researcher Karl Hostetler puts it this way:

> It is in the power of every researcher and educator to do something to improve the lives of people. Progress is not always easy, of course. It requires understanding, commitment, compassion, patience, and likely some amount of courage.[76]

For me, research is an experience in space and time, a connection between here and there, between the past and the future, with us living in the present, trying to make old dreams come true. The roots are always there, but our dreams may die. I hope this project will keep the dreams alive—not only my own but also those of others.

CHAPTER 2

Seeds of Fire

If We Want Light, We Must Conquer Darkness[1]

Before I was born, my parents had to leave the city where they grew up to work in the northern mountainous areas. During the Cultural Revolution, the Communist Party promoted the slogan that it was "better to be red than expert." Jobs were assigned by the government and often did not correspond to an individual's skills. My mother, who had trained to be an opera singer, was assigned to work in a factory packed with graduates from universities around the country. My father, who had just graduated from medical school, was sent to work in a different village hospital with "barefoot doctors."[2] Father could not come home every night, and Mother lived alone in a small room she had been assigned, which was near a prison.[3] Once a prisoner escaped and tried to break into Mother's room. She was scared to death. She was rescued by her neighbor, but she told me she was always afraid to be alone in darkness after that.

Later, Mother became pregnant and felt tired and could not perform her work as usual in the factory. She was accused of being lazy and was publicly criticized for not working hard for the Communist cause. She was told to kneel down to admit her mistakes. It was humiliating, but Mother was not the only one who had to do that. She told me many times later in life: "When you are struggling in darkness to survive, dignity and dreams become luxuries."

I would have been born in the mountain area if it had not been for Mother's physical condition. She was allowed to return to the city to give birth. On the day I was born, Mother's aunt walked her to the hospital. It took a while to get the news to Father. When Father finally received permission to return to the city to take the first glimpse of his newborn daughter, he gave me the name "Xiaoqing," meaning "clear dawn" in English, to express his generation's longing for light and justice.

We were soon back in the mountains. Mother became ill again, probably resulting from poor nutrition and overwork. She was operated on several times in the hospital. Father had to work and take care of Mother at the same time. I was left in the care of their friends. Unfortunately, I was not a popular girl because I cried all the time. Mother explained to me when I grew up: "I think you were hungry. I had no mother's milk to feed you. And we had no money to buy milk or milk powder. We later somehow managed to get some milk powder and mix it with other stuff to feed you, but then you had stomachaches and diarrhea all the time. It was so hard to raise you."

Father's aunt, San Gupo, came to our area to help take care of me.[4] San Gupo was the younger sister of my grandfather. Her husband had died shortly after their marriage and she never got married again. According to the Confucian moral code, a woman should remain chaste and faithful to her husband, even after his death. San Gupo was a kind and warmhearted woman. She lived in the same dark and shabby room, where she had first lived with her husband, for her entire life. After we left the mountain area, we invited San Gupo to stay with us, but she insisted that she did not want to leave her home. I could not understand then, and I don't understand even now, how a few months' memory could sustain her to be alone for the rest of her life. She looked so lonely and miserable in that small room. Maybe that room was San Gupo's root. She felt she belonged to that room. Any type of spiritual force, whether we agree with it or not, can be strong enough to move mountains.

It was cold in the mountain area—there was no heat, and no hot water. San Gupo did not wash me every day because of the cold. "You kept crying and crying and nobody understood why you were such a crying girl until one day we found out: Your right upper leg was all rotten because the string for the diaper was too tight and it went deep into your flesh. We felt so sorry for you. Father and I suddenly felt so helpless. We weren't sure if we could bring you up." Mother told me this story many times later on. The scar is still there on my right upper leg. I know it will stay there, like all the hardships carved in my memory; and it will never, ever, be gone with the wind.

Father and Mother decided to send me back to the city to live with my grandmother, my father's mother. I was too young to be sentimental about the separation, but Mother told me that my crying shook the world when I was taken from her arms. For the first time in my life, I left my parents and headed for a place that was strange and uncertain to me.

Grandmother was working in a sewing factory to support the family. My grandfather had died before I was born,[5] leaving behind my grandmother and four young children. My father was the eldest son in the family and my youngest uncle was only 12. Grandmother actually gave birth to five children, but one had died when it was still a baby. Grandmother told me that in those days not every baby survived.

Grandmother met Grandfather at the home of her elder sister, who was a concubine to a rich man much older than her. "It was most miserable to be a concubine," Grandmother told me when I grew older. "But what else could we do? If it had not been for my sister, our family would have been homeless and we would have starved. And I wouldn't have met your grandfather. He was such a nice man. When Seventh Aunt was in trouble, he told me to bring food to them." Seventh Aunt was Grandmother's younger sister, whose husband had been labeled the son of a landlord during the Land Reform Campaign.[6] After being repeatedly persecuted, he hanged himself and died, leaving behind Seventh Aunt and their baby son. Family members and acquaintances normally stayed away in such situations for they would also get into trouble if they ever showed any sympathy. After learning that Seventh Aunt and the baby had been locked up, Grandfather told Grandmother to find a way to bring food to them to rescue them, bringing them to the house where later I stayed with Grandmother.

Father said that Grandfather was an easygoing person with a good temper. Grandfather used to work for his brother, who ran a business. When the Communist Party took power in China, his brother's family fled to Taiwan. During the political campaigns launched by the Communist Party, Grandfather became a scapegoat for his "capitalist" brother. He was politically interrogated, condemned, and threatened. Grandmother told me: "Your grandfather became very sick; and he was timid. So later he died." I heard Grandmother mention many times that Grandfather died because he was timid. I did not quite understand why being timid was related to a person's death. I asked Grandmother what was wrong with not being brave. "Your grandfather had to confess and confess. He wrote materials (*xie cailiao*) to confess even things he never did. He wrote until three o'clock, four o'clock in the morning, but those people were still not satisfied. They said we were hiding things," Grandmother told me.

When I grew up, I came to understand that what Grandmother meant by "timid" was the fear inside Grandfather, the fear of being unreasonably criticized and getting his wife and young children into trouble. In a society without justice, fear is in the air.

Father almost decided not to go to college as he wanted to work to support the family. But when he was accepted by the best medical school in the area,[7] Grandmother said that he should go to the college to become a doctor. She told me later, "Your father was the most intelligent child in the family, and the baby who died was the most handsome one. Your grandfather always said that no matter how difficult it would be, we should give your father a good education." I was surprised that she still remembered what the dead baby looked like. Every child is irreplaceable and the best in the mother's heart.

It turned out that Father did exceptionally well in medical school although he had to walk two hours to school without shoes. Father told me it wasn't a big deal as few people had shoes to wear at that time.

Because Grandmother had to work, I was sent to a *tuoersuo*, a nursery center on our street. Every day, Grandmother would come and take me home in the evening after work. At night, I sat beside Grandmother watching her making soles of shoes to earn some extra money. Every night before going to bed, I asked for Father and Mother. Grandmother would recite the rhyme Father wrote for me: Papa and Mama go to work; Qingqing sleeps with Grandmother; No crying, no kicking off quilts; listen to Grandmother.[8] "If you remain a good girl—no crying—Papa and Mama will come back soon." Grandmother always told me the same thing. When I grew up, Grandmother told me that when she took me to the *tuoersuo* every morning, I never cried, but my eyes were full of tears.

I went to the same nursery center on and off over the years whenever I was left under the care of Grandmother. The so-called nursery center was actually just a room, a cold, dark room packed with kids from the neighborhood. The teachers told my grandmother that I was a terribly quiet girl: I sat next to the door without saying a word or making a move for the whole day. Sometimes Grandmother let me stay home by myself. I hated the darkness surrounding me. I did not turn on the light, as Grandmother told me many times that we could not afford to pay for the electricity. Once again I sat next to the door, waiting for Grandmother to come home. I rarely talked. Grandmother started to worry that I was dumb because my mother had suffered too much when she was bearing me. Grandmother kept saying I was a poor girl. I was not sure if I was poor or not. I wanted to be next to the door, waiting for the sunset, waiting for Grandmother. I missed Papa and Mama. I did not know where they were, why they did not come to see me. They left me in that cold dark room. I was scared. I wanted to see light. I wanted light.

On a cold winter afternoon, I was put into bed to take a nap at the *tuoersuo*. I shared a small bed with another child. The child took my blanket, the blue goldfish blanket that my parents bought for me, and did not share it with me. I was left in the cold but I did not speak out. When Grandmother came to pick me up after work, she found I was running a high fever. She sent an urgent telegram to my parents (there were no telephones), and Mother rushed back to see me. To make things worse, Mother was so worried when she arrived that she fed me the wrong medicine. She fed me the poisonous medicinal liquor for fractures, which had been put into an empty cough syrup bottle by Grandmother. Grandmother later described the scene to me: "Your mother was desperate when she discovered what she had done. She carried you and ran to the Children's Hospital. You know, there was no taxi, and it took a long time to wait for the public buses. I don't know how your mother managed to carry you to run such a long way to the hospital. We all thought you were dying."

Father and Mother decided to take me back to the villages. Before we left, Grandmother kept saying: "Qing should come back to the city to attend elementary school later. How can she climb those mountains to go to school? She looks so weak. She can't do that." When I first started graduate school in Toronto, Grandmother still mentioned in our phone conversations that she had been worried that I had to climb mountains to go to school. I told her that I did not have to climb mountains to go to school in Canada, but I had to walk in snow in winter. "Snow is better than mountains," Grandmother said.

"Why do you have to go to school for so many years? You should get married and have a home. Marry a nice man who will take care of you." In Grandmother's eyes, I am always that quiet little child. She wants me to have a home, a home that she hasn't had for a long time—too long for me to count how many years it has been.

I was back to the mountains and rivers of the wilderness. I started to make friends with other children in the area. I was happier there than before until one day I saw a doll. I had never seen a doll before. I went back home and told Mother about the doll I had seen: "It was beautiful, Mama. Can I have one?" I asked Mother. "We will buy you one later," Mother said. "But when?" I kept asking the same questions and went to see the lovely doll every day. I wished it were my doll, and I was unhappy with Mama for not keeping her promise to buy me one. Until one day, I suddenly "grew up."

One afternoon, while I was playing with my little friends along the riverside, I found something shining on the sand. I went over and saw a watch. I picked it up and recognized it was Papa's watch. I could not be wrong. It was Papa's watch. I had seen Papa wearing it every day on his hand. Papa must have forgotten his watch after washing clothes by the river. I put the watch in my pocket and hurriedly ran home. When I got home, before I had a chance to talk, Mother told me in a low voice: "Be a good girl today. Don't bother Papa. Don't ask about the doll. Papa is not in a good mood today. He has lost his watch." A watch was something precious during the Cultural Revolution. Father looked worried. "But I found Papa's watch," I shouted out. The rest of the story can be imagined: Father and Mother were excited and asked me where and how I had found it. I told them, feeling proud of myself. I did not ask for a doll after that, and I did not get my own doll until we left the mountains and settled down in a town. My finding of the watch is one of the stories that Father tells to this day.

Now, in retrospect, I can feel the pain that Father and Mother suffered during those days. Physical hardship may be tolerable, but spiritual deprivation is always harder to bear. Being exiled from home, Father and Mother, and many others of their generation, survived with broken dreams. As the exiled Chinese poet Bei Dao[9] puts it: "In an age without heroes, I just want to be a man." I never failed to feel the dilemma Chinese intellectuals faced under the rule of the Communist Party. In the eyes of those in power, intellectuals were a group suspected of being rebellious. Keeping them on the edge of survival was a means of control. Intellectual independence and human dignity could hardly be achieved without financial independence. How many human beings still have the heart to rebel if they have a little daughter at home, waiting for milk, waiting for a doll, waiting for light?

Father's spirit was never broken. Every night he taught himself English by reciting vocabulary from the English version of Mao's little red book; I saw him writing down English words on small cards and carrying them wherever he went. When I asked him why he did that, he explained in a very simple way that he wanted to learn English. What confused me more was that at night Father held our old-fashioned radio listening to a program called "VOA": Voice of America. He asked me not to tell people that he listened to VOA; otherwise we could "get in trouble." He looked serious when he said that and I made sure that I did not let out his secret.

The mystery is no longer mysterious today. For political reasons, Father did not get a chance to study English in university; instead, he studied Russian. Driven by a strong desire to know about Western culture, society, and politics, and most of all to update himself about what was going on in the world, Father embarked upon his dangerous English-learning journey. People growing up in a democratic society may find it difficult to understand how precious freedom is for those who are kept in darkness in a confined society.

Even now, I am amazed by Father's strong motivation to learn a foreign language under such difficult circumstances. What surprises me most is that using this primitive self-teaching method, he successfully mastered a large vocabulary and complex grammatical rules, which eventually enabled him to publish complex translations of research in medical journals later in his life.

Father's self-teaching was not limited to English. He taught himself how to write classical Chinese poetry (*jiutishi*), a type of classical Chinese literature. Classical Chinese is different from modern Chinese. Understanding the verses, rhymes, and allusions in those poems in classical Chinese is as difficult as understanding Old English for modern English readers, not to mention writing in these archaic forms of language. As an enthusiast of classical Chinese poetry, Father went to a bookstore that sold ancient books (*guji shudian*) in his school years and read there for hours. Once again, he had to walk without shoes from school to the store. It was under such conditions that Father taught himself the stylistic art of classical Chinese poetry. When Professor Yu Ying-shih at Princeton University wrote an introduction to Father's collection of poetry, *Lighting the Candles*, I felt very proud of Father: the world's leading critic of classical Chinese culture was praising Father's self-taught poetry writing.

The title of Father's poetry collection comes from a famous ancient Chinese household saying: "Zhou Guan [those in power] can feel free to set fires, while the commoners are not even allowed to light the candles." Father has lit the candles in my heart: whenever I am in darkness, I will think of his unbroken spirit, and that of many others of his generation, who have never given up conquering darkness for light. The seeds of hope they planted in my heart blossom, guiding me toward the light.

Because of Mother's special training as an opera singer, by the end of the Cultural Revolution, she was allowed to work for an opera group in a small town close to the city where she and Father grew up. The family was thrilled because we might be allowed to leave the mountains if Mother did a good job. Father and I moved from the area where Mother used to work to his work area. Father was on call for medical emergencies and I was often left home alone by myself. He left the door unlocked so that neighbors, friends, and colleagues could stop by to see me or to feed me. After a while, I was again sent to live with Grandmother.

One day Father showed up out of nowhere at Grandmother's home in the city. He first took me close to a building and spoke to someone, he then took me to an area where we could see the building from afar. "Wave to Mother, Qing, wave to Mother." I didn't know what was going on but I did as Father told me. It turned out that Mother had developed acute hepatitis while traveling with her opera troupe and was now being kept in the Hospital for Infectious Diseases. During her illness all Mother could do was to ask to see her daughter from the hospital window. For me, after being under the care of so many strangers at different places, Mother became a vague image of a woman waving from afar.

Father and I were at last permitted to join Mother in the town. We packed every little thing we had and got on the train. I was once again on a journey to a strange world. Father was assigned to work in the People's Hospital. He still needed to go to villages to treat patients from time to time. When Father published his book *Case Studies on Internal Medicine* years later, a journalist for a city newspaper where Father grew up came to our town to interview him. He called Father a "village doctor" in his report titled *Followers Blossom in Every Corner: A Village Doctor Writes a Medical Book*. We had a good laugh in the family because Father was regarded as a "village doctor" by his city fellows.

I started to travel with Mother and her opera troupe from one place to another. I was still a shy and quiet girl, but now I was being exposed to new people, new places, and new things. I saw people talking to Mother with admiration, saying she was a rising star on the opera stage. One day I went up to Father and talked to him seriously. I told him I didn't want to stay in the town any more. I told him it was boring living there. I wanted to go to the city, like the places I had visited with Mother. I wanted to get out of the town. I cannot remember the details of Father's reply. He said a lot. The only thing I remembered was that Father told me if I wanted to get out of the town, I should learn how to fly, like the free birds in the sky.

Father and Mother were both busy at work. I stayed at home a lot by myself. I did not like the silence and I was scared in our dark room. I usually put my small stool beside the door and held in my lap my best company—the old radio that Father had used to listen to VOA. Although there were no interesting programs available at that time, I liked to hear some sound. I watched people in the street and I could recognize almost everyone passing by day after day. I observed their clothes and facial expressions, trying to guess what was on their mind. I remember once I saw a young woman wearing a pink dress and earrings, something rare at the time. I thought she was beautiful and wished that I could dress like that. At the same time, I overheard people describing her as "a bad woman" because she dressed differently. In those days, everyone was shaped in the same mold and there was no room for being special. When individual differences were not allowed, anyone who behaved differently was condemned and despised. The love and appreciation of human nature for beauty became twisted and ended up being contradictorily associated with contempt.

I sometimes went to the home of our neighbor, my little friend Ming, to play. Unlike our family, Ming's family had been in the town for generations, so they had many family members around. Ming sometimes sang and danced with her young relatives on the street. When Mother was around, she would encourage me to join them, but I was so shy that they said I could only be their audience. I felt like an outsider.

Ming was the same age as me and her father was a driver. The adults always said that the three most admirable professions were doctor, driver, and pork butcher. But I felt that Ming's father had a better job than my father. Ming's family was the only one in the neighborhood that had a TV, a nine-inch black-and-white. That was a major attraction for all the kids in the area, but Ming's mother did not want too many children crowding their house. My parents too told me not to bother Ming's family, so I would be careful even though I wanted to watch TV. Every night I would keep an eye on Ming's family door—if the door was open, I felt it was possible that I was welcome to go in. I often waited in suspense and excitement. One day Father heard on the radio that there would be a Charlie Chaplin film shown on TV. "It is a very funny film, Qing. You should watch this one," Father told me. Father told me which channel it was on and made sure that my little brain would not forget it. It was like a special occasion for me. Mother cooked dinner early and washed me early. I did not have to shower myself, even though I was no longer a baby, because my parents were afraid that I would fall ill in the cold weather. They boiled some hot water to wash me every day.

Ten minutes before the film was scheduled to start—the TV programs were never on time in those days—Mother went with me to knock at Ming's door. "I wonder if Qing can come and watch TV tonight." Mother said some nice words and I was allowed in. I was reciting the channel number Father had told me. Ming was watching a different channel with some other kids. I watched the clock and wished they would change the channel. Half an hour passed, and they were still watching the same channel. I summoned enough courage and asked in a low voice: "Ming, could you change to a different channel? Father said there is a funny film." "No, we like this one," Ming answered. Actually they were watching something really boring. Perhaps it was just children's nature to try to be in control. I did not dare to ask again. I waited and waited, without saying a word. When Mother finally knocked at the door to take me home, I was disappointed. When I stepped into our door, Father asked anxiously: "Did you have a good laugh, Qing? Did you like the film?" I was already in tears and could not speak a word. It took quite a while for Father and Mother to figure out what had happened. I cannot remember the rest. Probably I was too tired or sleepy. Every time I recalled this, I felt sorry for Father and Mother. They tried to give me the best, but they did not have much to give me. I wish I had been stronger.

During festivals such as the Spring Festival (the Chinese lunar New Year), Father and Mother took me back to the city to see my grandmothers, uncles, and aunts. Every time we went, we would carry two chickens with us as gifts for my two grandmothers. In Chinese tradition, chicken for the New Year is like turkey for Christmas in the West. Chicken was a luxury at that time, so only during important festivals would we eat chicken.

The idea of going to the city was exciting, but the trip was terrifying. We first took the bus, and then transferred to a ferry. Both the bus and the ferry were packed with people—it was not just crowded. I was too small to be noticed. People often stepped on me and I cried out in protest. I kept telling Mother I could not breathe but there was nothing she could do, since it was impossible for them to hold me in their arms while the bus was moving. They needed both arms to stand safely. Once we got off the bus, Father and Mother had to run fast in order to find seats on the ferry, since seats were not assigned beforehand when the tickets were issued. Whoever ran fastest and fought all the way from the bus station to the ferry station would get seats. So actually we did not "find" seats—instead, we fought for seats. Father and Mother ran so fast that I was worried they would lose me. People pushed me in different directions and I was not sure where I was heading. I kept shouting, "Mama, wait for me. I am here. Wait for me." Mother would usually stop and hold me in her arms. Father sometimes would slow down as well to make sure we were all right. When that happened, we failed to get a seat and I had to stand several hours with the crowd. My little feet soon got tired, and Father and Mother had to take turns holding me in their arms. I looked into the sky—I wished I was one of those birds, flying freely through the sky.

When we got to the city, the first place we went to after we got off the ferry would be the bookstore street.[10] Mother joked that even if I got lost, I could ask the police to take me to the bookstore street and I would be able to find Father there. The public transportation in the city was crowded and inconvenient so we usually walked from one place to another. I didn't like going to the bookstores at all. Father would stay there for hours, carrying our heavy luggage and the two chickens we had brought for Grandmothers. I looked at those piles and piles of books and could never figure out why Father liked that place so much. I did understand that Father could not afford to bring those books home because buying books was a big deal for us. When we eventually got to Grandmother's home at night, Grandmother would ask me: "Did you go to the bookstores again?" I nodded my head and Grandmother would say: "Poor Qingqing. Your father is a bookworm."

There was one place that I enjoyed going to in the city—a museum, "the five-story tower," located inside a local park.[11] Once Grandmother took me to the museum and I was attracted by the things inside the exhibition glass boxes. When Grandmother told Father about my interest in museums, Father took me there himself one day. It was on that day that I first saw "foreigners" (*waiguoren*).[12]

China was a closed society at that time, so few foreigners traveled in the country. When I saw those two Western people, an old couple, I was curious.

"What is that?" I asked Father. Instead of saying "who are they?" I asked "what is that?"

"They are foreigners." Father seemed to be happy that I got a chance to open my eyes.

"What was that sister (*jiejie*) saying to them?" I was referring to a young Chinese woman accompanying the couple.

"She is speaking English. She is their interpreter," Father told me. That was the first time in my life that I heard the word "interpreter."

Father tried to explain to me that "English" is a language different from what we spoke and an "interpreter" was someone who knew both languages.

"You should learn English then you can go out and see the world!" I still remember Father's facial expression when he said those words to me. That sounded very special. At that time, ordinary Chinese would never dream of getting out of the country, but Father said that there was a "world" for me to see!

Ever since then, when people asked me what I wanted to do when I grew up, I would no longer say "teacher," "doctor," or "scientist" as I used to. I would say *"fanyi,"* interpreter. People would usually ask: "What? What is *'fanyi'*? This kid is full of strange ideas." My dream profession did change many times as I was growing up. However, believe it or not, some twenty years later, I was granted immigrant status to Canada as an interpreter.

When Mao died in 1976, Father invited his best friend to our home, closed the door tightly, and opened the only bottle of wine our family had. The next day, my parents brought me to the local memorial service for Mao, a compulsory political task. I saw people all wearing black armbands, a traditional sign of mourning. As a little girl, I was confused by the adults' facial expressions— everyone looked so sad in public while Father and his friend seemed to be full of joy the night before. Then came the time when all the plaster statues of Mao were torn down and I heard people constantly mentioning the word *"pingfan"* (rehabilitation)—a term used in connection with people who had been wrongly treated by the Communist Party.

I was growing up. Before I understood enough words to read, Mother read me lots of storybooks. Every night I would not go to bed without hearing a story. The *Collections of Fairytales* by the Danish writer Hans Christian Andersen was my favorite. I especially liked the story of the poor little girl who sold matches on the street on Christmas Eve. I often asked Mother to repeat that story for me. The match girl was so cold and hungry that she could not help lighting the last few matches she was selling. Each time she lit a match, she imagined she had turkey, warmth, and love. The next morning people found her body on the street. She died. Her helpless struggle and the longing for light left a deep impression on me.

Father and Mother started to teach me how to read and write Chinese characters. I was also required to recite three English words and one ancient Chinese poem each day as a condition to be able to go out to play with other kids. Those English words and ancient Chinese couplets were simply sounds to me; they did not make any sense. None of my little friends had the same task. However, I did as I was told, in order to trade with Father for playtime. Realizing that I needed a better language-learning environment and motivation, Father spent all our savings to buy me a tape recorder, the most luxurious possession we owned at that time. Father even managed to buy a set of language materials with a book and two tapes from Hong Kong. I was quickly attracted by the colorful textbook and the funny music played between the conversations. I tried to attach the English words to the corresponding pictures and figure out the sound of words spoken in the conversation. Even though I still could not spell a single English word, this learning process later proved to be extremely helpful. When I first started my formal English education in school, I found myself far ahead of others in terms of vocabulary and my ability to distinguish words in different contexts. Those ancient Chinese poems that Father made me recite have had a lifelong impact on me, too. They have shaped the way I remember and express—in images.

Father also bought me some colorful books of science stories. Unfortunately, I turned out to be slow in science. By the time I could read the newspaper, Father chose some articles which he thought were suitable for me. Every night at dinner time, we sat around our little dining table and discussed what I read in the newspaper. I was encouraged to voice my opinions. For most Chinese, chatting around the dining table gives a real sense of home and family. Our "home" continued until my parents divorced. Although we later had a nicer apartment, and although I later drifted from one corner of the world to another, those moments we spent in the crowded twenty-four-square-meter home keep coming back to me.

On the first day I attended elementary school, I embarrassed myself because the teacher found I did not write my name correctly. I wrote my name as "Xiao," which means "dawn" in English, with a dot in the upper-right corner. However, my teacher said that the dot should not be there. My classmates laughed at me when the teacher corrected me because they thought I was stupid not to know how to write my name. Now I view the missing dot in my name as the light at dawn. I struggle in darkness to search for my light, my dawn, and myself.

That was not the only time I embarrassed myself. I knew from hearing adults' conversations that Father was *youwenhua*, "a man with literacy/culture." In Chinese, we use the word *wenhua* to mean "education." In order to show Father that I started to acquire some "culture" after starting school, I told him at dinnertime about the writers, poets, articles, and history stories that I had learned in school. To my surprise, Father often commented differently on those authors and pieces. He would say things that I could not fully understand such as a "Mao follower," "a running dog of the Communist Party," "a writer with no integrity," or "a piece of propaganda." When I went back to school, I would tell my little friends things such as "my father said this writer is not that great." My friends would usually react with certainty: "Didn't you listen to the teachers? Didn't you read the textbook? He is a great writer! Your father doesn't know anything. Your father has no culture!" It was face-losing and confusing. I was not sure who was right and who knew better—my father or my teachers. I tended to believe the teachers because they were the authority in school. I sometimes thought maybe Father didn't have that much "culture." There was one time that I was sure that one of my little friends was wrong. One day my friend Yin suddenly said to me: "Who do you think is better-looking, Chairman Mao or Mao Zedong?"

"Are they referring to the same person?" I asked.

"No, I think Chairman Mao is Mao Zedong's brother. And Chairman Mao is more important because we only say 'Long live Chairman Mao' and we don't say 'Long live Mao Zedong," Yin replied.

"I think they are the same person!" I was pretty sure this time.

When I went home, I told my parents about Yin's question and they assured me: "Yes, Qing, you are right. Chairman Mao is Mao Zedong!"

It was not until many years later that I realized that teachers did not necessarily teach what they knew and what they believed—they had to teach what they were told to teach.

In school, I was greatly influenced by the Communist curriculum. I grew into an enthusiastic and idealistic young girl. I had dreams and I admired heroes. I believed in the principle of rightness—there was no gray area, only right or wrong. Political education was dominant both inside and outside the classroom, and it was meant to cultivate our spirits to sacrifice for higher causes. We were taught that in order to realize communism, we should be ready to sacrifice our happiness and even our lives. We studied hard in order to "serve the people." I spent lots of my spare time in elementary school doing "good deeds" with my schoolmates, such as sweeping streets. I joined the Young Pioneers in elementary school and the Communist Youth League in high school, a step before joining the Communist Party, all of which were regarded as real badges of honor. After school we lined up in formation in order to foster our collective spirits. Marching proudly out of our school campus, we sang together the *Song of the Young Pioneers*: "We do not fear hardship nor the enemy; study hard and struggle with resolve; toward victory we courageously advance. We are the heirs of communism."

There were blackouts throughout my school years. The electric power supply would go off at any time without any advance notice. We never knew when the lights would come back on. If I hadn't finished my homework, I would have to work by the candlelight. Father and Mother were worried that the dim light would affect my eyesight, so they would hold a flashlight by my left side while I was writing with my right hand. If Grandmother was staying with us, she would take turns as well. Gradually, I learned that I had better finish homework before it got dark so that I wouldn't have to worry about studying in the darkness.

Father was busy with his work and his writings. In order to spend more time with the family, Mother quit performing on the stage. She gave birth to my younger brother just months before the one-child policy was implemented. Father gave my brother a poetic name that carried the meaning of "looking up to the sky and looking forward to the future." My brother did not like this name, though, because it was difficult to write and other kids thought it was a strange name. The whole family, especially my grandmothers, was very happy that at last we had a boy in the family. Boys were considered more important. Everybody kept saying that my brother would have never come into the world if he had come a few months later—Mother would have had to have an abortion under the one-child policy. My family was one of the few among those of my parents' former college classmates that had more than one child. Unlike my parents, by the time their classmates returned to their professional jobs and settled down, the one-child policy had already been implemented.

It turned out that my brother liked stories as much as I did. He showed great interest in storybooks. Since he was too young to read any words, he asked me to tell him the stories in the children's picturebooks. I enjoyed doing that a lot. So, just as Mother had told me stories at bedtime, I told my brother stories during our playtime. We started to collect storybooks but our collection grew slowly. So I told the same stories over and over, but my brother seemed to enjoy them just the same. Even before we could buy a new book, we would walk a long way to the New China Bookstore, the only one in our town, to look at the books and discuss what we would buy next time. I still remember the excitement after we had saved enough money for a new book and we would run all the way to the bookstore. I cherish the memory of holding my brother's hand and seeing him trying to run fast on his little feet.

In school I participated in all kinds of extracurricular activities. I read books from Father's desk I found interesting and wrote my own diaries. I loved subjects related to the arts, but continuously failed all the science exams. Father said I was hopeless in mathematics. I knew Father did very well in mathematics when he was in medical school. I had heard him talk about DNA, so I told Mother that there must be something wrong with my DNA. My science teachers believed that my failure in science classes was a result of my spending too much time playing. Extracurricular activities were considered a waste of time. Since I did not prove to be a "focused student" in school, Father said I should learn some other things in my spare time. They found me a painting teacher and an English tutor through their circle of friends. For many years, I spent my evenings learning Chinese ink-and-water paintings at my teacher's home and my Saturdays learning English at my tutor's home.

My painting teacher Qu was a talented artist and writer, and he was also an "old Communist." When someone was called an "old Communist," it didn't necessarily mean that he was an old man. It simply meant that this person had been a Communist Party member for a long time. Teacher Qu was one such person. By the time he started to teach me, he had gone through various political campaigns and he was no longer that blindly idealistic. However, he still lived, wrote, and taught with passion, which might have had a lot to do with his artistic disposition. After the Tiananmen Massacre, Teacher Qu told us that the Communist Party was not like that earlier. "This is not the Communist Party I joined—we had good Party members and we worked hard for the people. It was a different Communist Party," he said with disappointment.

My English tutor, Teacher Chen, also had great influence on me in the small town. Teacher Chen had been one of the victims of the "Anti-Rightist Campaign" that Mao launched in the late 1950s when intellectuals were first encouraged to express their thoughts, and then cruelly persecuted. Teacher Chen was labeled a "rightist" and his wife had to divorce him. I heard my parents say that Teacher Chen and his wife loved each other when they were forced to separate. Teacher Chen was sent to work in a village and later he was allowed to live in the same town as we did. He rarely told me about his past, probably because he thought I was too young to understand. The only thing I remember was that he once mentioned he had to live with pigs in the village. By the time Teacher Chen was "rehabilitated" by the Party, his former wife had already remarried. I sensed that Teacher Chen still loved her. When I was young, I did not quite understand why Teacher Chen's wife did not wait for Teacher Chen but married someone else, but now I understand that in those days, people never dreamed of such a thing as "rehabilitation." To be reunited with someone you loved was too good to hope for. When human beings had to live like animals, all they would hope for was not to live with the animals, with the pigs.

Father continued his writing late every night, but the money he received for his publications was not enough to pay for the electricity. Knowledge was not worth anything. I overheard conversations among adults saying that Father could have been promoted to be the head of the hospital, which meant that we would have been assigned a bigger apartment and Father would have had his salary raised, if only he had agreed to join the Communist Party. But he refused. At that time, I did not understand why Father was so stubborn with his so-called conscience. In a young girl's eyes, a nice apartment weighed more than integrity and conscience.

That was not all. Like most Chinese intellectuals, Father took a nap every noon before he went back to work in the afternoon. Father said the nap helped him to work more efficiently and asked me to keep absolutely quiet at noon; however, there was one exception. Father asked me to wake him up if patients came to see him on Wednesdays. Father wrote them prescriptions and they left happily. Father was not paid to do that. In those days, even if a doctor saw 1,000 patients a day, he or she would be paid the same salary. I did not understand why those patients did not go to the hospital, but came to our home to wake up Father. Father seemed to read my mind and explained it to me:

Those patients live on their boats in some remote water villages. They come every Wednesday for my specialist services. They set out before midnight on Tuesday night and have to row for many hours to be able to get here at noon. If they had to line up in the hospital in the afternoon, they would not be able to get home until tomorrow. These people live a tough life. You are very much blessed. You should learn how to value what you have, and meanwhile, learn to understand others' difficulties. Learn to be compassionate, be warm-hearted. Live with conscience and integrity. I think you are old enough to learn how to be a decent human being.

When I grew up and came to understand the world better, I strongly felt Father's impact on me, even when I was like a boat drifting in the sea, and a candle flickering in the wind.

"At last, our country has hope!" Father shouted with excitement when the 1989 pro-democracy movement broke out across the country. "Long live freedom!" "Long live human rights!" I shouted with pride among the peacefully demonstrating crowd. We were so used to the slogan "Long live Chairman Mao!" that we still used the same Cultural Revolution language when we pushed for political reforms. Still, that was the first manifestation of my youthful idealism after years of Communist political education.[13] Sadly, our dream of greater freedom and political reform was shattered by the machine-gun fire in the center of Beijing on the night of June 3.

I went to school wearing a black armband. The news that "our army has won a glorious victory over a counter-revolutionary turmoil" was repeated everywhere. My teacher came to me and said, "I know what is on your mind. But if you don't take off that armband right away, no one will protect you from now on!" I took off the armband reluctantly while trying to hold back my tears. At that moment, I thought of Father's contrasting facial expressions of joy and sorrow when Mao died. For two generations, we were not allowed to express even our basic human feelings of sorrow and joy. I asked Father: "Where is dawn? And when is dawn?!"

Father started to burn the poems he had written during the movement and also urged me to burn my diary. One of Father's friends, Chen, wrote some poems to express his anger and sent them to a magazine in Hong Kong. The mail was confiscated and Chen was sentenced to three years' imprisonment. I found his prison's mailing address from Father's drawer and secretly sent him postcards. I did not leave a return address and Chen did not know who I was. But I did write on the cards my name and the name of my university. Many years later, I accidentally found out from another friend of Father that Chen had been searching for someone named "Xiaoqing" after he was released. He even went to check out dorms at my university to look for me. I was glad to know that I had done something meaningful. I never met Chen in person. Father told me that after being released from prison, Chen was dismissed from the government position he had held before and had turned to writing *wanlian* to the dead in a funeral home to support his family. *Wanlian* are traditional scrolls attached to funeral wreaths, which people use to express their feelings about the dead with classical poems, verses, and calligraphy. I always wished that I could send Chen hope again, as I did when he was imprisoned, but I didn't know what "hope" means for a talented poet working in a funeral home.

I got to hear many other stories about those who had suffered or had lost their family members. I felt a strong sense of guilt although I was not responsible for the massacre. Maybe that is what people call "survivor's guilt." I did not allow myself any entertainment or vacation. I considered it a sin to enjoy life with the thought that many others were suffering in prison or in exile. I later realized that I was not exceptional among those of the Tiananmen Generation. Ironically, we became the best illustration of the two central themes in Communist education—"sacrifice" and "idealism."

The year I was supposed to go to college, I was recommended by my high school to attend a university in the area. Being recommended meant that I did not have to take the stressful "once in a lifetime" national entrance exams that decided the future of every student in China—I would be admitted to the university that I was recommended to as long as I did well in tests on a particular subject. I took the English tests given by the university and received the top scores on both the oral and written tests. The whole family was happy and we took it for granted that I would soon receive an admission letter. I did not even go to school to prepare for the exam. Then the nightmare came.

One day, just a few weeks before the national exam, my English teacher sent my best friend D to see me in the late afternoon after school.

"Teacher C asked me to tell you to go to school for the evening study," D said in her always soft voice.

All high school students in our area starting from Junior One were required to go to school for "evening study" six days a week. But I had stopped going since I thought I didn't need to worry about exams anymore.

"Why?" I asked anxiously.

"I don't know," D answered without looking into my eyes.

Having known her for over ten years, I could tell that she was hiding something.

"Tell me. What happened? Does it have something to do with my admission?"

After urging her a couple times, D eventually nodded her head: "There is a problem. I don't know the details. Go to school tonight and the teachers will talk to you. Don't worry too much." Then she left.

I felt the sky was falling. Later I found out that my place had been taken by someone else, whose mother was in charge of the admissions office for our area.

Within a few days, Father started visiting some "powerful" people—the last thing he wanted ever to do in his life. One day he came home and talked to Mother quietly in the bedroom: "I need more money." "We have nothing left. You have taken all our savings."

Compared to powerful officials, we had so little. I kept crying until I lost my voice. One afternoon Father came to my room to talk to me. He sat by my bed and put his hand on my shoulder. He lowered his head, and said to me in a deep low voice: "Qing, I am sorry. I am so sorry." That was the first time in my life that I saw Father crying in front of me. I knew what was on his mind. He was sorry because he had sacrificed my future for his conscience. I wiped my tears and promised myself that I would never make Father feel sorry for me again.

I almost did not sleep during the weeks before the national exam. I surpassed my previous performance and was admitted to my first-choice university. That was the first time I passed the mathematics exam in senior high school. My mathematics teacher said it was a miracle.

After June 4, the Communist Party started to implement policies to boost economic development in order to build a new image, both domestically and internationally. Dramatic economic transformation and social changes were underway.

Upon university graduation, I left the city and went back to work in the small town where I had grown up. By then the town had become one of the most prosperous areas in China. It attracted graduates from top universities around the country. "To get rich" seemed to have become the only goal in the society. When I told people I would like to go back to graduate school, they thought I was stupid. My neighbor Ming had started to work after junior high school. She was envied by the families in the neighborhood because she had been making money for years. I felt life was unpredictable. When we watched TV together in the same room, we never imagined that our life paths could be so different. People say personality determines fate. I wonder if we are born with a destiny.

I worked for two state banks in the town and then returned to the city to work for two international financial institutions. Again, people said I was stupid to leave such well-paid jobs in a prosperous area. I started to think of the struggles Father and Mother had gone through when they were my age, but it must have been much harder. They didn't even have a choice. I had always tried to return to somewhere, since my early childhood, without knowing where I belonged and where my next destination would be. I sometimes feel I belong everywhere, and sometimes that I belong nowhere.

Every book of life comes to an end on its last page; however, the charm of our spirits can carry on forever, from one generation to another. It lights the candles for those in darkness, and moves mountains to make paths for travelers on their life journeys. "Life is too short for waiting when I see the setting sun, and I know again that I must carry on."[14] If we want light, we must conquer darkness.

Self-Exile: Home away from Home

Having been exiled during my early childhood, I decided to exile myself to Canada, the only country that was accepting professional immigrants from China. The decision was shocking to my friends and colleagues. In my mid-twenties I was an executive in an international company with a good salary and many privileges. People said that life as a new immigrant would be tough and that, as a first-generation immigrant, I would never be as successful as I was in China. I had no idea if I was going to be successful or not. I knew that I did not leave for a better material life like earlier generations did, although I wasn't able to articulate clearly why I left and what exactly I was looking for.

In March 1998, after going through all customs procedures at Hong Kong International Airport, I boarded a Canadian Airlines[15] flight. I had my long hair cut very short the night before, symbolizing a new life in a new land. Flying in the sky over the Pacific Ocean, I tried to search for my song of youth, but I could not sing. Heading for an exotic land with my dream of freedom, I was not excited. I knew I was leaving, leaving the land and the people I valued behind. I did not want to leave, but I chose to leave. I left what I love and I left because I love.

When I walked out of Vancouver International Airport, I had nothing but the two suitcases I was carrying. I started looking for jobs with my English name "Rowena" on my resume. I had given myself this name when I first entered college in China. Not knowing what "Rowena" meant and never having read *Ivanhoe*, I picked it simply because I wanted a name that started with "r" and ended with an "a"—the sound of it warmed my heart. I could have chosen "Rebecca," but somehow I felt Rowena was me, and I was Rowena.

I applied for all kinds of jobs and worked full-time, part-time, day-time, night shift, for a trading company, an immigration company, an education center, a tourism company, an advertising agency, and trade fairs. Many times when I at last opened the door of my so-called home after work, I found myself in tears. Waking up in the middle of the night I asked myself: "Where am I? Why am I here?"

One day, feeling weak, I happened to find a small quiet park near where I was living. Some children were playing on the swings. I had never dared to sit on a swing when I was a kid in China but somehow on that day I wanted to give it try—I wanted to be like those carefree Canadian children. I used my toes to touch the sand on the ground and started to swing higher and higher. For a moment, I was scared, but gradually I felt liberated. I was so close to the sky—a bright blue sky that I had never experienced in China. An inexplicable but unimaginably strong force, almost religious, hit me. I felt as if the dead of Tiananmen were watching me from heaven. I whispered to them a promise that I have kept ever since: I will not give up until truth is told and justice is done.

On a weekend afternoon I visited the public library in the neighborhood with my newly received library card. The library was small but cozy, with sunshine coming through the large windows, and people reading in different corners, relaxed. I went up to the librarian, without a second's hesitation, and asked: "Do you have any books on June 4 in China?" In those days, I had no clue that outside of China people didn't use the term "June 4" to describe the events of 1989. When the helpful librarian pointed me to the History Section, I found three books on Tiananmen. Ten years after Tiananmen, in 1999, in a small Vancouver public library, for the first time, I was holding in my hands books on a historic event that had had such a subtle but significant impact on my life. I checked out the books and burned the midnight oil to read them. "So people do know what happened to us and the world does care," I thought to myself. I wrote to all three authors, expressing my gratitude to them for their writing those books and also my frustration that historical truth had been buried inside my country. I never imagined that ten years later I would be teaching a seminar on Tiananmen at Harvard, listing two of those three books as required texts on my syllabus.

When I had saved up some money, I decided to do what I had been longing to do—apply to graduate schools. I couldn't make up my mind if I should apply for an MBA program or something else. An MBA degree seemed to be a natural fit with my background in business and it was a popular choice. But since 1989, I idealistically, if naively, believed that education was the key to a better China. Although I wasn't able to talk about education the way I do now—that institutional and constitutional changes might happen overnight, but it takes generations to change people's minds; that democratic mechanisms are a prerequisite, but they do not guarantee the establishment of a civil society—I believed in the power of education. I applied to education programs at five schools across the country. Worrying that no school would accept a new immigrant from an ordinary college in China, I worked hard to prepare for the Test of English as a Foreign Language (TOEFL), with the assumption that exam results were all that would count.

Whenever I didn't need to work, I buried myself in the Central Library in downtown Vancouver with a bottle of water and a lunch box, using their TOEFL preparation books. The day before the test, I took a day off from work; and on the day of the test, I got a ride to the test center. Hoping to perform better, I poured two packages of Chinese instant coffee in my mug and drank them up before leaving home. I almost got a perfect score in every single section, and I was accepted by all five schools.

Reading carefully those admission letters, I wished I had had someone to turn to for advice before making a decision. A friend who had lived in Toronto told me that the University of Toronto was a good school but I should probably visit all the schools before I made such a big decision. That idea sounded insane to me as such trips would be costly. It wasn't until I started to teach freshman students at Harvard that I realized that parents took their children for campus tours before they applied to colleges. I had never visited my college in China until I started school there; I had never been to Canada before I landed in Vancouver; and I had never been to Toronto before spending eight years in the city for graduate study. When you don't have a choice, you don't choose.

After spending two years in Vancouver, I was once again on the road. In 2000, I arrived at the Toronto International Airport, carrying the same two suitcases that I had carried from China to Vancouver. I traveled from one corner of the world to the other, searching for the key to my June 4 complex, for my lost dawn.

I ended up spending the next eight years at the University of Toronto finishing my masters' and doctoral degrees. I became deeply involved with generations of dissidents in Chinese diasporic communities, particularly in the Tiananmen student exile community, sharing the fate and experience of those who were punished for speaking truth to power.

I went to Toronto with hope and I initially proposed to write a thesis titled *Keeping the dream alive: The Tiananmen Generation's song of youth*. The title itself reflected my idealistic, romantic, and revolutionary sentiments toward the unfinished cause of 1989. I think from the very beginning I have been waiting for a happy ending. Despite all the obstacles along the way, I kept reminding myself not to lose faith in history—that justice will be done. But by the time I was supposed to conclude my study, I didn't see light at the end of the tunnel: I didn't feel that history had yet given me a fair ending. Unlike the darkness of 1989—a pure terror backed up by guns and tanks to silence the voice of a generation—this time it was a more subtle terror from a new generation that was programmed to treat lies as truth. I turned my concern into a postdoctoral proposal titled *Identifying with a "Rising China"? Overseas Chinese student nationalism*, and this brought me to Harvard in 2008. By the time my proposal to teach a seminar called "Rebels with a Cause: Tiananmen in History and Memory" was approved at Harvard, it had been twenty-one years since the massacre.

"Dr. He, why are you so passionate about this topic?" My freshman students, who had not yet been born in 1989, always asked me in the first class.

"Rowena, why are you still putting so much time and effort into teaching with all those teaching awards? It won't help your career." Well-intentioned friends who are successful in academics asked me.

"Xiaoqing, why are you still so stubborn about June 4? You were not even in Tiananmen Square. So many of us who were there have already moved on." I often got this question from other Chinese.

I was never eloquent enough to give a good answer. I didn't even know how to start or where to start. But I always ended my Tiananmen seminar with my favorite Chinese poem, one that is widely loved by the Tiananmen Generation: "I am a willful child . . . I want to paint windows all over the earth and let all eyes accustomed to darkness grow accustomed to light."[16]

Triumph and Trauma

CHAPTER 3

On the Road: Yi Danxuan

It is true that I am free here. But knowing that people who shared the same experience as I did are still being imprisoned for what they say and write, I can't be happy here, either. I hope I can be a free man—to live a normal life with normal freedom in the land where I grew up.

—Yi Danxuan[1]

It was a late winter afternoon at a Starbucks near Georgetown University in Washington, DC. I was meeting Yi Danxuan for our interview.

"Would you like to sit outside or inside?" Danxuan asked me. We had been to this same Starbucks with other exiled students in June, when we gathered for the candlelight vigil commemorating the Tiananmen anniversary. We usually sat outside in the summer sun.

"Let's go inside. It is getting cold outside. The sun is setting." I was trying to remind Danxuan that it was a different time of the day and a different season of the year.

The coffee shop was quiet although it was crowded with young people who seemed to be students at Georgetown. Some were reading alone and others were chatting softly with friends. After I had set up my tape recorder at a corner table, Danxuan came back with two large coffees.

"It is good that you are living in North America. You would have to be rich if you needed that much Starbucks coffee in China." Danxuan was addicted to Starbucks coffee, which in China is a luxury.

The Context of the Interview: Challenges, Opportunities, and Significance

When the 1989 movement started, Danxuan was an undergraduate student studying business management at Guangdong University of Business Studies.

He was elected vice president of the Guangzhou Patriotic Student Federation, leading over 200,000 students from 40 universities and colleges during the movement. The authorities didn't arrest him right after the military crackdown—they waited until the summer break when most students had left the campus. He was detained for twenty months before an official trial, at which he was charged with "disturbing social order" and sentenced to two years. Such "verdict first, trial second" practices were common for arrested student leaders and intellectuals in 1989.[2] Denied permission to resume his college studies after his release from prison, Danxuan applied for undergraduate studies at the University of Mississippi, where his sister was working on her PhD. He was admitted in 1992. In 1999 and 2001, he was elected for two consecutive terms as president of the Independent Federation of Chinese Students and Scholars, the largest organization formed by overseas Chinese students and scholars immediately after the Tiananmen crackdown. He continued his political activism for two decades, and during most of that period he resisted the idea of applying for American citizenship because he cherished the hope of returning to China. In 2008, after sixteen years of exile, he was allowed into China once, right before the Beijing Olympics; one year later, he tried to return again to visit his father, who had been diagnosed with cancer: this time, he was denied entry.

Compared with Wang Dan and Shen Tong, Danxuan was much less expressive; it took a long time for him to open up. However, even when he was quiet and didn't respond enthusiastically to questions, it didn't mean that he didn't have anything to say. He just did not often think aloud, and he was not a natural storyteller. So I tried to be patient and to ask more questions. At times I did become frustrated because so often I needed to read between the lines. But since we had numerous opportunities over the years to have conversations about activism, identity, and exile, I eventually came to understand his struggles and dilemmas as a political activist and as an individual.

From time to time Danxuan would become cautious about what he said to me because he was concerned that I might treat him merely as a "subject" in my study, and he didn't want everything he said to become "data." This problem became obvious at one point when Danxuan started to share with me his prison experiences. Since he rarely talked about his time in jail, I was curious, and I kept asking him for more details. All of a sudden he got upset and asked: "Could you stop thinking about your research for a moment when I talk to you?"

Danxuan's reaction was a reminder that, despite their political identity, my participants are, first and foremost, human beings. I had to develop more delicacy and sensitivity in our communications. I started to wonder if it was a good idea to reveal the identities of my participants; my original decision to do so had been based on the assumption that since the worst had already happened to them, using their real names would not put them under any new or unique risks of political persecution. But I realized that I was not simply interviewing them for a few hours about their perspectives as public figures. They were exposing to me many other aspects of their lives. Even people as socially active as Wang Dan or as media friendly as Shen Tong still want space—time off of the public stage. Danxuan was even more fiercely private: I joked that even in his dreams he probably makes sure that he does not give out detailed information about anybody or anything.

In our interview, Danxuan mentioned that he wrote to his parents only once during his entire prison term, because he knew that anything he wrote would be read and checked by the wardens. Wang Dan, too, tried not to show his emotions when he was imprisoned because he didn't want the authorities to think that he was defeated, but he failed to do so once when his mother visited him about a year after he was imprisoned. When he saw her graying hair and deteriorating health compared to just a year earlier, he could not hold back his tears. In order not to cry in front of the wardens, he bit his lips until they started to bleed.[3] (Only much later did Wang Dan realize that his mother had been jailed because of him.) I could empathize with this even though I had never been imprisoned. Fearing that my emails from abroad would be checked by the authorities, I had cut off contact with my friends and schoolmates in China. Even when I wrote to my family members, I did not expose my thoughts, emotions, memories, or any personal details about my life.

Danxuan would tell me to turn off my recorder during our interviews when he didn't want to answer my questions related to 1989, fearing that he would put others at risk. I could understand why he wanted to be careful: I myself too had subconsciously avoided revealing specific names, locations, and times when I wrote my memoirs, especially details related to my own experiences of 1989. In fact, Shen Tong shared the same concern: "I cannot say any more about how I left China. The lives of many people depend on it."[4] However, Danxuan's caution was associated with a sense of emotional disconnect that I was not able to name at the beginning. For example, he was lively when talking about his childhood but he became guarded and disengaged when asked questions about where he hid after the military crackdown. He was not absent-minded but at the same time I often felt that he was not really present. I observed a similar pattern, both verbal and emotional, when Danxuan communicated with others. I was puzzled for a while until he told me about how he had been interrogated after his arrest in 1989. He said the authorities had questioned him for hours and used all kinds of ways to make him divulge information on those involved in the student movement. "They told me that others had already confessed all my activities—they said that no one kept any secrets about me, so I had better tell them everything instead of assuming all the responsibility. They also told me that all the famous student leaders had run away to the United States and were enjoying good lives, leaving us to suffer in prison. I should confess everything to get a shorter sentence." Danxuan said that the authorities failed to get any information from him that led to the arrest of others. And of course I believed that: I still couldn't get him to talk even two decades later.

I could have concluded that he was just paranoid and couldn't get over his past trauma (which likely was a contributing factor), but my experience with the exile community had taught me that I needed to withhold judgment no matter how straightforward things appeared to be. For example, once I had been shocked to hear an exiled student leader, long known for his calm, rational demeanor, begin to advocate violence: "We waited for too long and we tried everything else; violent revolution is the only thing that we never tried." I later learned that, at the time, this man's mother had just passed away in China. Reading the letters she wrote from her sick bed, hoping to see her son one more time, I could then understand his desperation and his anger.

I had many occasions in the years that followed to realize that Danxuan was always on the alert. Once when we were having lunch, Danxuan received a phone call. I could tell it was something urgent and serious. It was an exiled student who had managed to return to China with her American passport—her English name on the passport had escaped the blacklist of the Chinese government. She had just started working for an American company in China when the police took her away for interrogation. Although the Communist Party wanted the world to forget about June 4, it also made sure that those who do remember know that the June 4 crackdown will never be over. She was concerned about her safety, so she wanted Danxuan to check on her at a certain time every day but she didn't want this to become public knowledge. Many activists at the time believed that if a person who was harassed, threatened, or interrogated alerted the Western media, the CCP would punish him/her more severely; most people preferred to remain quiet, hoping not to escalate the situation.

Because of his ongoing political activism, Danxuan had been in contact with many families of the June 4 victims, rights activists, and liberal intellectuals inside China. The CCP has been successful in marginalizing those people by accusing them of selling out their country to anti-China foreign forces; any support or contact with the exiles abroad can be used as an easy excuse to demonize those struggling inside the country. In order to protect these people, Danxuan and others like him kept absolutely quiet about anything they did. Even when exiles were criticized for being useless and doing nothing abroad, they still strictly followed their principle of not speaking. When Danxuan and his associates' mailing list was hacked, and people inside China were endangered as a result, I was reminded again that their painstaking secretiveness was not a game. I wish that I do not have to be vague in discussing Danxuan's activities and those of his colleagues, but I do not think I have the right to do otherwise.

Danxuan was probably the only one in the exile community who had more than one family member imprisoned in 1989. His cousin X, the son of his aunt, had been visiting Beijing during the night of the massacre. When X saw a soldier on the street beating an old woman with the stock of his gun, he was so angry that he grabbed the gun and asked the soldier to apologize to the woman. X was arrested as a "rioter" (*baotu*) and sentenced to five years in prison. Students tended to receive comparatively lighter sentences in 1989. Those who were not students were labeled "rioters"and faced more severe sentences, or even the death penalty. Danxuan was released three years earlier than his cousin. Two other students who were imprisoned for their participation in the 1989 movement in the Guangzhou area were Chen Wei and Yu Shimin, both of whom were students at Zhongshan University where Danxuan's father was a professor. Chen Pokong, a lecturer at the same university, was also arrested. Danxuan, Chen Wei, and Yu Shimin were all imprisoned for two years and released in 1992, and Chen Pokong was released in 1993.

While I realized that Danxuan had good reason to be secretive, it didn't mean that I was comfortable with it. What struck me most was that Danxuan's caution was nearly universal within exile circles. Distrust is often at the root of the discord and infighting among the cohort. Of course there is a distinction between precaution and distrust, but there is also a connection. Under the stresses and uncertainties of exile, some of these once-idealistic young people were fighting with one another, denouncing each other to their associates, and struggling to exclude those with whom they disagreed. I wonder, though, how many could have done better in their place, given all that they had been through, and all that they were still experiencing.

One of the advantages of working with Danxuan was that, compared with Wang Dan and Shen Tong, who were often interviewed by journalists and scholars and who had frequently published and spoken publicly over the years, Danxuan is not a high-profile Tiananmen student leader, and there is not much material about his experiences and perspectives. While the general public's understanding of the 1989 uprising is limited to Tiananmen Square in Beijing, because of the extensive coverage there by Western journalists, the Tiananmen movement was in fact a nationwide one that engulfed cities and towns throughout China. Even in Jonathan Unger's groundbreaking book *The Pro-Democracy Protests in China*, in which efforts are made to include events outside of Beijing,[5] the city of Guangzhou in Guangdong province is omitted. Danxuan's experiences as a student leader in Guangzhou offer a useful counterpoint to the better-known stories of Shen Tong and Wang Dan. Further, Danxuan's life experiences, particularly his experiences after the Tiananmen crackdown, seem closer to the reality of many other members of the exiled dissident community. After all, among the millions who participated in the 1989 movement and among the hundreds in exile, how many have been nominated for the Nobel Peace Prize like Wang Dan, or been included among *Newsweek*'s People of the Year like Shen Tong? Dissidents like Danxuan suffered imprisonment and exile like their more famous counterparts, enduring these hardships in anonymity and obscurity. Their voices deserve to be heard.

One common issue that Danxuan did not mention much in our interview was the struggles that low-profile exiles often face in their personal and professional lives. Once an exiled friend I highly respected was devastated when his wife wanted to leave him. "She married me when I was in prison. She really loved me and she knew what she was getting into. She said she was sorry but she really couldn't hold on to the kind of life we were living," he told me. He decided to let go—as much as he loved their child, he decided the child would be better off with the mother's new family. While prison could not stop love, freedom was not enough to sustain love. Unlike other first-generation immigrants who devote all of their time and energy to starting a new and better life in a new land, the exiles' minds and hearts are always somewhere else. For those who chose to continue their political activities, family life and a successful career may seem to be unaffordable luxuries.

Over the years Danxuan never talked about the possibility of giving up activism, and he never talked about those who chose to do otherwise, with only one exception. One year some exiled student leaders organized a press conference for the June 4 anniversary. One of the student exiles was angry when he learned that journalists had taken a group picture without him and his son who came with him. I felt embarrassed for him, thinking that his behavior would simply confirm the allegations made against exiled Tiananmen leaders that they care unduly about fame and money. When I visited this man's home the next day and talked to his son, I felt ashamed about my quick judgment. Actually, "talk" is not really accurate as the little boy did not speak any language I understood—either English or Mandarin Chinese. He was yelling and throwing things in frustration. My natural question was, "Where is his mother?" I later learned that before the little boy was born, his maternal grandparents had wanted to come to the United States to take care of his mother, but the authorities denied them passports. Fearful and under stress, the young mother had collapsed into depression. The boy was sent back to China to be raised by his grandparents and he ended up being unable to speak Mandarin Chinese. I never figured out where the boy's mother was on that day; I was told that she needed to be elsewhere for a while to rest. The exiled student had told his son that he would be in newspaper pictures with his father, and now he had disappointed him. When Danxuan told me that this student leader had given up his activism and had become successful in business, I was thinking about that little boy who spoke a language I didn't understand. People often asked me why those Tiananmen leaders gave up their activism. I did not have a clear answer, but sometimes I wondered: Did they ever really have any choice?

* * *

Formative Years: A Family Separated in the Name of Revolution

I attended primary school in Hunan province, middle school and two years of university in Guangdong province, and I received my bachelor's degree in the United States.

Before I was born, my parents were assigned to work in two different provinces. My father was teaching at a university in Guangdong province and my mother was working in Hunan province. I stayed with my Mom in Hunan and my elder sister stayed with my father in Guangdong. It was not until 1979, when China started its "reform era," that my family was finally reunited. By then, my parents had been living in two different provinces for twenty years. I spent my formative years in Hunan province without seeing my father and my sister much.

"Do you think your family reunion took place because of the loosening of political control and state policy in 1979?"

Of course. There was comparatively less control, and the rehabilitation (*pingfan*) was going on. My parents had always wanted to be together but it wasn't possible because of the household registration system[6]—people couldn't look for jobs themselves in those days. Without the government's approval, you couldn't move anywhere.

When my parents eventually managed to stay in the same city, a journalist from the *Nanfang Daily*, a provincial government newspaper, came to interview them. His article said that our family story was a good example of the effectiveness of implementation of state policy (*luoshi zhengce*), and it was thanks to the government that we could have a family reunion. Now in retrospect, it is ironic—it was inhuman for the government to separate so many families for so many years in the first place.

The government did things like that [separating families] in the name of revolution. I was not sure if my parents really thought that way. The reason I like the movie *Dr. Zhivago* is that it shows how unpredictable life can be, and that the fate of an individual (*geren mingyun*) is always connected to that of the society. On the surface, it may appear that individual life doesn't have much to do with society and you can still enjoy your life without caring about what is happening in the society. But in fact, as individuals, we can never escape the reality of the social contexts in which we live.

Danxuan's comment on the relationship between the individual and society was a response to the popular belief in Chinese society today that the middle class can live comfortable lives as long as they stay away from politics.

Father's Message: "Use Your Pen to Fight for Freedom"

"What was your life like after your family was united in Guangzhou?"

In those days housing conditions were tough. My father was still living in a dormitory building for singles even though he had been married for over twenty years. So when my Mom and I moved to Guangzhou, our family of three had to live in a small room—my sister lived in the dorm. There were no kitchens inside those rooms so all families in the building cooked in the public corridor. When you walked into the building, there were stoves everywhere.

Later I moved into a storage room which temporarily became available because my father's room was too small to squeeze in three people. It wasn't until years later when my father was assigned a small apartment that I had a chance to live with my family.

"When my family first moved to the town from the mountain area, we also lived in a small room in a building for singles, and the public corridor was also full of stoves. What was it like to be able to live close to your father after so many years of separation?"

Since my father taught comparative literature, I had the chance to read books of foreign literature that I found on my father's bookshelf, as well as those that he borrowed for me from the library. My father is a liberal intellectual with ideals, which is typical among his generation of intellectuals, but his generation had been suppressed too much. He was always concerned about my studies and my thinking. When I turned sixteen, he gave me the book *Spartacus* as a birthday gift.[7] On the cover page of the book, he wrote an inscription that said: "I hope you will use your pen, or even your sword when necessary, to fight for freedom and a better future for our nation."

A few years later, when Danxuan tried to put his father's advice into practice, he lost his freedom and later lost his right to return to the country for which he had fought.

High School: Between a "Three-Good Student" and a Human Being

Once at a Tiananmen memorial activity in Toronto to which Danxuan was invited as a keynote speaker, Danxuan was asked what had motivated him to participate in the 1989 student protests. He said that he believed the roots of his rebellion began in high school when he was not allowed to date his girlfriend. I asked him to expand on that.

I knew little about society at that time because of my lack of life experience and my limited access to information. The direct conflict I felt was more between individual freedom and social control, mainly reflected in our school lives. For example, we always had to stay late at school for self-study classes (*zixike*) and we were never given time for physical exercises in the afternoons. Also, there were restrictions on hairstyles and clothing, and we would be punished if we looked different. Everyday we were required to do morning exercises together. When I saw all the students moving the same way on the playground, I felt that we were all being shaped in the same mold. I am not saying that I understood much about freedom at that time. I think it was just human nature to feel suffocated. Anyone who has ever lived under that system knows how individual freedom was suppressed.

"Did you get into trouble because of your hair and clothes? I got into trouble in school for wearing my hair in a ponytail."

No. I never wore strange and exotic clothes (qizhuang yifu).

I couldn't help laughing after hearing Danxuan's answer. Actually in those days, there was no such thing as "exotic clothes." The term "qizhuang yifu" was an expression created by the authorities, who decided on their own what was "strange" and what was "exotic." Wang Dan and I used to joke with Danxuan, telling him that he always dressed formally, as if he were ten years older than his actual age. I started to think that maybe Danxuan's style of dress had something to do with his high school experience.

In those days, even university students were not allowed to have boyfriends or girlfriends, to say nothing of high school students. So when I started to have a girlfriend, the principal and the teachers all came to talk with us and attempt to stop us. Now in retrospect, I believe they did that out of good intentions and that they really wanted to help. They did believe it was bad to have boyfriends or girlfriends as high school students. When you look back, you find that funny. It reflected the values in those days, although we could see values changing as society progressed. In an authoritarian society like China, absolute obedience was required. To use today's language, "standardization" was required. But I think love is a natural feeling of human beings. I believe it would have been better if we were given guidance instead of being punished for dating.

I was confused. Anyone who has been in love knows that love isn't something that can be easily controlled as you wish. My girlfriend and I had to suppress our feelings because of the constant pressure. The good thing was that we were not expelled from school. I didn't think I did anything wrong, but I was severely criticized as a young man. For students, schools and teachers had absolute authority, and the authorities disapproved of my behavior. So you can imagine how stressful that was. Of course at that time I couldn't reason as I can now.

Our teachers gave us lots of negative examples about how students' futures were ruined by dating. Those stories were mainly from the media, also controlled by the government of course. For example, we heard that students who had been dating were expelled from school because they had violated the school rules and regulations. So it was not that the students who dated dropped out of school—they were forced out. The problems were not due to the dating per se, but due to the stress and values imposed by the school and society. Our teachers thought that my girlfriend and I were very good students and it would be a great pity if we ruined our futures because we were dating.

"When you said 'good students,' what exactly did you mean?"

We were "Three-Good students" (*sanhao xuesheng*).

All three of my participants were "three-good students" in China. The "three-good" student honor system has been in practice since the 1950s. It promotes and rewards students with good morals, high academic achievement, and robust health. Although the idea of all-round moral, academic, and physical development may seem straightforward, the Communist Party had unique criteria for "good morals," as Danxuan pointed out:

In the Communist context, "morals" are closely linked to your political stand points—whether you are in line with the government's political indoctrination. This is reflected in the exams we took for our political education classes—the exams were mainly tests of our loyalty to the regime. Everyone had to write and say what the government preached in order to pass exams.

"What do you consider to be important moral principles?"

I think it is important to be consistent and to have faith. I mean, we should be true to ourselves. What we say and what we do should be consistent. I don't mean that we should always be the same or that we are always correct. I understand we are constrained by our limited knowledge and experience, which consequently affects our judgment. But at least we should do what we believe to be right. Being consistent means you practice what you believe. What you do must be consistent with what you say.

"What were your peers' attitudes toward you and your girlfriend?"

I never talked to them about this at the time. But I could feel that they were supportive or sympathetic. It wasn't until many years later—when I just got out of prison and one day ran into a high school classmate. He said that he thought my girlfriend and I were very brave, and that my girlfriend should be the model for women to learn from in modern China. But he dared not tell me these thoughts when we were still in high school.

Danxuan was smiling happily when he said that. It must have been reassuring to him to receive open support from a fellow classmate years later.

"You mentioned earlier that the media were controlled by the government. Did you read newspapers or watch TV news?"

I didn't read many newspapers. I only read sports news. I found the official news boring—it was all about the Party's meetings and the leaders' speeches. I don't think people were consciously resisting the news from the official media at that time, but not many people showed much interest in the news. They may not have been able to express it in abstract terms as "freedom of press" or "government control," but they would tell you that the news was meaningless so they didn't read the papers. People didn't need to be very knowledgeable or logical to make decisions like that—they could rely on their nature and instinct to make such judgments.

Leadership in the 1989 Movement

"What made you first become involved in the movement?"

There are several reasons. First, I think most Chinese were politically enthusiastic in 1989. It was not that we were born with such enthusiasm—it was simply because we had been suppressed for too long. As students, we believed that it was time that we shoulder the responsibility for our nation and the people, which was what we had been taught throughout our education. "Every man has a share of responsibility for the fate of his country" (*guojiaxingwang pifuyouze*). We were idealistic. At the beginning we cherished the hope that the government would make efforts to improve and to fight against corruption. At a personal level, as I mentioned earlier, I had felt conflicts between individual freedoms and social control when I grew up. I was dissatisfied with the social reality.

I was living on the university campus where my father taught and I had many friends. When we heard the news that Hu Yaobang had passed away,[8] we started to post *dazibao*, big-character posters on campus.

"Dazibao," big-character posters, were large pieces of paper on which writers expressed their views using ink and brush to make large-size, easily legible Chinese characters. As the common mode of political expression during the Communist era,[9] big-character posters were "one of the few outlets of expression available to Chinese who desired to make a dissenting political statement or to raise a personal grievance." Big-character posters were also used to denounce people during the political campaigns in the 1950s, the 1960s, and the 1970s. So they were instruments of individual expression as well as suppression. These posters were usually posted at prominent sites such as university bulletin boards or city walls. During the 1989 protests, big-character posters went up on campuses all over the country. The most highly concentrated poster sites became the gathering points for student demonstrators.

"What role did you play during the movement?"

We had meetings in our dormitories and then we started to take to the streets. All universities and colleges in the area sent representatives to attend the meetings. Among this group, members were elected to the newly established Guangzhou Patriotic Student Federation. I was elected vice president of the organization. I organized hunger strikes, demonstrations, and other activities. The first formal demonstration took place on May 4.

May 4 is a historically significant date in China. On May 4, 1919, students demonstrated in Beijing against the provisions of the Versailles Peace Treaty, which made special concessions to Japan regarding the former German possessions in Shandong province. Since then, the well-known "May Fourth Movement," has been broadly symbolic of democracy, modernization, and leadership by intellectuals. On May 4, 1989, journalists from nearly every major Beijing-based newspaper and news agency went to Tiananmen Square carrying signs reading: "We want to tell the truth; don't force us to lie."

"What role do you think students played during the movement?"

We saw our role as students to express and to speak out for the people and to push for reforms. We had no intention of overthrowing the government. Of course after the military crackdown on June 4, things changed.

Anger and Fear under Martial Law

"Were you afraid when you became active in the movement? Did you ever worry about what would happen later?"

Not really. Not until the declaration of martial law.[10] We were holding our Standing Committee meeting when we heard about the imposition of martial law in Beijing. I should say that we were not very much worried, but we were angry. We decided to return to our own universities (which we were representing) to organize demonstrations. When we were saying goodbye to each other, one of the committee members hugged me. You know, in China we rarely hugged. We didn't know what was going to happen. We had never experienced something like that before. You would only see such scenes in movies. We were uncertain about the future and we didn't know if we would have any chances to meet again.

I had almost forgotten this hugging scene that Danxuan described until I attended a small celebration when he received his MBA degree from George Washington University. As a surprise, a friend of Danxuan, Z, flew in all the way from the West Coast late at night to join the graduation party. They talked about the hugging scene. Z had also been imprisoned after the movement.

"What happened on the night martial law was declared?"

When we returned to our campuses after the committee meeting, we found students had already self-organized spontaneously and had gathered outside the provincial government building. By midnight all campuses were empty because all the students were on the street. So the government's announcement of martial law actually resulted in more anger among the students, and it was the direct cause for the large-scale demonstration in Guangzhou the following day.

When Martial Law was officially imposed on May 20, citizens in Beijing took to the streets to make sure the army would not enter the city to harm the students. Martial law signaled the central government's attitude toward the movement.

"What was your general impression of the students? Were they afraid?"

We felt that we were doing something right. We weren't afraid because we thought we were doing what we had been taught to do—to shoulder the responsibility for the society and the nation. After I was released from prison and I talked to older Chinese overseas, they said that you young people were not afraid in 1989 because you didn't understand the nature of the Chinese Communist Party. These people of the older generation had already experienced the political campaigns of the 1950s and 1960s. They had witnessed the cruelty of the Communist Party so they were less optimistic. I don't know what difference it would have made if in 1989 we [students] had better understood the nature of the Party.

Reactions of Parents, Teachers, and the General Public

"What were your parents' reactions to your participation in the movement?"

My parents were of course worried but they didn't stop me. They were very supportive of the students. They didn't have any chance to talk to me—I only went home once throughout the movement to change my clothes. I spent most of my time on the square where the students were hunger striking and demonstrating, in student dormitories where we held our meetings, and on other university campuses. My father told me later that it took my mother a long time to wash my clothes because they were so dirty.

The "square" Danxuan refers to here is Haizhu Square in Guangzhou city of Guangdong province. It is different from Tiananmen Square that Shen Tong and Wang Dan referred to when they talked about the "square." During the 1989 movement, students and citizens gathered in the public squares in major cities across the country to express their views. Ironically, in China, as in other Communist countries, many of these squares had been created by the regime itself as public spaces to host demonstrations by citizens forced to participate in memorial parades and other shows of mass support.

When I visited Danxuan's mother on the university campus where his father teaches and where the family lives, she told me exactly the same story about washing her son's clothes. She said Danxuan only returned home once during the movement and it took her a long time to wash his terribly dirty clothes. Washing her son's dirty clothes seems to have become an un-washable memory.

"Did your teachers support the students? What about the general public?"

There were different reactions among the teachers—some supported us and took part in demonstrations; some tried to convince us not to participate because they were worried about us; others working as political counselors tried their best to stop us; and a handful simply thought that we were wrong to demonstrate.

In general, people were supportive. We received donations and letters. We set up a broadcast station on the square and there was free speech time. People from all walks of life came up to speak. Bands also came to play and to show their support. I think 1989 was very different from the Cultural Revolution. Although the society in the 1980s was far from what we call a "civil society," different ideas and voices did exist.

Both the broadcast station and the big-character posters provided spaces for free expression. During the movement, students' broadcast stations were set up in Beijing and other provinces as well. It was an important way for us to express our opinions and to allow the public's voices to be heard. The demonstrations were also a means of expression. There was no other way to freely express oneself. The broadcast station also provided a space for people to share information. People didn't trust the official media because they were tightly controlled by the government. News from informal sources was regarded as more trustworthy than the official news.

When I asked Danxuan to tell me more about the setting up of the broadcast station, he told me to turn off my recorder. He said he would not get into any more details that might cause problems for the students involved. So many years after the military crackdown we still could not openly and freely talk about the setting up of the broadcast station, a symbol of freedom of speech in 1989.

"Why do you think the movement was supported by so many people?"

That had a lot to do with the social reality at that time. It had come to the point that social conflicts were becoming acute and people were dissatisfied with the government. Students were like the spokespersons for the general public. Let's put it this way: if you are not allowed to express yourself and someone else will speak out for you, of course you would support him or her.

The public's support for the movement was reflected in a massive demonstration in Guangzhou on May 23. I wanted to know more about this demonstration from Danxuan's perspective as an organizer.

The demonstration was jointly organized by students from Guangdong, Hong Kong, and Macau.[11] By then the movement was no longer only a student movement. It had become a mass movement with participants from all walks of life. News reports in Hong Kong estimated that over one million people participated on May 23. The Chinese official media reported with a more conservative estimate of half a million.

"I too participated in that demonstration. My memory of walking and shouting slogans together with the other protesters on that rainy night remains fresh in my

mind. On my way to the demonstration, I told the mini-van driver that I was going to demonstrate and he said that he would give me a free ride. Those mini-vans were privately run and they normally bargained to get more money. I was really touched."

I think that happened everywhere throughout the country in 1989. In the early stage of the movement, one of our members of the Standing Committee fainted on the street because he hadn't slept for several days. A car quickly stopped to give us a free ride. Things like that occurred a lot in those days. We got free rides from people we didn't know at all. When drivers saw that we were students, they didn't ask anything and dropped us off wherever we requested.

The Tragic Ending of the Movement

My friends and I never thought that the government would order the army to open fire although early on my father had said that would happen. This showed that we didn't understand the nature of the regime well. We hadn't experienced as much as the older generations so we were still naive. We had been taught during all our school years that the government was the people's government and the army was the people's army. How could the people's government harm its own people?

"How did you feel when you heard that guns had been fired in Beijing?"

I was angry and confused. I didn't understand why things had turned out like that. I felt as if I had been deceived by the government. When I say I was deceived, I don't mean only in 1989. I felt that I had been deceived since birth. The government had lied to us. This wasn't the kind of government that we had been told it was. It was a betrayal.

College students of 1989 grew up during the "reform era." The government propaganda instilled in us the idea that our generation was growing up in sweet water under the Communist Red Flag. We had little knowledge or memory of the country's past. In such a context, we trusted the government and believed in the lies of the regime. However, the gunshots on June 4 woke up our entire generation. The gunshots actually stripped away the veils of lies that the government had been preaching. We came to realize that the government would use any means whatsoever, including the use of violence, to maintain its power.

Danxuan's reflection was shared by Wang Dan. Both felt that, until the moment that the shooting started, it was impossible for their generation, growing up in the 1980s, to associate the post-Mao Chinese Communist Party, represented by Hu Yaobang, Zhao Ziyang, and Deng Xiaoping, with killers. Even those who had experienced one political campaign after another during their entire lives had not anticipated that the government would open fire on its people.[12]

"What did you do after June 4?"

We tried to break the news blockade and helped to hide those intellectuals and students who were in danger.

"So you didn't consider yourself in danger? Were your parents worried about you?"

Of course, especially my mother. The government's attitude before June 4 and after June 4 was very different. It was obvious that any activism after the military crackdown would lead to severe punishment. Still, my parents couldn't stop me from continuing.

"Am I right to say that you felt there was something more important than your parents?"

You can say that.

"What made you decide not to give up?"

I was young in 1989 and I couldn't articulate why I wanted to continue. I simply felt that the task was unfinished. As a student leader, I couldn't just leave it. I had a responsibility to continue. I believe that was the basic thing to do for my conscience.

"Why was conscience so important that it even outweighed your life and family?"

That's a religious question. I can't expand.

I tried to get Danxuan to give me more details such as where he hid, how he was found, and what happened after he was arrested. He refused to answer my questions and told me to move on to the next one.

When I visited Danxuan's mother, she took me to a building where Danxuan had held meetings with the student representatives during the movement. She told me that after the crackdown, the building was taken over by the authorities. After the crackdown, she spent lots of time in the area, and whenever students returned for information or to find their friends, she told them to run away. She told me that Danxuan disappeared for almost two months after the military crackdown; she had no idea where he was or whether he was even still alive. Meanwhile, the police went to their apartment and searched Danxuan's room.

A Trial without Defense

Danxuan was detained for twenty months before he was given an official trial.

"Can you tell me about the trial? Did you defend yourself?"

No, I didn't want to do it because I knew it would be a waste of time. The trial was supposed to be open but even my parents were not allowed into the court. After I was sentenced, I was taken into a police van. From the window on the back of the van, I saw my mother and her colleague who was accompanying her. I smiled at them. After I was released and saw my mother's colleague again, she told me that she was impressed by my smile on the day when I officially lost my freedom.

When I visited Danxuan's parents in China, his mother showed me some pictures taken on the day of his trial. I saw the police van Danxuan had mentioned. It was a van with no windows except the one in the back. In one of the pictures, the police van was driving away. That must have been the moment that Danxuan described. Danxuan always made light of emotional scenes. I wonder, though, if such levity could ever make the heaviness any lighter.

Wang Dan describes in his prison memoir a similar scene inside a police car. When the police drove him back to prison after his only meeting with his mother, he saw from the car window that his mother was walking with difficulty and he couldn't hold back his tears.[13] Wang Dan's parents didn't tell him at that time that his mother had been imprisoned as a result of his political activism. She had developed problems in her leg while in jail.

"Do you feel any guilt toward your parents?"

Yes. I didn't think I did anything wrong but I felt very guilty toward my parents. They suffered a lot because of me. My mother got sick—she developed stomach problems; she accidentally broke her leg; and she was hospitalized. My family didn't tell me all these things because they didn't want me to worry. When I later learned of this, I was very upset. Parents are always parents. While I was in prison, they worried about me every day, especially before I was sentenced. They were not sure what my sentence would be.

Life in Prison

Danxuan barely mentioned his life in prison. I wasn't sure if it was because he didn't think it was significant or because he didn't want to recall it. So I tried to get him to tell me more in the interview.

"Who else was with you in prison? Were you the only student there?"

Different kinds of criminals. Some had been sentenced to death and were waiting to be executed. I knew there were other students there, but we were not put in the same cell.

"Could you describe to me what the cell was like? How big was it?"

Let me see...About 4.5 meters in length, and 2 meters in width. It was less than ten square meters, and usually seven to eight prisoners were kept in one cell.

It was very crowded. We all slept on the floor, and each person had about half a square meter of space. So we were forced to sleep on one side and we could not stretch our bodies.

That was all. I later got a chance to hear a more descriptive account from him when we went together to an event organized by Chinese immigrants. A well-educated young Chinese couple who knew little about what had happened in 1989 asked Danxuan what it was like to be in prison in China. This time, instead of giving mere numbers to describe the cell, Danxuan compared prisons of the Communist Party with those of the Nationalist Party (KMT). Although most Chinese knew little about the Communist Party prisons, we had all been repeatedly exposed to stories and movies that described the intolerable conditions in the KMT prisons before the CCP seized power. Generations of Chinese were familiar with images of Communist Party members being tortured by the KMT. Danxuan said the CCP prisons were even worse than those of the KMT. He said that Communist movies such as "Red Rock" described how when the revolutionary characters were taken out to be executed, their revolutionary comrades could see them from behind the bars and together they shouted revolutionary slogans. However, Danxuan's prison cell was all covered up like a coffin and he had no idea what was happening outside.

"Did other prisoners know why you were arrested?"

Yes. They did.

"What was their attitude toward you?"

They were mainly sympathetic and supportive.

"Did you feel discouraged to see the ending of '89? Did you feel your values had been challenged?"

For a period of time, I felt confused (*panghuang kunhuo*). I spent a lot of time thinking in prison, but I never thought that I did anything wrong. That was important for me—the belief that I did nothing wrong. I think there are certain things in human nature that no one and nothing could suppress.

"You told me before that when you were in prison, you didn't write any letters to your parents. Why?"

The Laogai system (reeducation through labor)[14] in China was created with the goal of changing your mind through labor. The authorities also wanted your family to influence you. I think letters to my parents should be something personal and I didn't want to share my feelings openly with others. But I knew that all the letters would be examined and checked. So I only wrote one letter to my parents while I was in prison.

"What did you write in that letter?"

My question was followed by a long period of silence. Similar situations later arose during my interviews with Wang Dan and Shen Tong. Those moments were unpredictable and I always found myself unprepared. I didn't know what to say or what to do. Danxuan answered my question in a different way:

When I was in prison, "I Want to Have a Home" was my favorite song. I really wanted to have a home.

"I Want to Have a Home" was a popular Chinese song in the early 1990s and it had been one of my favorite songs as well. I started to sing the song: "I want to have a home—a place that doesn't need to be luxurious. When I get hurt, I can turn to it. . . . " I stopped when I noticed the pain on Danxuan's face.

"Your mother told me that while you were in prison you had a fever for a long time. The authorities didn't take you to the hospital until your parents voiced strong requests on several occasions. Can you tell me more about that experience? Did you ever wonder if your activism had been worthwhile?"

I never asked myself the question whether it was worthwhile. Maybe that was not an issue for me. When they took me to the hospital, I was handcuffed and my feet were fettered. There was a long corridor that I needed to walk through before I got to the doctor.

I didn't push for any more details. Having to walk down that long corridor in the crowd as a criminal being watched by police must have been humiliating for a proud young man.

Expulsion from College

"So were you officially expelled from your college?"
Yes.

"Were you informed orally or in writing?"
Of course not orally. The school authorities never visited me in prison. They sent a letter to my home.

"Did your teachers and friends visit you in prison?"

They tried to, but none of them were allowed. No one was allowed to visit me except my parents. Actually, even my parents were not allowed to visit me until after one year. But my friends did visit my parents. My parents even received flowers sent by strangers.

"What happened after you were released from prison?"

I wanted very much to finish my undergraduate studies, but I wasn't allowed to. I felt helpless. There wasn't much I could do under such circumstances. So I applied for a student visa and came to the U.S. I didn't expect to stay for such a long time though. I just wanted to complete my undergraduate degree and then return home.

Danxuan's response here did not show how reluctant he was to leave China, which contrasted with the impression I had formed over the years about his eagerness to return home. But again, I had learned to read between the lines. Student activists from the 1989 movement were punished in different ways, with imprisonment being only one. Several of Danxuan's friends were assigned jobs unsuited to their abilities or sent to work in remote areas.

Life in Exile: An Ordinary Life or a Great Cause?

"Did you start your undergraduate studies right after you came to the United States?"

Yes, but for only one term. I needed to pay a high tuition as an international student and I couldn't afford it. My sister was trying to support me, but she was a student herself. So I decided to temporarily leave school. I didn't go back to school until I had saved up some money after working for several years.

I tried to look for different jobs, like any other Chinese students abroad. I didn't have a car so I walked around the neighborhood where I lived looking for jobs. Many students worked in Chinese restaurants because English language and skills were not required. I also tried to get jobs in restaurants but they didn't hire me because I didn't wash the dishes quickly enough. Later I got a job as a Chinese tour guide.

"Did your university know about your experience? Did they give you any scholarships?"

My university knew, but I think few '89 students got scholarships at that time. Most of them were like me, having to work hard to support ourselves.

Student leaders and intellectuals who escaped from China soon after the Tiananmen crackdown received much more support than those who came later. There was not as much attention to the event by the time Danxuan was released from prison and came to the United States. Those who left in 1989, even if they did not receive financial support, were taken care of in a better manner because of the strong moral support from the general public.

"Did you have a support group of other '89 students?"
Of course friends would help with certain things such as finding a place to settle down. But as you know, everyone was working hard to survive.

"How did you feel when you could go back to school again in the United States?"
I was very excited! At last I could return to school again.

It must have been great as Danxuan rarely used expressions like "very excited."

"Did you start as a freshman?"
I had some credits transferred from China, but I took more courses than required. So I graduated with more than enough credits for the degree.

"Now that you have studied as an undergraduate in both China and the United States, can you share with me your thoughts about the two systems?"
I think they differ significantly. The undergraduate curriculum in the United States is more comprehensive and it covers broader areas. It is more comprehensive, deeper, allows more choices, and it is more up to date. And of course you have more personal freedom when attending schools here.

For example, there would not be a new-semester convocation (*kaixue dianli*) warning you not to date during your school years. Of course, there are things like ethics and codes of conduct, but the school would not gather students together to tell you what you could and could not do. The school rules and regulations are commonly accepted as moral or academic standards. Schools here are places for you to learn and grow, not places to control your life. In China, we have a traditional concept of home and country. When you are kids, you are subject to your parents' discipline (*guan*); when you grow up, you are subject to the CCP's discipline (*guan*). Schools are considered like a big family and are responsible for the students' personal lives.

I talked about this when I was interviewed by a journalist after I first got to Mississippi. I said that things people are born with or take for granted here may be things that people in other parts of the world have been fighting for, at the cost of their freedom and lives, but they still haven't achieved them. So it was a big contrast for me to live in the new social environment.

When I saw young people having the opportunity to live normal lives as human beings, I began to think a lot. When I say "normal," I mean you live in a stable environment and you can make plans for your future. You have choices. However, I first lived in a system with no freedom; then I experienced June 4, and then started a new life in a strange land trying to learn a new language. Many people have asked me why I am still carrying on the cause of 1989 now that I am living in a democratic country. I think the major reason that keeps me going is that I do not want the next generation in China to have to repeat what I've been through. If I have children in the future, I hope they will live a better life.

"You can raise your children in the United States."

Of course, I can. But I feel our cause is not completed. I am connected to the people and the land in China. When I left China, I was already over 20 years old. It is not possible to take away the scars carved on me by Chinese society and the experience I lived through. I can't disconnect myself from them.

"When you say you can't, do you mean that you are not able to or you are not willing to?"

I don't want to. That was why for many years, I had only two suitcases and I was ready to return home anytime. I didn't have much furniture either. My basic principle for living in the United States was that I kept a minimum of daily necessities.

Danxuan's two-suitcase concept was shared by Shen Tong later in our group discussion.

"Why is it so important for you to hold onto China instead of settling down to live an easier life in North America?"

I don't enjoy settling down in North America. I won't feel happy.

"Is it because you didn't really want to leave China when you left?"

That is part of the reason. Of course, they didn't force me to leave but there wasn't much I could do under the circumstances.

Danxuan's answers were becoming briefer. I had the feeling that he wished to avoid my questions.

"What role does June 4 play in your decision?"

June 4 is of course something important in my life. But there are Chinese students who choose to return to China after their studies. These are personal choices. Different people can give you different reasons. For me, June 4 is part of the reason, but not the whole reason.

Danxuan certainly should have known that his situation was different from the other overseas Chinese students with whom he compared himself.

"When you were a child, your parents were separated from each other by the Party. When you were a teenager, you were not allowed to date your girlfriend. Now at last you can make your own decisions in a democratic society, but you still want to return to China?"

I value the freedom here, but I grew up with the memories of Chinese society and Chinese people. I think all immigrants who settled in North America also grew up with memories of their own society and people. Wouldn't it be wonderful if I could return home and have freedom at the same time?

It is true that I am free here. But knowing that people who shared the same experience as I did are still being imprisoned for what they say and write, I can't be happy here. I hope I can be a free man—and to live a *normal* life with *normal* freedom on the land where I grew up.

"Right after September 11, you shared with me your thoughts on the danger of sacrificing human lives for a cause or a goal, no matter how noble it is. But now you are going to sacrifice your rights to live an ordinary life for a cause you believe in?"

It is dangerous if you encourage people to sacrifice their lives for a cause or a goal. But you can choose what kind of life you would like to live for yourself.

"You mentioned the next generation just now. If you choose to return to China and if the CCP does allow you to do so, but the political situation remains the same, your children will have to live in an authoritarian society. How do you justify your decision?"

When we talk about making changes, there are two levels—the personal and the social. I will try to improve my personal situation. At the same time, I would like to do something for social progress. The personal and the social are always connected. When the tsunami occurred in Thailand, you can say that it was not the business of other countries, but people all over the world lent their hands because we don't want to see others suffer. When we talk about the happiness of the next generation, it is always connected to the broader social contexts. We all live in the same world. Individuals are not free from the broader social contexts. If I can make up my mind to settle down in North America, I would be happy for myself. But for the time being, I simply don't want to do that.

"Democracy Is Not a Big Slogan, but a Way of Living"

"How do you think your experience in the U.S. has revised your dream of 1989?"
I don't like your using the term "dream." It is too romantic and dramatic. Don't use "dream" in my profile.
"'Dream' here is referring to our ideals and hope. It is my word, not yours."

Alright. To get back to your question, my experiences in the United States have provided me with the opportunity to experience and understand personal freedom in a deeper sense, which made me value personal freedom even more. In 1989 we as students didn't have a concrete understanding of freedom and democracy. We just understood it conceptually and we longed for it. But after living in the U.S., I have learned it through life; I live in it. I think the ultimate goal of a democratic system is to protect an individual's freedom. So I think democracy is not a big slogan, but a way of living.

The greatest thing destroyed by the Chinese Communist Party was the traditional culture in China that they uprooted during all the political campaigns since 1949. We can see the consequences of such destruction in the Chinese society now. It has become a society with neither traditional Chinese values nor universal democratic values. The government has been silencing different voices in the name of maintaining stability, but a real stable society doesn't have to rely on political control. It is more important to have social order based on shared values with which people identify from the bottom of their hearts. Unfortunately, the Communist ideology has dominated Chinese society. The nation has become rootless with little to hold on to.

"If you could return to China tomorrow, what do you think you would do?"
I will start working and fighting for changes for myself—to improve my situation. I will try to be a free man. I believe social changes start from each individual. I think my life will be more complete if I return to China.

"Suppose you were put in prison again, do you still think your life would be more complete?"
Yes, but that is an extreme case.

*   *   *

The issues with which I struggled while speaking to Danxuan became obvious during my interviews with Shen Tong and Wang Dan, and during our group discussions. They all were struggling between sacrificing for an unfinished cause and living an ordinary life. This conflict and confusion was closely related to their experiences in China, crystallized by their participation in the 1989 movement.

By the time our interview ended, it had become dark outside. I thought we made the right choice to stay inside the coffee shop. Although the warmth from the heating was different from that from the sun, at least the room provided us with a shelter from the cold and the wind. But Danxuan might not have agreed with me. During those hours in Starbucks, we saw young people coming in and out. Those who were working on their assignments had long finished and left, while Danxuan and I were still there, talking about an incomplete, if not impossible, task.

One of Danxuan's favorite movies is "Saving Private Ryan." He told me that he used to be a big fan of the Chinese revolutionary movies when he was a child. When he watched more war movies outside of China, one difference was very obvious to him—the Chinese revolutionary movies tended to project heroes as faultless and flawless human beings who were ready to sacrifice life and family for the nation and a higher cause. I decided to watch "Saving Private Ryan" to try to understand its impact on Danxuan. The movie is about a mission in World War II to find a young soldier named "Ryan" and return him home safely. Ryan's three brothers have all been killed in battle. The mission is led by a Captain Miller, who commands a platoon of men who have mixed feelings about risking their lives for Ryan. Eventually Ryan is saved, but Captain Miller is killed near the end of the mission. Before he dies, he tells Ryan: "Earn this. Earn it." Danxuan was very touched by a scene in which Ryan visits Miller's grave with his wife and children to tell the Captain that he had led a good life, and that he was a "good man," and thus worthy of the sacrifices by Miller and others.

When asked about his attitude toward life, Danxuan will tell you that it is important to live a healthy life. He also says that those who were killed in 1989 would like to see us living a good life. However, his ongoing political activism makes it difficult to realize a truly healthy and happy life. Unlike those who died in 1989, Danxuan is the "Ryan" who survived. At the same time, he is like Captain Miller, who wants to save more "Ryans," even though he believes that those who sacrificed their lives for him and for China would like him to lead a normal life.

Danxuan appears unflappable most of the time, but I know that once I mentioned the song "I Want to Have a Home," he became emotional no matter how hard he tried to hide it. When he was a young boy, the CCP separated his family forcing them to live in two cities. After 1989, the CCP separated them with prison walls. Now, they are living on separate continents. Sometimes, when I look at him, I think maybe it would have been easier for him to die in 1989 rather than to have survived and carried on.

CHAPTER 4

No Direction Home: Shen Tong

It was a rainy Saturday night in the middle of New York City. Through the car window and the rain I was trying hard to read the names of the streets. Like any traveler on the road, despite the maps and directions on hand, we still get lost during our journey. Drivers honked impatiently, reminding me that I didn't belong there although I was physically present. The city was as strange to me as I was strange to it. It was in this city that Shen Tong had chosen to set up his home.

Earlier that week, in Washington, I had taken part in the memorial activities for the Tiananmen anniversary, and then left for New York to interview Shen Tong. Knowing it was going to be several hours' drive from DC to New York, he thoughtfully suggested that I stay with his family on Saturday night so that we could start our interview early Sunday morning.

By the time I found Shen Tong's building in SoHo, it was already late in the night. Shen Tong came downstairs to greet me and showed me to the elevator. When the elevator door opened again, I found myself in a tastefully decorated living room. There, Shen Tong introduced me to his wife, a young woman with a pleasant disposition, and to a second woman, their friend, who, as I realized only later, was a movie star.

Challenges: A Controversial Leader and a Well-Known Author

Shen Tong was an undergraduate student studying biology at Peking University in 1989 and co-chaired the Student Dialogue Delegation to engage the government in dialogue during the movement. Before the movement erupted, he had already been admitted to Brandeis University in Massachusetts, which made it possible for him to apply for a Chinese passport, an unusual document for Chinese citizens to hold in those days. Six days after the June 4

Massacre, he managed to board a plane at the Beijing airport with valid travel documents. Among my three participants, Shen Tong is the only one who was not imprisoned immediately after the 1989 crackdown.

Shen Tong was named one of *Newsweek's* People of the Year in 1989, and in 1990 he published his autobiography, *Almost a Revolution*. He founded the Democracy for China Fund not long after coming to the United States and remained an active dissident until the late 1990s, when he started his own business. He has studied at Brandeis, Harvard, and Boston University.

When I interviewed him, Shen Tong had disappeared from the dissidents' circle for over a decade. Unlike Wang Dan and Danxuan, he rarely showed up for events organized by the exile student community during my research years. Although we had known each other for a long time and he was always supportive of my projects, we had participated together in only one event – a telephone memorial service after former General Secretary of the Party, Zhao Ziyang, died in January 2005. Zhao had been expelled from the top leadership in 1989 because of his support for the student movement and had lived under house arrest until his death. The student exiles regarded Zhao as a man of conscience and upon hearing of his death they shared their sadness and feelings of helplessness. When Zhao's predecessor, Hu Yaobang, had died on April 15, 1989, students had taken to the streets in mourning, thus triggering the Tiananmen Movement. When Zhao died, students were exiled and scattered all over the world and there was nothing they could do other than to organize a telephone memorial service in his memory

During the service, Shen Tong offered a perspective different from the largely positive views of other exiled students. He argued that Zhao had been part of the CCP system in 1989, and the students were protesting against corruption within the Party leadership, including the notorious cases against Zhao's sons. Shen Tong must have anticipated disagreements from the group, but that didn't stop him from expressing himself. That was the Shen Tong I had come to know—although personally, I didn't think that the memorial service was the right time to engage in criticism of Zhao. After all, Zhao was the only one among the top leadership who chose to stand on the side of history in 1989. In his 2009 memoir he made it clear that he knew his decision would end his political career:

> By insisting on my view of the student demonstrations and refusing to accept the decision to crack down with force, I knew what the consequences would be and what treatment I would receive…I knew that if I persistently upheld my view, I would ultimately be compelled to step down.[1]

In the middle of the memorial service, Shen Tong told us that he had to get off the phone early because he had a baby girl to take care of. We were all surprised to hear that he had already become a father. Usually news about one's marriage or having children would spread fast among members of the exile student group. At that time, the death of Zhao and the birth of Shen Tong's daughter didn't present an obvious contrast to me, but later on, the themes of life and death would become prominent during our interviews and group discussions.

Shen Tong has resumed his political activism in recent years. In 2011, after leaving the software company that he had founded, he participated in the Occupy Wall Street Movement. In 2013, he joined efforts to seek the release of Nobel Peace Laureate Liu Xiaobo, who is currently serving an eleven-year prison sentence in China and whose wife has been put under house arrest since her husband received the Nobel Prize.

Shen Tong and Wang Dan had both been undergraduate students at Peking University in 1989, and both their families were associated with the university. Shen Tong's father and sister were graduates of Peking University, as were Wang Dan's parents. The university, colloquially known in Chinese as *Beida*, was the center of the 1989 movement. Founded as the Imperial University of Peking in 1898, it had hosted and educated many prominent thinkers. Known for its liberal tradition and encouragement of progressive thought, *Beida* had been at the center of the country's political debates and was considered the cradle of democracy. In particular, the "Triangle," a jumble of bulletin boards erected to form three sides at a point in the center of the campus, historically had been a symbolic space for free expression. Throughout the course of the 1989 movement, the Triangle became a marketplace for information where leaflets were often distributed. Surrounded by big-character posters, students, teachers, and ordinary citizens would gather to express their opinions and to learn of the latest developments. The various opinions expressed on the bulletin boards were emblematic of the university's reputation for tolerance and openness. In 2007, the authorities demolished the Triangle despite opposition, especially from the university alumni of the 1980s. Wang Dan commented that it was "a stupid abandonment of the school's democratic tradition" and that the Triangle was "an unforgettable place for every student inspired in the 1980s by the democratic spirit."[2]

From the very beginning, I was aware that it would not be easy to write about my research participants. This was particularly true of Shen Tong, who had been a controversial figure. In 1992, he tried to return to China and was seized by the authorities at his mother's Beijing residence. Seventy-four members of the U.S. Senate signed a letter to Chinese premier Li Peng calling for his release.[3] After being held by Chinese authorities for more than six weeks, he was released and immediately expelled from the country. Thereafter, those whom he had contacted prior to his arrest were placed under surveillance and some were even imprisoned. Shen Tong faced criticisms that he should have known that while he had the whole world to protect him when he got into trouble, those whom he had contacted during his trip would be left unprotected and vulnerable. For his part, Shen Tong explained the reasons for his trip in a public statement:[4]

> For three years, I have been yearning to return to the land of my birth, the land I was forced to flee in the wake of a bloody confrontation between tanks and people. I have come back to touch, taste, and smell the wonders of my native land. I have come back with the same dream of democracy and freedom my friends and I struggled for in Tiananmen Square.
>
> I have returned without malice or ill intent. I am inspired only by a love for Truth. I do not know what will happen to me in China, as my journey continues. But I do know that no gun, no tank, nor any attempt to buy people off by consumerism can destroy the need of the human spirit for freedom.
>
> I am extremely grateful to the American people for the support they have given me over the last three years. They provided a home when the door to China was slammed shut behind me.
>
> Exiled dissidents have accomplished much since 1989 to keep the dream of a democratic China alive, and will continue to accomplish more; but the time came for me, this one dissident, to return to his homeland.

Several years later, in 1999, Shen Tong expressed his pessimism about the prospects for Chinese democracy in an interview with a journalist on the tenth anniversary of the Tiananmen movement:

> We all thought that the Cultural Revolution was the worst that could ever have happened to the Chinese people…it couldn't be worse.…Then came the Tiananmen Square shootout. We all thought that the 1980s were the best years we ever had and things could only change for the better. But things do not necessarily change from good to the better. It could change from good to very bad.[5]

Despite this, Shen Tong announced his determination to carry on: "Why I haven't given it up? It's like asking me, 'Why live?'"

In 2007, eight years after his "to live is to not give up" statement, Shen Tong was featured in a *CNN Fortune Small Business* magazine story whose header read, "A Tiananmen Rebel Turns Capitalist: After Fleeing to the U.S., an Entrepreneur Returns to Do Business with His Former Oppressors." In the article, Shen Tong justified his decision to give up activism by saying that he could have a greater influence as an individual by bringing technology to Chinese society. He confirmed that his visits to Beijing were "on condition that he stays out of Chinese politics," but denied the accusation that his company sold software to the Chinese military or to state security agents.[6] Shen Tong explained to me later that there was no factual evidence supporting such speculation—his company sold media organizing tools, not censoring software.

There have been criticisms that Shen Tong abandoned the cause of democracy for money. It is true that his decision has provided a more stable life with a financial security greater than that of most members of the exile community. Very often I have heard comments that the Tiananmen exiles are stuck in democratic activism because of their poor English language ability and lack of other skills: there is nothing they can do other than continue their activism. But in 1989 most of these exiles were studying at China's top universities. If other Chinese students and immigrants can survive and prosper abroad, the exiles should be able to do the same, if not better. Shen Tong is a good example. In this chapter, I attempt to understand the controversy surrounding Shen Tong based on his life experiences and the connections between the various episodes in his life. I hope that this narrative account will foster reflection and prompt further dialogue and stories.

Another challenge that I faced while crafting Shen Tong's profile was how to handle his views on and experiences of conflicts within the dissident community, which were closely related to his decision to give up his political activism. On the one hand, it is true that splits and fights have become part of the reality of the exile community;[7] on the other hand, the CCP has worked to manipulate public perceptions of the exile community through state-controlled media. By emphasizing the schisms and infighting among dissidents, the regime seeks to further justify the 1989 military crackdown. It is not uncommon, especially among the younger generation in China, to believe that the trouble-makers in 1989 would have led the country down the path to chaos had it not been for the government's crackdown, despite having no idea about the challenges faced by exiles. I do not want to be part of a discourse that dismisses the exiles' efforts and struggles, but nor do I want to ignore this issue either.

A third challenge in writing about Shen Tong is that he has published an autobiography and has been interviewed by journalists all over the world. In 1990, Shen Tong published his memoir, *Almost a Revolution*, with the help from former *Washington Post* journalist Marianne Yen. The book, the first autobiographical account by a student leader of the 1989 uprising, starts with a self-introduction:

> My name is Shen Tong. I was born on July 30, 1968, a time when all of China was awash in a sea of red...My given name, Tong, is a word used to describe the redness of the sunrise. Many children born in 1968 were named Tong because the word was also used to describe Chairman Mao Zedong, the supreme leader of China. But my parents didn't give me this name for its connection with Chairman Mao. They chose it because Shen Tong sounds like the word prodigy.[8]

Described by one scholar as "a compelling personal narrative and a valuable historic document,"[9] *Almost a Revolution* has been widely cited in studies of the 1989 protests. This chapter might be viewed as a continuation of the autobiography, shifting the focus from Shen Tong's socialization in China prior to 1989 to his experience in exile. Readers will find in this chapter Shen Tong's firsthand reflections about his life in exile with respect to his prior experiences in China as well as new perspectives on each episode of his life that were derived from the interview and group discussions. Unlike other studies on the Tiananmen uprising that mainly focus on the causes and progression of the uprising, here I am concerned with the full lives and struggles of these exile students from their own personal perspectives.

One significant change in terms of perspective concerns hunger strikes: Shen Tong was among those student leaders who opposed staging a hunger strike in 1989, and his views remained unchanged for over two decades. After witnessing the Arab Spring, however, he started to think that 1989 might have had a different outcome if the students had sought a real revolution: an overthrow of the government. So while Chinese officials and some outside observers continue to blame the student leaders for staging the hunger strike on the grounds that it was too radical and led to an impasse with the government, Shen Tong told me that he now believes that he should have supported the hunger strike:

> Just look at all the regime changes in the past quarter century. 1989 is unique in that there were such prolonged street protests calling only for reform. While that might be one of the reasons it lasted so long, had there been greater demands, such as regime change, other possibilities might have become real, regardless of their chances of success. But without the students' blessing, no other forces could have the political buy-in of the protesters, and by proxy, the populace.

My interview with Shen Tong began on a Sunday morning. His wife was busy preparing breakfast for us, and Shen Tong was feeding his daughter as he talked with me. Although we had been communicating with each other for years regarding my studies he began the interview by raising questions related to my topic and methodology. Since he said he was comfortable speaking either English or Chinese, we ended up switching between the two. Shen Tong is a good storyteller. His narratives were like water coming out of a pipe—once I turned on the tap, they flowed nonstop. However, as he pointed out, recollection itself can be problematic sometimes. I later found a few historical mistakes in his narrative, as well as contradictions between the information gleaned from the interview and the material in his autobiography. In such situations, I would refer to a third source to decide what to include in the profile.

*   *   *

Growing up in a Police State

Unlike many other children in our city, who grew up in the government agency residential compounds in their parents' intellectual circles, my immediate influences were our neighbors who were common workers. However, because of my parents' background, my upbringing was greatly influenced by my father and his intellectual friends.

I did not understand the distinction Shen Tong tried to make here until I read Wang Dan's memoir explaining that children in Beijing were divided into two groups: those growing up in a residential compound (dayuan) *and those growing up in a small alley* (hutong). *The former were from families who worked in government agencies or military units, and the latter were, generally, ordinary citizens. The two groups formed their own circles and rarely mixed with one another.[10] Wang Dan had grown up in a compound whereas Shen Tong had grown up in an alley.*

When the 1976 Tiananmen Incident happened, I was seven. My family always thought that I was the one who remembers the most. During that period, all my relatives—my elder cousins, my uncles and my aunts, and my father's best friends—all came to our home. Then they would go to Tiananmen Square, and then return to our home. Most of the time they took me as well, but sometimes I didn't go and one adult would stay at home with me and my sister. I knew it was for the death of Zhou Enlai—to mourn Premier Zhou.

The 1976 Tiananmen Incident, also known as the April 5th Tiananmen Incident, was triggered by the death of Chinese Premier Zhou Enlai. Historically, mourning the death of a leader in China was not only legitimate but even officially sanctioned and organized.[11] Zhou was considered by many Chinese as a morally upright and politically moderate leader at that time. His death unleashed the first spontaneous mass movement in China since the CCP had seized power in 1949. Hundreds of thousands[12] of people filled Tiananmen Square to pay tribute to Zhou and to vent their political dissent.

My family members—my parents, my grandmother, and my uncles took turns taking me to the Square. I actually wanted to stay home to play with my friends, and I wondered why they wanted me to be there. We took Bus No. 10. We went two or three times a week. It first started in January when Zhou died. It went on and on until April, around the time of the Qingming Festival.[13]

I saw all those people walking around in the dark. It was always in the dark. They were in big heavy coats. They all looked so solemn. They were making speeches, copying big-character posters and small-character posters, reading poetry, and there were also paintings—little paintings on scrap paper. That [form of mourning] isn't talked about so much. I don't remember clearly. Recollection itself is a problem. But it wasn't so much about the substance, but how serious people were and how many people there were, and the heaviness and bizarreness of the scene both in the Square and back home.

The grown-ups would have discussions at home. I didn't know exactly what they were talking about, but obviously it was something serious—about what was happening in the Square. One of my uncles used to come to our home to listen to the English program on the radio, but during those few months, they no longer listened to those programs. Instead, they would listen to the news and commentaries. The grown-ups also shared what they had copied down from the posters in the Square. Things continued like that until the government crackdown on April 5.

On the day of the crackdown I was with my mother and my grandmother. I remember that day clearly. We were walking around the Square. My father, uncles, and my father's friends were in other parts of the Square copying posters. All of a sudden my mother clutched my hand and told my grandmother that she had caught sight of the People's Militia running in columns trying to block the Square. We ran and tried to get out. But when we got to the perimeter of the Square, it had already been blocked by the militia. Probably because they saw that we were two women and a kid, they let us out.

I knew something serious was happening. My mother and my grandmother almost dragged me home. We didn't know what was happening to my father's group. It was like June 4. And there were no cell phones or pagers at that time—nothing. It took us more than twenty minutes to run home. When we got home, my father's group was already home worrying about us. Obviously they had left the Square on their bicycles before us. I didn't understand why we hadn't taken a bus instead of running.

Thirteen years later, Shen Tong again ran for his life from Tiananmen Square, but this time he was not running toward his home. He had to run away from his home and from his home country. While no machine guns and tanks were used during the 1976 Tiananmen Incident, the 1989 uprising ended with the People's Liberation Army firing AK-47s and explosive bullets at unarmed civilians.

Immediately after the crackdown the radio news kept repeating that a counter-revolutionary movement in Tiananmen Square had been crushed, and that anyone who had collected the subversive writings needed to turn them in, otherwise they would face imprisonment. People were told to expose (*jiefa*) their neighbors. We lived in a small alley (*hutong*)[14] with five or six residential compounds. Our neighbors all lived close to one another. The people on the Neighborhood Committee[15] would drop by unexpectedly at night to check on us. So we had to destroy all the writings that we had copied from the Square as quickly as we could.

"Did your family burn those copies at home?" I asked this question because my father had burned his writings after June 4.

No. We couldn't. The smoke would have been noticed if we attempted to burn anything and we would get into trouble. The grown-ups thought of another way. Since most of the papers were written with ink pens, they filled all the containers we had at home with water. Then they soaked the sheets in the water. Afterwards, they flushed them all down the toilet.

"You already had a toilet at home in those days?"

No. It wasn't a private toilet. It was a public toilet in the courtyard. That is why we had to wait until it was late and others were already asleep, and that it was late enough that even the members of the Neighborhood Committee would not suddenly appear. When the time was right, the grown-ups would go to the toilet. It took a long time to soak all those sheets of paper. The biggest headache was those papers written with ballpoint pens that were the most difficult to destroy.

"So your parents did let you know what was going on at home? I mean, they didn't try to hide it from you?"

Our home was very small. They couldn't avoid it! There was nowhere to hide!

"Did your parents tell you and your sister not to tell others?"

No. They didn't at the beginning. But when the whole thing went on a bit longer, they emphasized that we couldn't tell anyone what had been going on in our home. We knew it was very serious so we didn't tell anybody. That was the whole concept of lying. I never thought of that before this moment. It just happened that way. It was like everybody was looking over your shoulder. Anyone around you could be an informant.

There were so many secrets we had to keep. It was very confusing. At home, we were taught good values. When we got up in the morning, the first thing we did was to greet the elders. We would greet Papa, Mama, and Nainai (grandma). We would not be punished when we broke glasses or negotiated for allowances, but we would be punished severely if we told a lie. But then this happened: in 1976, we had to keep a secret from the Neighborhood Committee and from our school.

"Once a professor told me that 'lying' wasn't a good word to describe my behavior after June 4 and she suggested that I use a different word because it was not right to lie."

She was so naïve. Everybody did [lied]. That is the basic reality of living in a police state. You live a huge public lie. We don't need many theories to understand this. She should read Havel's *The Power of the Powerless*.[16]

I think there is a difference between being formal and pretending. Being formal has an element of pretending—it is like when we go to a party. In my family, my mother did the tailoring work herself. In the 1970s, even early 1980s when we were growing up, everybody's clothes were worn out, you know. My mother always added a dash of color to our clothes to make them look better. It was very important that we presented ourselves well when we went out. And that felt good. Therefore, for me, being formal, being presentable, and being respectful in a polite society is very different from how things are in a society where public doctrines determine what you can and cannot say. You are not allowed to speak freely or to show your emotions freely. You simply have to act and speak exactly what the public doctrines require.

"My grandmother also tried hard to get a piece of cloth to sew clothes for me too."

Having new clothes was a big deal in those days. We had to wait until the Chinese New Year to get new clothes.

As children, I think both Qing [Shen Tong's elder sister] and I were comparatively sensitive and that had a lot to do with our father's sensitivity. My father was a very sensitive person. He was intellectually and emotionally sensitive about what was happening around him. After work, he would sometimes bike to the Zhongnanhai Compound[17] to watch the petitioners, the *shangfang*[18]—people from outside of Beijing who would come to the capital to lodge appeals with the high-level authorities. He would stand at a distance and watch from the beginning to the end, unless the police came. But he would not participate. He always stressed that he would be concerned (*guanxin*) but he would not participate. Actually I didn't quite understand that. I am an action-oriented person. If I have an idea, I want to put it into action. My father basically lived his life in fear. Of course now in retrospect, we can understand what happened, but as children, we would think that our parents, especially our father, knew everything and that he was a hero.

Shen Tong mentions in his memoir that his father once told him to stay out of politics:

"You should be concerned about your country and understand what's going on," he said in a calm voice. "But don't participate in anything."[19]

My father was always depressed. He didn't even have a place to read. Not until 1989 did they [the Beijing Municipal Government where his father worked] assign him a room in a two-bedroom apartment. He had to share the apartment with another couple. It was before the movement started. I was attending university and I remember that I went to the apartment to help him decorate his room. He took his collections of books out from the boxes where he had kept them for years and put them on the bookshelves [in his newly assigned apartment].

"Were you confused as a child about what was happening around you?"

I didn't think much at that time, but if we are going to analyze, that was what happened. I think my family education was very good, to the extent it could be. We were relatively coherent and warm, and very straightforward. Even when we were little, when my parents made relatively big decisions for the household, like buying a piece of furniture, they would talk to me and my sister, and they would ask "What do you think?" They didn't have to—we were just five, six, or seven years old. We didn't contribute anything, but they made a point of doing this. For us, it was just the way our family was. But I found out later that this kind of open communication and participation was uncommon in Chinese families at that time. After I grew up, my father told me that they had intentionally let us participate in decision making on important things at home to train our ability to think independently.

However, once we got out of the family environment it was a different story. We had to learn certain public behavior—this part was beyond just being formal, but we had to pretend, which was a necessity. The pretending in the society was implicitly and explicitly reflected at home. For example, we were told not to say certain things. Even if we had not been told, in 1976 we could tell from the fear in the atmosphere that something bad might happen. So there was a pretense in the whole society, in the neighborhood, in workplaces, and in schools. My family was a safe haven for me to act more spontaneously. To a certain extent, Qing and I were provided a shelter [in which] to express our opinions more freely. However, because of the social conditions, conflicts and confusions were also very present.

I think I had a reasonably normal childhood. For a period of time when I was in Grade One, I didn't go to school for one semester. I became self-isolated (*zibi*)—I totally lived in my own world. I was told that I didn't need to go to school those days—I guess probably because I behaved strangely at home. I knew there was something wrong with me. I had all different types of strange thoughts and wild imaginations. I thought of lots of inventions and I wanted to put them into action. I would describe them to my family members. I don't remember exactly what happened. I can't expand today. I think I was a sensitive kid.

Another thing is that I didn't go to kindergarten—instead I started primary school right away. So I kind of became not very sociable—*buhequn*. I never thought about it until it became very apparent. For example, right after June 4 when I first came out [of China], people said I acted like a *duxingxia* (loner). If you put it in a positive way, I am independent; if you say it negatively, I am self-centered. You can see that I am not closely associated with the exile group. I think that has a lot to do with my upbringing.

But I was very popular in the neighborhood. Everybody knew me. Our family members were addressed by referring to their relationship to me—as Yuanyuan's [Shen Tong's infant name] mother, Yuanyuan's father, and Yuanyuan's grandma. So you see I was very popular among Chinese when I was young, not like now.

Shen Tong laughed as he mocked himself for not being popular among Chinese now.

Although my father tried to create a free family environment for us, he was rather timid. I think the fact that both my sister and I are disciplined has a lot to do with my father always being cautious.

I am never satisfied. I am always very harsh on myself. I think this has a lot to do with the influence of my family and Chinese society. When we were kids, we were taught to admire those harsh revolutionary figures and to be harsh in action. We were told to take cold showers during freezing winter mornings and to get up very early to jog, etc. We did all those hard things and we thought those were the right things to do. Even the songs we sang during our childhood were all harsh songs. For example, [songs about] driving the Nationalist Party [KMT] soldiers into the rivers and cutting off the heads of the Japanese. It was all about hardship and determination. The whole environment was like that.

I have to say that before Yanyan [Shen Tong's daughter] was born, during the fifteen years since I came to the States, I was never really happy. When I was in senior high school and university, I was pretty happy most of the time. Of course I had the growing pains of youth for a few years. But most of my time in the States, I was struggling. For example, my company has been in operation for five years. For the first four years, I was struggling really hard. It was unbelievable. It was very important for me to save face. I never thought this way. [Shen Tong was murmuring to himself when he said that.] I am very hard on myself and part of that is for *timian* [to keep up appearances].

"What do you think of your mother's influence on you? I used to think that my father had a great impact on me, especially intellectually. It wasn't until recent years that I began to realize how much of an influence my mother had on my life. For example, her passion, her kindness, and her perseverance have had a very subtle influence on me. I just didn't feel it directly before."

I am glad you raised this question. My mother didn't come through very clearly in *Almost a Revolution*. But actually her influence was tremendous. She had a lot to do with my action-orientation and pragmatism. She would always make things work no matter how harsh it was. She was very different from my father—that was why my father tended to be depressed and he died early.

For example, when our neighborhood had conflicts, my father thought that because he was working for the Municipal Government and he would like to join the Communist Party, he shouldn't get involved in those conflicts. He would find ways to avoid the conflicts. But my Mom would try to solve the problems, which was bizarre as my father was supposed to be the man of the house. Also, when my father was working in the factory, if he was not treated fairly, my mother would go to my father's supervisor to negotiate for my father. This happened a couple of times before my father went abroad to study.

My father was sent abroad to study for four years. My mother had to take care of the family all by herself. My protective environment kind of dissolved. I only communicated with my father through letters. He came back only for a short period of time each year. So I started hanging around with bad people. I shoplifted once. If my father had been around, it would not have happened.

Shen Tong's father had majored in Korean language at Peking University. He was assigned to work in a factory during the Cultural Revolution. He later worked for the Foreign Affairs Office of the Beijing Municipal Government. Shen Tong describes his father's absence in his memoir:

"I was about to turn eleven that summer in 1979. I didn't know then that the next four years—my passage from boyhood to young adulthood—would be a time when I needed my father the most."[20]

My mother has a pragmatic and optimistic approach toward life. Our home was very small. My sister and I had to live in my parents' bedroom. During weekends, my mother asked her brothers to find some construction materials such as sand and bricks at construction sites nearby. They built a small room for me and my sister.

For a period of time, I liked jazz very much. Jazz originated from the blues. Blues send the message that no matter how tough life is we can always find a way out. I would think of my mother and her optimism toward life. She had a clear pragmatic approach combined with optimism, which was very different from my father's intellectual depression. If you were purely pragmatic, you would be depressed too in Chinese society. But she had her optimism. She could somehow re-invent her life.

My mother and my grandmother didn't care that much when I participated in the movement in 1989, while my sister and my father were more supportive. My mother had common sense. If she thought it was dangerous for me, she would think that I had better not do it. She said in the TVB[21] interview that she stopped caring about politics after my attempted return to China in 1992. What happened afterward was a big blow to her. She almost collapsed. I didn't even know; in all these years she never told me.

College Years: Becoming a Student Leader

"Danxuan mentioned in our interview that he participated in the 1989 movement because he wanted to fight for his personal freedom. When he had a girlfriend in high school, the school and his family were opposed to it."

I remember someone said that sexual behavior is anti-government. I can't remember who said that. Sexual self-expression is probably the most intuitive and significant individualist act in a social environment that is repressive both politically and culturally. Youth angst is both enhanced and satisfied by the forbidden fruit that in China in the 1980s included free love and sexual affairs. And physical romance and romanticizing political and social movement converge. I had sex with my girlfriend when we were young. Sex before marriage was pretty common in my university. The change of social norms in the eighties started with sexual liberation. It was the reflection of the generation's relative individuality and spontaneity, but of course the movement of 1989 was one of great collectivity.

It [the change] was especially obvious in *Beida* (Peking University), but it wasn't so much the case in Tsinghua University. For example, on the *Beida* campus, there are different *pai* (groups), such as the TOEFL groups, the majiang[22] groups, and the dancing groups. Campus life was *duoyanghua* (diverse). I won't call that "pluralistic," because it wasn't pluralistic, *duoyuanhua*, yet. In those days, I participated in lots of campus activities as a member of the Student Union and I went out dating a lot.

Another thing I believe had a big impact was the adoption of the one-child policy. It was a campaign. Abortion became very easy in China although it was supposed to conflict with traditional values. Because of the state policy, it was much more convenient for young people to be sexually active. It was convenient because it was easy to have birth control and to have an abortion. Because of the population control policy, condoms became highly available in a conservative society that used to have strong controls on sexual behavior. Abortion became something like, I don't know, as easy as having a small operation.

"Don't you have to have a marriage certificate to have an abortion?"

Still, that was very easy. You just need to have some kind of connection to do it, since the ultimate goal is to reduce the population.

"The implications of this reality are profound: abortion became a government decision, not a personal choice, in the name of population control."

Relationships between state policy and individual values and an individual's beliefs regarding human life... Even if you were married, it was the same. If you hadn't been given the quota to have a child in your work unit, you still couldn't have a baby. Some people decided to get married when they got pregnant before marriage, but if they didn't have the quota to give birth, it was still a problem.

The society was in concert trying to prevent population growth, so everything became easy. The ready availability of condoms made a big difference. For example, it used to be a big headache when I went with my buddy Dakun[23] to buy condoms at pharmacies. We were very shy and we would look at all counters pretending that we were just looking around. Then we pointed at the condoms and pretended to ask in surprise: "What's this?" But with the gradual development of the birth-control campaign, things got much easier. So the one-child policy politically and practically affected the sexual behavior of our generation.

"I think here we have a problem of the ends justifying the means. As long as the CCP can achieve its ultimate goal, then nothing else matters. This is how we were always educated. Generation after generation, in the name of a noble goal, the government could think up a reason to justify anything they wanted to do."

Gandhi once said: "The means are equally important if not more important than the ends." I think we can expand on this a bit. This not only has something to do with the Communist police state, but it also has a lot to do with Chinese culture as well, for example, the Confucian way of ruling a state.

"Isn't it also true that it had a lot to do with the antihuman nature of the CCP culture? The regime always judged human beings from a moral high ground. Human nature, such as sexual desire, was regarded as a sin. Everything was black and white. There was no gray area."

We have lots of problems. In fact, our ideology—the righteousness that we projected on ourselves in 1989—was especially reflected by the image of Chai Ling.[24] It was a populist nature (*mincui*).

"Did you think this way in those days (in 1989) or are you thinking it now only in retrospect?"

I was in a dilemma in 1989. There were many contradictions and dividing moments, such as the April 19 beating of students at Xinhuamen. I was surprised. I couldn't understand how come the politically indifferent students all of a sudden became so passionate and committed. I knew the campus hadn't been like this before—it used to be very difficult to organize activities. So when Wang Dan and I were elected during the April 25 election, I didn't even participate in the election because I felt that the students' enthusiasm would not last for long. Also, I thought that if we considered ourselves as student leaders, our biggest task and responsibility was to try to bring about a good ending—not to get too many students into trouble (*shou chongji*). So I didn't want to be elected. But according to the rules, candidates could be self-nominated or nominated by others, so I was elected anyway. I talked about this in my book.

The Xinhuamen Incident started on April 19, when students staged sit-ins in front of Xinhuamen and demanded that government leaders come out to meet with them. Confrontations between students and police took place in the early morning of April 20, 1989. Witness accounts called the confrontation a "bloody incident." Yang Guobin describes the incident as "the first critical emotional event" that "changed the course of the movement." After the incident, a deep sense of shame and anger prompted students to organize the very first independent student organization.[25] The incident also led to the declaration of class strikes and students' camping in the Square on April 21. The April 25 election that Shen Tong mentions here was the election of the Preparatory Committee of Peking University.

Another incident was on the night of May 12, the night before the hunger strike. I remember that night I had to go home. My sister's boyfriend, on behalf of my father and the rest of our family, came to my dorm to take me home for dinner. Chai Ling was crying downstairs giving a speech at the Triangle.[26]

After Chai Ling's speech, the number of students signing up for the hunger strike rose to about three hundred.[27] Chai Ling's speech later became the core of the students' Hunger Strike Statement.

When I went back to campus, my friend told me that it had been decided to launch a hunger strike. He told me it was a premature ejaculation. The reason that I mention this incident is that it serves as an example to show the impact.... I felt I was too cynical.... I didn't realize students were so sincere.... Many students wrote their wills before they went on the hunger strike. I felt that my political awareness (*juewu*) was insufficient—I was too pessimistic and negative. Based on the previous experience, I felt that the government would punish us (*shoushi*) soon, and the students' enthusiasm was not reliable. I was living with those thoughts so I was constantly being educated. I started to think that maybe other students were become more devoted to the cause than I was.

I read articles in Hong Kong magazines about people's power and about the Polish Solidarity movement. I should say, we, or, at least, I was influenced by the international trend of democracy. It wasn't something that I imagined. It had a direct impact.... So I thought we could do it in China as well. When I saw the changes in other students, I felt that they had educated me.

My point is that in those days, I had a relapse in my thinking. There were times when I wasn't very optimistic. I was confused by others and by myself as well. But I should say that at that time I reflected on the movement more than most other students. Leftist nationalist thinking had had a strong impact on us, while we were not clear about rightist individualism. There was lots of populist thinking involved. Anti-corruption is a good example. Zhao Ziyang was responsible for the corruption, but how come all of a sudden we respected him as a god?

Life in Exile

For fifteen years, between June 4 and Yanyan's birth, I had violent nightmares almost every single night. That's unbelievable. Most of the time when I woke up, I was fairly unhappy.

It was all about murder. It was pretty graphic. Either I was killed or others were killed. There were bullets, knives, gushes of blood. It was a slow-motion killing things. I never had such dreams before June 4. I don't know why.

For a decade and a half, I had nightmares every day. The problem ended after Yanyan was born. I didn't solve the problem on my own, but about one week after her birth it (the nightmare) was gone. It never came back again. I have become a reasonably and relatively content person in the past six months.

"Some exiled students told me they had nightmares about running for their lives and escaping from China. Did you have that type of nightmare as well?"

For me it was not that much about running away—it was vivid images of killing scenes. Actually when I got to the United States, I got lots of good opportunities to write and speak privately and publicly to relieve myself psychologically. When I wrote, most of the time I was calm. However, whenever I had individual in-depth interviews, I couldn't stop sobbing. In the past (before Yanyan's birth), in private interviews about the details of June 4, I couldn't help sobbing.

For example, last year Kaixi was shooting a documentary on exiles and he brought over a team. We were having the interview in the corridor outside my study-room. Kaixi was sitting behind the camera on one side and I was sitting on the other. Because he was the one interviewing me, and we were familiar with each other, for the whole time I couldn't stop sobbing. I couldn't stop my tears.

When Shen Tong said "Kaixi," he was referring to Wuer Kaixi, another prominent student leader of the Tiananmen protests. He was a Uyghur student studying at Beijing Normal University in 1989, subsequently listed second among the twenty-one most-wanted students. After the crackdown, lengthy film clips of him were shown on TV throughout the country so that viewers would be able to identify him and turn him in. He fled to Hong Kong with the help of Operation Yellowbird. He first went to Paris and then moved to the United States. He now works in Taiwan as a political commentator. During the past few years, Wuer Kaixi has tried to turn himself in to Chinese authorities—in Macau in 2009, in Tokyo in 2010, in Washington in 2011, and in Hong Kong in 2013, but all without success. His parents have been repeatedly denied permission to leave China, and he has not been allowed to return, so he has not seen his parents since 1989. His teenaged sons have never met their grandparents.

For the fifteenth anniversary of Tiananmen, Kaixi traveled to the United States from Taiwan to shoot a documentary about the exiles. I met him and his cameramen in Washington DC, along with some other exiled students. Shen Tong was not with us that day, but Wang Dan and Danxuan were there. Among many other memories, one of my deep impressions about that day is that we were all extremely hungry at night. Over the years it had been the practice that the exiled students would not go out for dinner after the candlelight vigil in order to maintain the solemnity of the event. Going without dinner was particularly hard that year because we had had a full day of activities, including organizing a press conference at the National Press Club. By the time we finished the candlelight vigil, large-framed people like Kaixi were famished. We ended up eating slices of pizza in a crowded hotel room. Many of us had to sit on the floor because there were not enough chairs or beds to sit on. I was rather sad that night, watching them eat pizzas sitting on the floor, enthusiastically talking about China, their home country that no longer welcomed them home.

I had the feeling of being reborn (*congsheng*) after Yanyan was born. All of a sudden I realized that there was something subconscious about my nightmares. Although I had lots of chances to relieve and express myself, in my subconscious there was still a huge problem. I think this was like a metaphor—the birth of a life. That kind of loss (in 1989) needed to be balanced by the birth of a life.

Shen Tong's remark reminded me of something that had happened to a dissident exile who had spent so much of his time and energy working for the democratic cause that his personal life fell apart. When his wife became pregnant, they couldn't afford to keep the baby because of their financial situation. They both became depressed afterward and his wife challenged him with the following questions: If the lives of those victims in 1989 should not have been taken away, then why should we give up the life of our own baby? Those who were killed in 1989 died on our behalf so we could have a better life, why are we sacrificing our future to fight for justice for those who were killed? If there is any sacrifice that should be made, why is it always us who have to make such a sacrifice?

Infighting: From Comrades to Enemies

I think I am more like my father—always being harsh on myself, and I can't forgive myself for failures. For example, I feel that I have devoted lots of effort and have done lots of practical work for the democratic cause. For about ten years, I spent most of my time on it. Actually, I like my major but I didn't have time for it—I spent less than 40 percent of my time or even less [on my studies]. The rest of the time I worked for my foundation. But in the Chinese community, how could they...? After I returned from China in 1992, the betrayal was unbelievable. They tried everything to destroy you. It was really unbelievable!

Shen Tong shared with me his experience and feelings of being betrayed by some well-known dissidents. He mentioned in particular one incident. In the late 1990s, representatives of the exile groups, including both of the pre-June 4 exiles and those of the post-June 4 exiles, were attempting to merge to form a common front for overseas democratic activism. They signed a document confirming their alliance, and Shen Tong was responsible for the actual operation. Shen Tong said that he used all the political credentials and resources he had accumulated over the years to work on this. In the end, the leaders who had signed the document denied that they had signed it. Instead, they asserted that Shen Tong had presented a fake document.

I cannot comprehend why that happened. The very fact that my peers, and the exile community in a broader sense, had such a strong negative perception of me—I simply cannot understand that. I tried to pretend that I didn't care, but I just couldn't take it. After I left China, the biggest blow to me was not the difficult situation or the pressures from China, but the problems originating from the dissident groups. Of course I recognized the fact that the situation was getting harder on everyone. First, we were becoming irrelevant to China; second, U.S. policy toward China had changed. In these contexts, where the resources dried up, it became more and more difficult to survive. The ecosystem had disappeared.

I survived those (betrayals), but I will not forget them with the passage of time. You see how I remember things—I remember everything. I blame myself, just like my father had blamed himself. When my grandparents passed away, my father was at the military school and he was not allowed to return home for the funeral, but he blamed himself. I also tend to blame myself. The reason that I am a survivor has a lot to do with my mother, with her "pragmatic optimism"—that's a perfect phrase, but I never realized that before. Somehow life goes on.

When Shen Tong's grandfather passed away, his father was not allowed to return home to attend the funeral. When his own father died, Shen Tong was living in exile and unable to return.

Because of those betrayals by the dissident community I had a major identity crisis. As we discussed over the phone, I wonder whether I should be a public intellectual, an academic intellectual, a political activist, a social activist, or a media professional. At the same time, I had all these choices at that time. The challenges in the democratic community were not derived from external hardships, but from our own colleagues and comrades. I could handle external hardship, but not an internal betrayal. And it seemed to me that this wasn't just a one-time betrayal. That was the way it was going to be.

My academic pursuits were being challenged as well—my dissertation was not approved. That was another blow for me. It was true that my dissertation wasn't perfect but it should have been good enough to pass—it was a thesis of 700 pages. I then cut it to 400 pages. The major reason that it was not approved was that I failed to maintain a good relationship with my supervisor. Also, I had always thought that things were going well in school so I didn't pay too much attention. Working for the democratic cause was my primary task at that time, and writing provided my emotional relief. Academic work was a different track, and it wasn't my priority. So at that time both my academic pursuits and my political pursuits faced insurmountable problems. I somehow still pulled through.

After the betrayal in 1998 and 1999, I realized I had to do something. I clearly remember that in April 2000, I was in New Orleans for a jazz festival. I decided that I really needed to take a break. I was basically depressed. All alone I had been a student relying on scholarships. The funding for my foundation had dried up after that incident. The foundation basically collapsed, so my colleagues all lost their jobs. I borrowed money from my credit card and went with my friends to New Orleans. One day, after a few drinks in a bar, I made a bet. I said I would spend the next seven years to build a business. Since I had always been interested in the media, I thought I would turn media into a business, a very big business. In the 1990s, Internet companies like Yahoo! could easily be listed on the stock market. However, I didn't know much about IT nor did I know much about business at that time. What I had done with the media in the past was related to culture—it was talent-intensive and not capital-intensive. I was a complete layman in terms of doing business.

"How does it feel now to be a businessman?"

I can't really accept the fact that I have become a mere businessman. I don't mean that I look down upon businessmen, but being a businessman is not my thing. But now I am learning to appreciate it and to be reasonably content as an entrepreneur. For me, to have both intellectual and political pursuits and dreams, not just politics, I mean, to be an "action-oriented idealist"—that's a good term—is much grander than just being an entrepreneur. Being an entrepreneur is very hard—don't get me wrong—trying to build something from scratch. I think I have pulled through in the past five years. Again, I think my mother's pragmatism has something to do with that.

A few of my close friends observed that I have become more materialistic over the past year. For example, I couldn't accept that I lived in SoHo before—I preferred to live in the West Village. Of course this doesn't make any difference to non–New Yorkers. The point is that the West Village is less commercial. I am rather biased against commerce in favor of intellectual work (*qingshang zhongwen*). Let me give you another example. My sister specializes in fashion. For many years, I looked down upon her profession. At our dinner table, I always joked about cosmetics and fashions. In 1989, when I first came to the United States, the media called me "blue jeans." I tried to make the point that: (1) I didn't spend my time making money; (2) I didn't pay too much attention to clothing styles. I resisted anything materialistic. For me, it is not a virtue; it is a problem. At the same time, I cared about my face. So I tried to be outstanding and unique. This is important. I think it has something to do with my relatively isolated childhood (*bu hequn*).

"Now in retrospect, how do you feel about those conflicts?"

It is a relief for me to feel disgusted by the dirty politics involved in the dissident circles. For this reason, I started not to look at those things so politically. Now I can tell you the details (of the betrayal) as if I am telling a story. It is like when I told you the story about shoplifting when I was a kid. I don't need to be in a safe environment to share things like this anymore. It may not be a good story or good thing to tell, but I can talk about it with a sense of balance (*pingchangxin*). This is a good start. I don't think it is normal for such things to happen. But I was harsh on myself and I felt a lot of bitterness when I talked about those things before. So to start with—the only thing I can do—is not to look at such things politically. Of course this will not help me to solve the problem, but I can start to look at those things from different perspectives.

"I find it difficult to present this type of information."

You don't need to cover up anything. When I wrote my book, some people didn't like that I revealed the in-fighting and problems of the movement. But I think it is a better book than *Moving the Mountain*[28]—not because it was written in better language. I think it (*Almost a Revolution*) is a better book for its readership—the general public and the young college students. If one describes things as close to the fact as possible, it will be more accessible. People understand things better if they are accessible. This has actually been a problem in many of my later writings. I am so wrapped up in my own ideas that I make things less accessible. However, accessible things will be closer to home. Our problems may have particularities that common people can't imagine, but they also involve human emotions and human weaknesses that everyone can relate to.

You should be able to openly talk about the conflicts in the community. It is still an unfolding story. Our lives are now less dramatic. However, in terms of long-term impact, how do we know? Most of the exiles had become irrelevant. The word "exile" itself can be problematic. What exactly does it mean? What does it imply about our current lives (*shengcun zhuangtai*)? Who are we? The strong political connection we have only exists in our subjective world—we consider China as our cultural center, intellectual center, and life center. The previous generation of dissidents—the generation before the 1989 generation— had basically lived split lives (*shenghuozai fenliezhong*). Psychologically and intellectually speaking, their center is in China, but physically they are overseas. They are disconnected from the society of today's China. Our generation of exiles is basically the same except for the fact that maybe some of us can choose to live a comparatively normal life in a foreign country (*yiguo*).

I happened to be in contact recently with one of the student leaders on the most-wanted list. He had disappeared from the public eye for many years. We went on vacation together with our families. He is now quite successful as a businessman in finance. We had some arguments during the trip. He tried to stress two points: first, he said June 4 and what we did thereafter overseas was all bullshit; second, he said he had no moral bottom line. However, I don't think and I don't believe that he meant it. I argued with him by saying that maybe what we did in 1989 wasn't as great as we had believed at the time, which is also a main point that I have been reflecting on all these years. I keep asking myself what exactly was it all about in 1989, and how I can recover the facts and feelings instead of presenting memories based on reinterpretation or even misinterpretations. But 1989 was certainly not bullshit. Afterward, I kept thinking about what he said.

I think that his outlook may have something to do with his personal experience, if you look at the fact that not many student leaders have actually received a lot of public attention after they became exiles. You can name the names [not many]. His point was that you might think that we had had great influence, but actually our impact was limited—we were just some members of the cheering squad. I disagreed with him. When I participated in the movement in Beijing, for me it was both an experience and an experiment as well.

But I can relate to him in the sense that I had to overcome serious psychological obstacles when I first started to do business. How could I give up this [democracy work] and start to do that [business]? I felt that I would never forgive myself for that [giving up]. I needed to come up with some kind of explanation for myself. However, I couldn't really find one—it wasn't that I didn't care about this [democracy work]; it wasn't that I thought the mission had been accomplished; and it wasn't that I thought it was not meaningful to continue—none of that. I couldn't accept the fact that I had stopped doing this [democratic work]. This was painful for me. That's how I could relate to what he said. He had provided himself with an explanation. It is like the blues—no matter how harsh life is, it finds a way out. I think his extreme perspective was how he provided an explanation for himself. Another interpretation might be that he had somehow glorified the cause, but it turned out to be not that glorious after all, so it was bullshit. It also could have been that because it was not worth working with the other members of the community. This is like the case in Taiwan. The current beneficiaries of the Democratic Progressive Party (DPP) are not those who devoted and sacrificed for the Party in the early years—they just happened to be members of the same political group.

"Still, you didn't make up excuses like that (to give up the democracy work)."

For me, the decision was comparatively easier because I had great interest in the media and I had some background in the media. If I had taken up finance, that would have been very difficult, unless I could become like Li Lu or Chai Ling[29]— and just to become a capitalist. I am not morally criticizing them. I admire them for being able to do that.

"To get back to your friend's perspective, it might be true that his thoughts had changed but it didn't mean that he necessarily thought the same way in 1989. It was just a different perspective at a different time."

That is your interpretation. He believes in his current ideas and he thinks that June 4 was wrong. The same perspective can have different interpretations. You are too emotionally involved in the event so it is hard for you to accept his perspective. We all have this problem. What happened during our telephone memorial service made me disappointed and angry.[30] But when I calmed down, I was glad that I started to put things into perspective. There is no way for us to keep June 4 in perspective because it is too close. So the only perspective is a nonperspective—it is only an emotional attachment. This is the opposite of when we say in English "to put things into perspective." About June 4, we think that it is too big—it is like Niagara Falls. It is just larger than individual life and it should be larger than every individual life. In other words, we tend to think that it is larger than individual life and it should be larger than any one individual's life. That is not a proper perspective.

"Still, 'to put things into perspective' doesn't mean to call it 'bullshit.' I don't think that is the way to put things into perspective."

I think I can start to put things into perspective to some extent by keeping some distance. Of course this is worth analyzing. It is like you have a great love relationship with someone but then you are dumped. It would be very painful of course. However, after many years, I can put things into perspective and we can remain friends. It is a good thing but it is also a sad thing. You come out of that extreme passion and attachment.

When I first read that information several years ago, I had interpreted it as an indication of his "unrequited love"—neither his love of the cause nor his love of China had been answered. In a sense, he became a homeless drifter, a man "always on the road" living in "a home for the homeless," as he described himself in our group discussion. In his autobiography he writes:

In this great international family that I now live in, there is only one door that remains closed to me—the door that leads to my native country, China . . . [Behind that door], there is my family, that splendid earth, and my people. There is my dream and my friends who wait in prison for that dream to come true.[31]

When I re-read Shen Tong's comments on putting things into perspective, I started to think that maybe what he was implying here was that he was ready to think about 1989 from a different perspective and to reconcile with the Chinese government. My speculation was clarified after a long phone conversation with him, in which he made it clear that he remained critical of the Beijing regime.

I have kind of disappeared from the democracy community in the past five years for two reasons: first, I was not very gregarious [in the community]; second, I couldn't deal with the fact that I wasn't doing something related to my ideals, even though I was doing what I was professionally interested in. I believe that I should pursue our goal in a way I am familiar with, by doing things I am interested in. I believe only in this way can we achieve it in an effective and normal way. However, it is true that the media have nothing to do with our ideals.

We can classify Chinese intellectuals as a knowledge class. In the Chinese context, the concept of "class" is useful. It is related to social status. For example, university graduates will become cadres once they graduate—their salaries and rankings are based on that as well. Intellectuals are classically defined by Edward Said as "outsiders." In this sense, they have a strong social function, cultural function, and value orientation (*jiazhi dingwei*).

A Son's Guilt

"You did not mention much in the book about the pressure your parents felt during the movement. Could you tell me about that?"

For my father, the impact was direct. During the movement, his work unit, the Beijing Municipal Government, put lots of pressure on him. I was the most active among the children of the officials in the Municipal Government. They had videotapes to monitor what was happening on the Avenue of Eternal Peace during the movement, and I could be seen almost every day—I was among the group. They all knew that I was the son of Old Shen. My father couldn't sleep every night but he kept saying that he couldn't betray his son. My family didn't tell me this until after he passed away.

Shen Tong's father was admitted to the hospital a few days before the military crackdown on June 4. Shen Tong describes his visit to the hospital on June 1 in Almost a Revolution:

I stayed for only five minutes, but on my way out of the hospital I looked up and saw my father, wearing the light blue hospital-issue pyjamas, staring out the window while my mother held his hand. I had never seen my parents touch each other or show any affection before. I should have known then that my father was gravely ill, but I didn't think about it. I wish now that I had known the truth; if I had, I would have spent every minute with him at the hospital.[32]

Shen Tong's father passed away shortly after Shen Tong fled China.

Soon after I got to the States, I found out from my host family that there was a holiday called "Fathers' Day." My father was in the hospital and there was no phone at the hospital. It was difficult for me to find out what the situation was at home. I missed home a lot and I was worried about my family. I didn't have any money to do other things so I bought a card and sent it to a friend's place and asked him to pass it on to my father—it was impossible for me to send mail home directly. That was the first and the only Fathers' Day card I managed to send to my father before he passed away. My father was very happy. He asked friends and relatives whom he trusted to listen to foreign radio broadcasts to get news about me. After he learned from the news about what I was doing, he said he was proud of me. Before that, he didn't want me to continue my political activism.

"Why do you think he changed?"

I think that before, he was worrying about my safety so he didn't want me to participate in the movement. But after June 4, the worst thing had already happened. He didn't need to worry about me when I was abroad.

Shen Tong found out later that his father's superiors in the Beijing Municipal Government had asked his father to spy on his son. His father told his mother: "I have

always done what the Party has asked of me, but I will never betray my son." Shen
Tong sighed that "Only now do I understand fully what my father went through in
order to protect me."[33]

In order to protect the rest of the family, my father wrote a will. In his will,
he said: Number One: "I didn't educate my son well." He didn't say that he
would disown his son. Number Two: He wanted the work unit to assign the full
apartment to our family.

Disowning family members was common during political campaigns in China.
People were expected to formally announce that they had disowned family members
who were politically incorrect. As Shen Tong explained earlier, before the movement
started, his father had been assigned a room in a two-bedroom apartment, to be shared
with another couple. His father was asking the Beijing Municipal Government to
assign the other room in the apartment to his family so that they could move out of
their old 15-square-meter home.

"Did your father show his will to the government, or just to the family? The
government didn't have the right to read others' wills."

So what? This had nothing to do with laws in China. The authorities would
read it! He was a Party member! It was lying. It was nothing else. **My father was
actively, consciously, explicitly lying while on the brink of death in order to
protect my family.**

My family tried not to tell me about my father's will because they were afraid I
would become upset if I heard that my father said that he hadn't educated his son
well. I WAS upset, but not because I thought my father didn't understand me. I
know he was trying to protect me; and he was trying to protect my mother and
the rest of the family. I felt very sad. I felt sorry for my father.

I tried to get Shen Tong to tell me more about his feelings when he learned of his
father's death. He became silent for a short while, then, with tears in his eyes, he said:
"It is too late to get into emotional things at this time of the day." Our interview ended
in silence. That was the only time throughout the research process that Shen Tong
refused to answer my questions.

The epilogue of Almost a Revolution *might help address the unanswered question,*
but I know no words are adequate to replace those moments of silence:

I could not attend my father's funeral, and I never had the chance to say
goodbye to him. I thought about all the lost opportunities when he was in
the hospital during the last days of the movement, when I hadn't sat at his
bedside and talked to him or comforted him. For a while I was determined to
go home.... I slowly came to realize that my father's death had given me more
strength to carry on the pro-democracy movement in exile. He would not have
to worry about me anymore, and I felt even closer to him. We are no longer

separated by the continents and the oceans. I feel his presence often, wherever I am.[34]

*   *   *

By the time I left Shen Tong's apartment in the evening, I had almost forgotten that I was in New York City. My mind was full of images of a young boy being dragged home by his mother and grandmother from Tiananmen Square, and the young man who didn't get to attend his father's funeral. I almost forgot about all the criticisms of Shen Tong. I could understand why he wanted to provide a good life for his loved ones—for his mother, his wife, and his baby daughter. At the end of the day, we are all ordinary human beings who simply want to have a home, a real home.

CHAPTER 5

Living Somewhere Else: Wang Dan

A few weeks after my interview with Shen Tong, I was once again in New York City. This time I was not in Manhattan, but in Queens. Walking among the crowd I heard the sounds of different Chinese dialects, saw innumerable signs marking Chinese stores, and smelled the aromas wafting from Chinese restaurants. This New York street could have been in China—but somehow, similar smells, sights, tastes, and sounds are not enough to give us the feeling of being home. Instead, they reinforce our sense of homesickness. This is especially true for the person I was meeting that day: Wang Dan.

I had planned to fly to Boston to interview Wang Dan, but he had moved to California to take up a postion as visiting scholar at UCLA while completing his Harvard dissertation. When he told me that he would be in New York for an event and was planning to get together with some exiled students in the area, I suggested we take the opportunity to combine our interview with a group discussion.

We had planned to meet at Starbucks. Unlike the one in which Danxuan and I had conducted our interview, this Starbucks in Queens was crowded and noisy. Several years earlier when I had first interviewed Wang Dan in Cambridge, we had also planned to meet at Starbucks, but decided to leave when the noise became unbearable—we eventually held the interview sitting on the grass inside Harvard Yard. There was no such tranquil refuge this time. Sometimes we have no choice but to stay wherever we are, whether we like it or not.

An Activist in Public and a Child in Private

Wang Dan is probably more of a symbol of the crushed democracy movement than anyone else. In the words of one journalist, he "has maintained an integrity that perhaps no other top dissident enjoys."[1] His life story would make great raw material for Hollywood scriptwriters, but it is far too dramatic for any normal human being to wish to experience. Before the 1989 protests broke out, he had been an undergraduate student studying history at Peking University and an organizer of a "Democratic Salon" on campus, which gave students a chance to listen to and discuss unorthodox viewpoints. After the June 4 crackdown, he topped the most-wanted list because of his leadership role in the student movement, but on the list the authorities had changed his age from twenty to twenty-four; perhaps the Chinese government thought it was unconvincing, or embarrassing, to claim that a twenty-year-old boy was a leader of such a "counter-revolutionary" conspiracy. When the authorities questioned Wang's uncle whether Wang Dan was his nephew, his uncle answered, "I do have a nephew who is studying at *Beida* but he is twenty years old. So, the one on the wanted list is not my nephew."[2] Wang Dan's mother recalls in her own memoir that it was rumored that he was in a van on the way to cross the Yellow River to his father's hometown of Yancheng so police secretly gathered around his uncle's house at night hoping they would catch him. His uncle was kept inside the house and all he could do was to listen to Voice of America (VOA) and hope that Wang Dan had escaped. When the other villagers heard these rumors, they sent young people to the major entrances to the village to make sure that Wang Dan would not enter. They also tried to think of ways to hide him if he were to ever show up. As a historian, Wang Dan's mother said that the story reminded her of those scenes from over fifty years ago, when Chinese villagers tried to protect the soldiers in the Communist army from the Japanese.[3]

Wang Dan was arrested on July 2, 1989 and remained in custody for nearly two years before his official trial in 1991. He was charged with "counter-revolutionary propaganda and incitement" and sentenced to four years in prison. His sentence was comparatively mild compared with those given to other political prisoners at the time, possibly due to his high profile and the fact that he was a student. His mother was also jailed for fifty days for the sole reason that she was the mother of a "counter-revolutionary." Wang Dan was kept in Qincheng Prison, a maximum-security facility located in the northwest suburbs of Beijing that was built in 1958 with help from the Soviet Union. The majority of its inmates are political prisoners. In Wang Dan's published prison memoir (*Wang Dan yuzhong huiyilu*), he recalls that Qincheng was packed with students after the military crackdown, and every day the young prisoners would spend their time studying. Even the experienced wardens at Qincheng were overwhelmed by the fact that the prison had become a college library.[4] Wang Dan describes his fellow prisoners as his "Qincheng alumni."

Released from prison in 1993, Wang Dan was detained again in 1995. The authorities held him for seventeen months without charging him. Then in 1996 he was officially sentenced to eleven years in prison for "subverting state power." These charges against Wang Dan were based on claims that he had published articles in the overseas press and had enrolled in a correspondence course at the University of California at Berkeley. "Subverting state power" is a crime the regime frequently uses against human rights activists. For example, Wang Dan's good friend, the 2010 Nobel Peace Laureate Liu Xiaobo, was also charged with "subverting state power" in 2008. He is currently serving an eleven-year sentence.

On April 19, 1998, the Chinese and American governments struck a deal to release Wang Dan on medical parole just prior to President Bill Clinton's attendance at a planned summit in China. Wang Dan was taken directly from prison to the airport and headed to the United States. He has been banned from setting foot in mainland China ever since. He resumed his university studies in 1998 at Harvard University and received a masters' degree in East Asian Regional Studies in 2001 and a PhD in East Asian History in 2008. He is currently teaching in Taiwan.

A *Time* story describes Wang Dan's situation in the following way:

> Not all of Wang Dan's fellow exiles have remained so dedicated to—or obsessed with—their homeland. . . . Wang Dan has no quarrels with them for moving on from 1989, but he cannot. His work is what he considers his duty, his destiny. "I know the reason I am in America is because people died on June 4," he says. "If I stop my activities, then I will be dishonoring their memory." For that reason, he can never go home. . . . The tragedy for Wang Dan is that enduring exile has not nourished the movement back home; he is hardly a Nelson Mandela who inspired antiapartheid protests even while spending 27 years imprisoned on Robben Island. Instead, Wang Dan's journey from Tiananmen Square to Harvard Square has brought an increasing irrelevancy, a feeling he articulates as "having to keep so much distance when I want to be so close."[5]

Wang Dan is proud to have been a student of *Beida* (Peking University), his *muxiao* (alma mater), as he calls it when he refers to *Beida*. His father had studied at *Beida* and then taken up a position there as a professor of geology; his mother, also a *Beida* graduate, worked at the Museum of the Chinese Revolution. Wang Dan has repeatedly expressed in public his "little ambition" to become president of Peking University. When asked during a PBS interview what he would do as president of Peking University to promote his ideals, he answered:

> [All] universities produce ideas more so than technically skilled people. And Peking University is a bastion of liberal thinking in China. And so if it trains these people and they go out to serve as important people in every sector of society that would be an ideal of mine.[6]

In a public statement regarding the 1989 crackdown Wang Dan stated that while the government is guilty, the students also made mistakes (*zhengfu youzui xuesheng youcuo*). He admitted that along with the government's responsibility for the 1989 events, he also shares some of the responsibility. Some responded with concern that such a declaration would be used by the Beijing regime to discredit the Tiananmen movement. Wang Dan later clarified his statement in an interview:

> Some have misinterpreted my statement. I am not responsible for the blood-shed. My responsibility is to the dead who lost their lives for our struggle. My responsibility is to continue the efforts to bring about democracy. No one, nor history, can hold students responsible for the massacre.[7]

As a three-time nominee for the Nobel Peace Prize, Wang Dan has been interviewed by journalists all over the world. In the *New York Times* alone, he was featured in 44 articles in the ten years between 1989 and 1999. He has published extensively in Chinese, most recently in 2012 when his Chinese memoir came out in Taiwan. The University of Toronto libraries alone hold twenty of his published books. When he was exiled in 1998, a *New York Times* article described him as a dissident with "too much fame and freedom."[8] What else could I possibly still write about Wang Dan that has not already been written or said? I handled this challenge as I had in the case of Shen Tong. I focused my interview with Wang Dan on his formative years as the basis for his later life, one aspect of his life that has not been studied extensively.

Beyond the difficulty of building on the already extensive literature and reports, an even greater challenge in studying Wang Dan's life lay simply in getting him to open up and talk about himself. This may sound similar to the challenge I faced with Danxuan, but it was actually quite different. Having known Wang Dan for years, I had learned how different he can be on stage and in private. Probably because of all the interviews he has given, he seems to have trained himself to automatically shut off part of himself around recording devices—once I turned on the tape recorder, it was difficult to draw him into sharing his inner feelings and thoughts with me. It was not that he did not speak, but that he knew exactly what to say in public. As he himself puts it in a media interview: "Every year we do the same speeches, and I know everything they are going to say, every joke," he says. "Of course, they know what I am going to say, too."[9] Such a standard canned answer was certainly not what I hoped to get out of the interview.

Along with this potential for "diplomatic speech," Wang Dan can be defensive. He was understandably ready to fight to protect his privacy. Between the age of twenty during the 1989 military crackdown and the age of twenty-nine in 1998 when he was sent into exile, Wang Dan was either imprisoned or living under close surveillance. He was followed everywhere by police. In just one home search, the police reportedly took away eight bags of his books and belongings.

The methodology that I chose helped to address these challenges. Although the narrative profiles may appear to readers as simple oral histories, in fact, they are not. The researcher-participant relationship plays a significant role in the crafting of these profiles. I did not go to Wang Dan as a stranger, to record and to analyze him for a report. I present his words as well as his silences. And I do not record only what he said during the interview or present what is available in the literature—I offer my own understanding of Wang Dan based on my interactions and communications with him over the years. In other words, I did not merely listen to his words or read his writings. I "read" him as an individual in order to come to a fuller understanding of the person. This would have been impossible if we had not been involved in any collaboration beforehand. This was also the case from Wang Dan's perspective. When he addressed my questions, he knew the contexts and he understood where I was coming from. As a result, I believe he was less inhibited and we were able to have more open discussions than would have been the case otherwise. However, a close researcher-participant relationship is not perfect. There are also certain drawbacks. It was probably because I knew Wang Dan so well that he did not feel that he had to make a formal presentation when speaking to me. He could get bored when answering my questions. For example, he bargained with me by asking, "How many more questions do I have to answer?" or "Let's go and join the others. I am hungry." I don't think he would have done this had he been participating in a more formal or impersonal interview.

Wang Dan appears as a mature and calm leader in public, but in private he can behave like a child. Although Danxuan and Shen Tong have similar tendencies, their behavior was more restrained than Wang Dan's. Once after speaking at a fund-raising dinner for the Tiananmen Mothers, the audience that packed the grand hall of the restaurant gave Wang Dan a standing ovation. While I was still immersed in his compelling and thoughtful speech, as soon as we left the venue, he spoke with excitement: "See? I did a great job! I am good at this!"

He can be childishly honest, but in a positive sense. For the fifteenth anniversary of the uprising, he traveled around the world to give speeches. To use his own words, he "lived at airports" during that time. Despite the fact that he was an inspiring speaker, he asked his good friend Liu Xiaobo to draft a speech for him—probably because he was too busy and too tired to write so many speeches. If it were me, I would have been embarrassed to tell others about it. Instead, Wang Dan told a group of us around the dinner table that he had to make sure that he would receive the draft from Liu Xiaobo. "Otherwise I won't know what to say." It sounded as if he was making an amusing announcement. He asked me to keep the copy of the speech for him as he was talking to people before the event. I bet that he had forgotten the draft of his speech until it was nearly time to give his talk. He was looking for me in the crowd and seemed relieved to find me: "Do you still have my talk?" This time, he whispered, quietly, like an adult.

Like Shen Tong and Danxuan, Wang Dan began introducing himself by saying he was born during the Cultural Revolution. The Cultural Revolution is like a birthmark for those of the Tiananmen Generation. In fact, all three of my participants are very close in age. Danxuan was born in 1967, Shen Tong in 1968, and Wang Dan in 1969. Both Wang Dan and Shen Tong referred to the neighborhood committees in Beijing when they described the political context of the Cultural Revolution. Compared with Shen Tong and Danxuan, Wang Dan seems to be more proud of his success in surviving within the CCP system. He mentioned more than once during the interview that he had been a "three-good student" and a student cadre. In fact, he submitted his application to be a Communist Party member when he was in high school.[10] One of Wang Dan's high school teachers once said that if all Chinese students had been like Wang Dan, communism could have been realized in China. Wang Dan later joked: "If everyone in my generation was like me, communism would have ended."[11]

Wang Dan frequently used the official terms of expressions of the CCP in daily conversations, as he did in his speeches and writings. Shen Tong would sometimes use them as well, but in general, his vocabulary tended to be more Westernized. Compared with Shen Tong and Wang Dan, Danxuan didn't use much CCP language, which may have had something to do with his mother tongue: Danxuan's mother tongue is not Mandarin Chinese, the official national language. He speaks two other dialects—Hunan dialect and Cantonese. Wang Dan and Shen Tong both grew up in Beijing so they only speak Mandarin. Despite the differences among the three individuals in terms of their language backgrounds, they all reverted to using the Communist Party jargon when describing their experiences and thoughts related to the Cultural Revolution. I was glad that I had brought from China my father's old Chinese-English dictionary published in 1976, right after the Cultural Revolution. The old dictionary helped me tremendously with the translation of some of those old terms, which don't necessarily appear in the more recent dictionaries.

Wang Dan was the only one of the three participants who directly named the revolutionary movies in the interview, although both Danxuan and Shen Tong indirectly mentioned the impact of those revolutionary stories. At Danxuan's graduation party, the guests sang songs from the movies, including some of those that Wang Dan had referred to. Although he seemed to have good memories of the films, he rarely sang any of their songs. When we got together with other exile students, we sometimes would sing karaoke; Wang Dan enjoyed singing what we call "campus folk songs" from the 1980s, especially those from Taiwan, but not the revolutionary songs.

Along with the revolutionary movies, Wang Dan also mentioned the scar literature (*shanghen wenxue*), a genre that emerged in the late 1970s, soon after the death of Mao. The scar literature portrays the human suffering during the Cultural Revolution and the earlier political campaigns. Though the scar literature focuses on trauma and oppression, love and faith remain its major themes. Most writers of scar literature were not opposed to the Communist regime, but retained a faith in the ability of the Party to rectify its past mistakes. Scar literature came under attack by conservatives within the CCP leadership as early as 1979. Eventually, the government began to crack down on the genre as part of a wider campaign against "bourgeois liberalization" launched in the early 1980s.[12] Liberal General Secretary of the Party Hu Yaobang was blamed for his "laxness" in fighting bourgeois liberalization and in January 1987, he was forced to resign from his position. If we consider the significant influence that scar literature had on the Tiananmen Generation, it is not difficult to understand why, among other reasons discussed in Chapter One, students reacted so strongly to Hu Yaobang's purge in 1987 and why his death in 1989 triggered the Tiananmen movement.

* * *

Growing up in a "Political Society"

I was born during the Cultural Revolution. Now in retrospect, the society was very political. But of course, as a kid, I would not have called it political at that time.

"Why do you say the society was political?"
I lived in a residential compound belonging to the Museum of the Chinese Revolution in a *hutong* in Beijing. There were neighborhood committees. They (the committee) often organized activities to promote the government policies. As kids, we would go with our parents to attend those activities. I think some people are born with a great interest in public affairs, while others have no interest—I belong to the former type. So my childhood memories include the activities organized by the neighborhood committee, and the Criticize Lin Biao, Criticize Confucius Campaign.[13] Other than that, I don't even remember where my kindergarten was located or anything about the other children.

The neighborhood committee often organized theatrical evening parties (*wenyi wanhui*). All the courtyards were required to send representatives to perform. Our courtyard would ask the children to perform. I still remember how we had our rehearsals, and how we put on lipstick for the performances. I don't really remember much else about it. My general impression is that it was an environment that put a lot of emphasis on collectivism. We always had to live in a collective context and I was averse to that.

I studied well in school, and my family didn't put much pressure on me. They gave me lots of freedom and I made friends with other kids. I had always been a "three-good student" and a student cadre. My family didn't have a strong political or ideological background. We didn't discuss politics at home. But since both my parents are *Beida* [Peking University] graduates, I had quite a special attachment to *Beida*. Other than that, what was happening in the society didn't have much of an impact on me. So I never had much sense of defeat.

"Can you give me an example of your parents' giving you lots of freedom at home?"

When I was in primary school, *wuxia* (martial heroes)[14] fiction was very popular. My friends in our class all loved to read *wuxia* romances. You know, children like to imitate after they read a lot about something they are interested in. So seven or eight of the boys in our class decided to organize a gang (*bangpai*) and set up a stronghold (*shantou*). We established a Chinese Chivalry Party. Actually we had no idea what a (political) party really was, but we knew that it was something often mentioned in the *wuxia* stories. We were so serious that we even made a seal for our party. Each of us received a party membership certificate that was stamped with our own pictures and the party seal. We made a party constitution in which it was written that we were all sworn brothers. I was in Grade Five.[15] That was just childhood fun, you know. But two of the kids' parents were working at the Ministry of Public Security. They lived in the residential compound belonging to the Ministry of Public Security, which was next to our courtyard. One of the kids threw around all the stuff about our party at home and this attracted his parents' attention. In those days, the Ministry of Public Security was very leftist [politically]. I didn't know how the incident was reported to the ministry. It really wasn't so serious that it should have been reported—it was simply because some of the children of the staff at the ministry were involved. It was said that within the courtyard of the Ministry of Public Security, a group of children were establishing a political party. One kid was questioned and he disclosed the names of the other kids in our group. I was told to go to the Ministry of Public Security. My father went with me and he waited for me outside. We were both confused and had no idea what was going on.

I was questioned. The officer asked me "What is this all about?" and "What do you plan to do?" As a kid, I had no idea. So I said this was about *wuxia*. I imagine if this had happened in other families, the parents would have become nervous and beaten their kids. But when we got home, my Mom asked me what it was all about. I told her "We were playing *wuxia*." Then she said, "Go to bed" and that was it. My mother's reaction left a deep impression on me. I felt that my life really didn't have any pressures. I had been really frightened, but when I saw that my parents didn't care, I was relieved.

"Did you ever think about this incident after you grew up?"

No, not at all. It isn't a big deal in my memory. I think it is important for parents not to make a fuss (*dajingxiaoguai*). Otherwise, their children will have to endure a lot of stress.

The society was tightly controlled. This was right after the fall of the "The Gang of Four"[16] (*sirenbang*). I think such a funny incident like our party could only occur in a tightly controlled society.

"Did you feel any conflicts between home and society? Danxuan and Shen Tong both talked about such conflicts."

The atmosphere in the society was tense but my family was comparatively relaxed. And it was exactly because of the intensity of the pressure in the society that my family tried to protect me. That was why I can say that my childhood memories are bright and positive.

In China, trying to establish a political party can be serious enough to cost someone their life. Chinese writer Zha Jianying has published an essay in The New Yorker *about her brother, who helped to start an opposition party—the China Democracy Party—in 1998: "It was the first time in the history of the People's Republic of China that anyone had dared to form and register an independent party."[17] As a result, her brother was sentenced to a nine-year prison term for "subverting the state" and he was labeled an "enemy of the state." Wang Dan and his family never could have imagined that in 1996, Wang Dan, the little boy who survived the Chinese Chivalry Party incident, would be sentenced to eleven years in prison for precisely the same crime—"subverting the state."*

"In your prison memoir, you talked about reading revolutionary stories. Can you tell me more about that?"

I have enjoyed reading revolutionary stories since I was a child. My Mom specializes in the history of the Chinese Communist Party, so she would bring home revolutionary books about the Party. Some of them she had bought, but others had been distributed by her work unit. They were all about Party history. I would read those books at home. I read stories about the Nationalist Party [KMT] as well as stories about the CCP. So I grew up with a good understanding of the CCP.

"What made you so interested in those books?"

I had nothing to play with and our family had lots of books. All that I could do was to read. Every day after dinner, my parents would read books. My sister had to do her homework. I couldn't go out to play with other kids at night. No one played with me so I had nothing else to do. There was no TV at that time.

I had the reputation of loving to read even when I was a child. I was a good student at school. I didn't study very hard, but of course I wasn't lazy either. I wanted to do some extracurricular readings after school, but there was no library when I was in primary school. My father's field is geology. I had no interest in his books and I didn't understand. So I read my mother's books instead. Of course, the so-called "Party history" was simply the CCP's version of history, but some of the tales were like storybooks. I enjoyed reading them. I think what I read had a lot to do with my family background—those were the only books available for me. So I grew up reading that type of books... I can't remember what my teacher taught me at school, but my extracurricular reading is the major part of my memories about growing up.

Wang Dan describes in his prison memoir how those revolutionary stories stimulated his interest in learning foreign languages:

I read many proletarian revolutionary stories, such as the story about Lenin using milk as ink to learn foreign languages when he was kept in prison. It was such stories that influenced me early on to think that prison was a good place to learn a foreign language. It is really funny that I started to study foreign languages when I was kept in prison by those who had started to learn English when they were kept in prison before. Such a repetition may be a comedy in the context of history, but it is unfortunately and definitely a tragedy for the nation.[18]

"What is the impact of those revolutionary stories on you? Did you admire heroes who sacrificed their lives for the Communist cause?"

Of course, I did. I think we grew up in a kind of social context in which all the teachers and schools were indoctrinated with the values of socialism and communism. I was a "three-good student" and I was a student cadre. I worked hard to be outstanding politically[19] (*zhuiqiu jinbu*). I read storybooks about the former Soviet Union such as "The Story of Zoya and Shura"[20] as well as stories about the anti-Japanese war—about how children themselves organized into a children's regiment (*ertong tuan*) to fight against the invading Japanese. As a child, I looked up to those revolutionary heroes. I always imagined that I was in an anti-Japanese War situation. I wanted to act like a hero and I wished I could become one of them. I think it is just natural for children to think in that way.

In those days, our school would organize spring outings to places such as the Summer Palace and Fragrant Hills. When we biked to those big hills, I would tell my classmates that this would make a great place for guerrillas to hide. When I saw the big hills, I naturally thought about the guerrillas. I think that had a lot to do with my readings and my worship of heroes.

When I look at the younger generation today, I think there is one thing that, unlike our generation, they have never experienced. That is the work-study program. We were required to work on a farm or in a factory attached to our school. We regularly went to a farm to cut wheat. It was a new experience for us because we were all city kids. That was the first time that I saw a donkey roll over (*lü dagun*).

I had rarely seen donkeys, to say nothing of seeing a donkey rolling over. I found that very interesting. The very few images I still remember from my primary school years are the images of the rolling donkeys, working in the factory, and cutting wheat in the field. I can't recall the names of many of my classmates but those images made a deep impression on me. I still talk about them from time to time.

"What were your parents' views about your working in the factory and on the farm?"

There was little room for their opinion—they could be either for it or against it. All students had to go. It was required. It was a compulsory school activity. They just prepared food for me.

I think it was a good experience—to be in the vast world. It is a good personality-tempering experience (*taoye xingqing*). Psychologically, it made me realize how big the world is (*guanghuo tiandi*), and how different the countryside was from the crowdedness that I was used to in the city. Everywhere there were trees in the countryside. I guess I was sensitive even as a kid. It is hard to describe exactly how I felt, but I was impressed by the vastness.

The above is a good example of Wang Dan's frequent use of official CCP expressions. In a talk Danxuan once gave on social changes in China, he talked about the importance of eliminating the impact of the CCP culture. I asked Wang Dan what he thought about Danxuan's idea.

It is hard to eliminate it, though. I think the CCP culture is in our blood because it was part of our upbringing. For example, in our conversations, we always use terms such as "leadership" (*lingdao*) and "fighting on the frontline." These are results of the CCP education. Of course we should try to eliminate it, but I think it will be very difficult.

"You just described the vastness of the farm. Did you start writing poems at that time? I know you have published collections of your poetry."

No. I was just a kid then, but maybe that somehow showed that I had an aptitude for literature (*wenxue qingxiang*). I guess other kids just thought it was fun to play on the farm, but I was really touched by the vastness. I can still remember how moved I felt when I got off the bus and saw all the fields around me. That was a new life experience for me.

We went to the farm on weekdays. The whole class liked going to the farm because we didn't have to stay in the classroom—no more classes! We could have fun outdoors. Also, our families would usually prepare better food for us because it was rare that we would go for a trip, especially considering the fact that we needed to do labor work there. We used to compare and see who brought the best food from home. We were all very happy.

"Who took care of you on the farm?"

Our teachers, cadres of the production team (*shengchan dui*), and the peasants. They told us to line up, and then they showed us how to harvest the wheat with sickles. We also collected wheat heads in the field. I thought it was a lot of fun. It was like going on an outing.

I can't recall anything particularly negative about my childhood. I think my childhood memories are positive and sunny. That is why I enjoy writing nostalgic articles. I find the dark and gloomy articles by others interesting, but I don't recall any of those kinds of experiences from my childhood. I can't remember experiencing any sense of frustration or defeat (*cuobai gan*) during my childhood.

I think everyone's childhood has a bright side. But when people recall their childhoods, some tend to remember the dark side, whereas others remember the bright side. I think childhood is really all the same for everyone. It is just the ways that we remember our childhood that is different. Childhood itself is not different—everyone's childhood should be as sunny because that is the golden time of our lives.

That is my theory (of childhood). To put it more simply: childhood doesn't mean where you attended kindergarten or whether you had enough food to fill your stomach. For me, childhood represents a stage in life. We later experience adolescence, middle-age, and old age, all of which are built on the foundation of our childhood. I think childhood is the purest period of time in our lives. Whether we are happy or not at each later stage of life has a lot to do with our interaction with the outside world. In this sense, childhood should be the happiest time in life—it doesn't matter whether or not you went hungry because one's childhood is the least interfered with by the outside world.

"I think childhood is different not because the ways in which we remember it are different as you put it, but because the experience itself can be different, in different social, historical, and personal contexts."

It is true that we can't choose the historical contexts in which we live, but we can always choose how to remember. I think people's life attitudes have a lot to do with their ways of remembering childhood. If we want to change our worldviews and values, the first thing we need to do is to change our childhood memories.

"If we can't relive our childhood, then how can we change our memories about it?"

No matter what someone has been through, childhood represents hope and the future. Those who are elderly may have money, families, everything, but they don't have a future. In this sense, childhood should always be the happiest period of life because you have hope and a future.

Based on this part of the conversation, Wang Dan believes that memories can change if we can change how we regard them. However, in later discussions about his experience of exile, he seemed to imply the opposite—there is no way to change our memories of the past because that is where we come from and those memories are in our bones. Wang Dan's ideas about childhood may have a lot to do with his own experience—he had been living in the public eye since he turned twenty years old. His personal life and even his sexual orientation have been topics of public discussion. Probably that is why he feels that he was happiest when he was a child and his childhood was "least interfered" with.

"A Fish in Water" in the Collective System

"Am I right in saying that you were comfortable within the system at that time?"
Yes. I was like a fish in water.

"So you were a three-good student, a student cadre, and you enjoyed reading revolutionary books…"
Even before I finished my sentence, Wang Dan jumped in to complete the list:

And I accepted education about heroism…All these [experiences] made me realize how easy it is for humans to be influenced by collectivism; how easy we can lose ourselves to the collective. Of course this is my current thinking—I never thought this way when I was a child. I fully understand what it is like when you are influenced by collectivism—it makes you feel as if you have taken sugar-coated pills. We so much enjoyed being a part of the group that we would accept and do whatever we were told.

I would call this vanity (*xurong*), but not glory (*guangrong*). As kids, we didn't have much to be proud of. So what was most important for me as a kid was to be praised by the adults and to be accepted by my peers.

The longing for recognition Wang Dan describes may not just be characteristic of children, but also of adults. It is natural for individuals to long for approval from people whom they care about. Unfortunately, the exiles have been cast out by the system that instilled those heroic values.

"When did you start writing poems?"

In primary school, I remember when I first started writing poems my teachers gave me very positive feedback. I think the major reason why I was able to continue writing and publishing poems later in life has a lot to do with the encouragement from my teachers when I first started. Of course when I re-read the first or second poems I wrote, I did not find them to be good. But my teachers' encouragement gave me confidence and nurtured my interest.

"Shen Tong was greatly influenced by Western literature..."

Again, before I finished my sentence, Wang Dan jumped in:

I am more interested in classical Chinese literature. I spent two years of my spare time studying classical Chinese literature in a Children's Palace. It was located on my way home from school. This Children's Palace had been an imperial garden (*wangfu*) in the past. It was a very nice place with lots of trees. I got to know many other students who were also interested in classical Chinese literature. We would sit inside the palace (*dian*) and learn. That is a beautiful childhood memory. So my early experiences were influenced by traditional Chinese culture, not by Western culture.

Wang Dan and Shen Tong had had a competitive relationship dating back to their time at Beida. *They had organized two different on-campus democracy forums at Peking University. The "Democratic Salon" organized by Wang Dan, the "Olympic Science Academy" organized by Shen Tong, and the "Confucius Study Society" organized by Wuer Kaixi at Beijing Normal University are considered the most important on-campus forums before the 1989 protests.*[21] *In Almost a Revolution, Shen Tong hints at the competition between them on various occasions. Based on my interactions with Wang Dan and Shen Tong over the years, one thing that strikes me is that unlike the other infighting among the various dissidents, they, Wang Dan and Shen Tong, never became angry with each other; instead, it was more like two young men having fun competing with each other.*

"Shen Tong talked a lot about how Western literature and culture influenced his thinking and values. He recalled that he felt very much encouraged after reading about Martin Luther King and Gandhi. He believes that his later political activism is related to such readings. Was this the case for you?"

I read a lot of translated Western novels as well. They did have an impact on me, but I don't think they had anything to do with my political participation.

"So what were the influences you think led to your participation in 1989?"

The period that influenced me the most was the time when I had just started senior high school. Since I was a league cadre,[22] I was rather active politically in school. I read the selected works of Marx and Lenin. For example, I read the Leninist classic *The State and Revolution*. I studied these works seriously and took notes. I don't think I believed in socialism at that time, but I was at an age that I had a desire to learn. The only theoretical system that was accessible to me at that time was Marxism and Leninism, so I dashed off to study them. It was for the sake of learning, not because of any beliefs (*xinyang*).

"In an interview with Beijing Spring,[23] you said that you believed in Marxism at some point:

> *In middle school I became interested in politics. I was given the title of a 'model pioneer' by Beijing municipality and led many political activities at school. I believed in Marxism and during a certain period, I would wake up every day at 4:30 am and read the selected works of Marx and Engels."*[24]

I was wrong then. This is not true. Maybe I intended to say I would have liked to become a Marxist. But the reading was more for learning than because of any belief.

I remember once I saw a book in the school library called *A Collection of Essays of Soviet Dissidents*. The book includes historical accounts of Stalin's purge of his rivals. I was rather shocked after reading it because I had been studying the works by Marx and Lenin that stressed the positive aspects of socialism. All of a sudden I was reading about the dirt under the positive and the glorious. I was shocked by the cruelty. How could this have happened? I started to question what I had been reading and to pay more attention to works that expressed different points of view, such as the writings by Professor Fang Lizhi.[25]

Of course, attending *Beida* was a turning point in my life. I had many opportunities to interact with professors, to attend public lectures, and to discuss things with fellow students. Those experiences gradually led to changes in my thinking.

I can't recall any dramatic experience that led to a dramatic change in my thinking. I am not the type of person who would make any radical changes overnight. I changed gradually as I accumulated more knowledge over time.

Revolutionary Movies and Scar Literature of the Eighties

"You have stated in your writings and speeches that the 1980s was an era of idealism in China. Can you elaborate?"

It [the eighties] was a time full of hope. People were talking about what the future would be like. Many new things and ideas emerged. For example, we had been watching lots of revolutionary war movies such as *The Railroad Guerrilla*[26] (*Tiedao youjidui*), *Tunnel Warfare*[27] (*Didao zhan*), and *Li Xiangyang*[28] (in *Guerrillas on the Plain, Pingyuan youjidui*). Then all of a sudden, there were movies like *The Back Alley* (*Xiaojie*) and *Romance on Lushan Mountain* (*Lushannian*).

There was a cinema next to our home. There was no wall between our courtyard and the cinema so we always went there to watch movies. I watched *The Back Alley* when I was in junior high school. That was the first good movie that I saw in my life—the first movie that I ever saw that had a human touch (*renqingwei*) and didn't have much political preaching. It was just wonderful! For a long time, I remained immersed in the plot.

The Railroad Guerrillas, Tunnel Warfare, *and* Guerrillas on the Plain *were all household names in China about the Chinese fighting against the Japanese invaders during World War II.* The Back Alley *and* Romance on Lushan Mountain *came out in the early 1980s; both are examples of "scar literature."*

The Eighties Was a Golden Era in China

The whole country was watching *The Back Alley* at that time. Before that we didn't have many choices [of movies]. But then lots of new things started to emerge. People became hopeful and positive. You rarely heard complaints. In my memories, people were all smiling, very different from now. I think the eighties was the golden era in China, not because we were eating good food or wearing nice clothes, but because we had hope for the future. That is something that was nonexistent in the nineties. Although in the nineties people were wearing better clothes, eating better food, and they were richer materially, they were not richer spiritually

Wang Dan had been using the word "hope" when he talked about his childhood and his formative years during the eighties. Such views of the eighties are common among Chinese intellectuals who see the 1989 military crackdown as a watershed that has led to an economic boom but also a society with no values. The crackdown not only crushed the pro-democracy movement but also crushed the hope and faith of the people. However, dissidents from the Democracy Wall Movement may disagree with Wang Dan's description of the eighties. In late 1978, activists began posting news and ideas in the form of big-character posters along a long brick wall in the western side of Beijing, now known as Democracy Wall. Wei Jingsheng, one of the most well-known activists, posted his famous essay titled "The Fifth Modernization," arguing that democracy should be added to the list of the Four Modernizations advocated by the government, namely, modernization of agriculture, industry, national defense, and science and technology. As a result, Wei was sentenced to fifteen years in prison.

The lack of generational continuity between democracy movements in China, as a result of tight political control and censorship, has been noted by observers both within and outside China. For example, in 1979, Peking University student Hu Ping wrote an article titled "On Freedom of Speech," in which he discusses the role of oppositional forces in China. Ten years later, Wang Dan wrote his own piece on the subject. Wang Dan's piece is described as "inferior" to Hu's earlier essay in terms of both content and style.

That is not surprising, because Wang, like most of the younger activists of the late 1980s, was ignorant of Hu Ping's work and the dissident activities in the late 1970s.[29]

Sociologist Craig Calhoun has also noted the destruction of historical continuity:

> *It is no surprise, then, that the students of 1989 were not well informed about the Democracy Wall Movement or even about the Cultural Revolution. Copies of Wei Jingsheng's discussion of democracy as "the fifth modernization," for example, were hardly in circulation or available in school libraries. It is significant, in this connection, that the student protesters' demands were almost identical to those of the intellectuals whose open letters and petitions had helped start the protests in late winter. The main exception was that the students hardly ever mentioned Wei Jingsheng or called for the release of political prisoners.*[30]

Wang Dan said it wasn't until after the brutal suppression that he "woke up":

I think my memories of society prior to 1989 are positive. And it was because of my positive attitude that I participated in the student movement. I didn't even have a negative impression of the CCP. I just thought that our country should have freedom and democracy, and I hoped that we could achieve it. So I participated in the 1989 movement not because of *hatred*, but because of *hope*. This is an important point, which might have been mistaken by outsiders. We weren't trying to overthrow the government (in 1989). We wanted to improve it. The tragic ending woke us up. What I am trying to emphasize here is that it wasn't something negative that led to my involvement in 1989.

Danxuan expressed a similar opinion during his interview. He said that the goal in 1989 was not to overthrow the government but to push the CCP to reform and to improve. It was the cruelty of the crackdown that changed his views about the nature of the regime.

Perspectives and Retrospectives on 1989

"Can you share with me your reflections about your involvement in 1989?"

I think it is human nature to prefer to live in a free environment. When a social movement like June 4 happens, it triggers people's longing for freedom. However, human beings all have reasons other than emotions—most people will do the calculations. For example, they will calculate: what might happen if I participate; I might lose my job, etc. However, there are a small number of idealists who tend to be more perceptive and to be less calculating. I think I was born to be the latter type.

I am against totalitarianism and I long for freedom and democracy. Don't misunderstand me. I am not indicating that I am an elite. I believe most people have similar feelings. To be frank, in this sense I didn't have a clear idea about myself before June 4. I could feel that there was something deep in my heart, but I wasn't exactly sure what it was that excited me. June 4 was a turning point. I became clear in terms of my viewpoints. I should say that the awakening process has not ended even up to this very moment: it is an ongoing process. Now I have clearer ideas about concepts such as socialism, communism, and totalitarianism, and I have better answers to questions and phenomena that I couldn't understand before. I don't think I had the answers to these questions in 1989. In 1989, it was more as if I was acting out of instinct. But I know that I will not look back. Rather I will look forward to search for things that are important to me.

I think 1989 was the time that brought out the best parts in the human nature of the Chinese people, but then we had to face the reality of the military suppression. For a small number of people like me, we will not turn back. After experiencing imprisonment, exile, and so forth, there is nowhere for me to turn back to even if I wanted, and there is nowhere for me to hide even if I wanted. Things happen and situations develop naturally. It is a process of searching for answers and searching for human instincts. That is why I manage to remain a calm person.

"You said earlier that your thinking never changes radically overnight. Did the 1989 movement result in any big changes in your thinking?"

No. The 1989 movement didn't directly result in any significant changes in my thinking because the changing process had started long before 1989. I know many people's thinking started to change in 1989, but that is not the case for me. It is true that 1989 occupies an important position in my life, but it is not as important as others assume.

"Why isn't it as important in your life as others assume?"
Well, if you ask me why June 4 is important in my life, I can't give you a good answer, which shows it isn't really so important for me. I really can't answer the question—probably I am not eloquent enough. Of course, being imprisoned is part of it, but other than that, I can't expand.

"What about the movement's impact on your beliefs and values?"
I don't have a clear belief.

Post-Totalitarianism and Lying

"Have you ever wondered why those soldiers who were about the same age as the students opened fire?"
Those who opened fire were no longer human beings in a real sense. Biologically, yes, they were human beings; but psychologically, no, they were not. Their human nature had been twisted by the system. The animal nature was brought out by the system and had overcome their human nature. They were no longer human beings in a real sense. Opening fire was neither a conscious decision on their part nor a hobby, but the result of their minds being twisted by the system.

"If it were you, would you have opened fire?"
I probably would have done the same. I would have faced execution if I didn't obey military orders.

"What about those of the later generations who support the CCP's argument that the military crackdown in 1989 was necessary and a just decision?"
I think that has a lot to do with the social context. You have to analyze how real those attitudes truly are. As Havel puts it, one characteristic of post-totalitarianism is lying. This is common sense. Such attitudes are not real. They are lies. Those people may appear as if they are serious and that those are their true feelings, but that isn't really the case. They are lying subconsciously and when they lie, they don't even realize it. Some people know they are lying, such as some of the CCP officials, but not most ordinary people. Lying can become a subconscious behavior. The reason that post-totalitarianism is successful is that it can make people lie subconsciously. In capitalist societies, the authorities try to convince you to accept certain ideas; but Communist states make you lie subconsciously, as illustrated in Havel's *The Power of the Powerless*.

Shen Tong also mentioned Havel's The Power of the Powerless *when we talked about lying in authoritarian societies.*

"Can you give me an example about this lying phenomenon?"
About how I lied? I rarely lied.

"No, I don't mean that. I would like to hear a personal story about this phenomenon of subconscious lying."

Once I was invited to give a talk at Cornell University. The student who organized the event was also a Chinese student. He was a younger student but he had a clear mind. We went for lunch together before the talk. Then it started to rain heavily. He said he would go back to his dorm to get umbrellas for us. When he came back, he came back with only one umbrella. I asked him how come he only got one. He said he only had one umbrella, and he had tried to borrow one from another Chinese student, explaining that Wang Dan was on campus to give a talk and we needed to borrow an umbrella. That Chinese student said: "What? Wang Dan? Is that the guy from June 4? No way! I am not going to lend my umbrella to a counter-revolutionary." Then the organizer sighed as he told me this story. I was thinking to myself. It is raining hard. He must have lots of hatred toward me that he didn't even want to lend me an umbrella. He must hate me very much. You can't say that his hatred was just pretending, because he really didn't want to lend me an umbrella, and the organizer was his good friend. Just imagine: a good friend, borrowing an umbrella, on a rainy day. If it had not been for lots of hatred, such a refusal would not make any sense, right? However, I asked the organizer, do you think your friend ever read or watched anything about June 4? "Definitely not," he said.

I kept in touch with the organizer after the talk and he told me that he had later had some discussions and debates with that Chinese student [who had refused to lend me an umbrella]. When the student heard that I had been a student at *Beida*, he asked with surprise: "So Wang Dan was from *Beida*? What actually happened on June 4?" It was obvious that he knew nothing about June 4 and he knew nothing about my political views. If he knew nothing about me, where did all the hatred toward me come from? If it wasn't a lie, what else could it have been? So obviously the hatred was not real. But he did hate me. This is a typical phenomenon in a totalitarian society. When you grow up in such a society, you are taught to hate those whom the government tells you to hate. You blindly accept. That Chinese student was a victim of such a system. His hatred was not real but he really hated me. It is paradoxical.

Even in the eighties, when you said "Down with the CCP!" people around you would advise you to be cautious—telling you not to say things like that or you would get into big trouble. I think that is the kind of mechanism that helps to produce the lies. After living in that type of atmosphere for a long time, you gradually become trapped to believe that it is dangerous to say "Down with the CCP!" You may not know exactly where the danger comes from but you become scared and think that it will be dangerous [if you do or say certain things]. In the U.S., who cares if you say "Down with Bush!" A post-totalitarian society is a society of lies. Nothing is real. It is like the emperor's new clothes. So now I have learned not to be angry with such people. They are simply victims and they don't know what they are doing.

"You were taken from prison directly to the airport and forced into exile. What was in your mind when all of a sudden you were put on a plane leaving China for the United States?"

I think lots of heroic touching stories are not real. Now I am a well-known figure and I know many famous people. To be frank, I don't believe those heroic stories about touching moments such as walking out of prison and being forced to board a plane to leave your country. I don't think those stories are real. Based on my own experience, I had no special feelings and there is nothing worth mentioning.

"You had no feelings when you were forced to leave China?"

No, neither excitement nor sadness. I had no idea what was going to happen in the future. I was very confused. I am being honest with you.

"Isn't 'being confused' a type of feeling?"

It is, but it is neither heroic nor noble as many others described in their stories.

"Different people may feel differently even in the same situation."

Probably, but I felt nothing. I didn't know what was going to happen to me. I talked to the person who was accompanying me on the plane. Afterward, I got tired and I fell asleep. When I woke up, we had already arrived. Then all types of activities started, blotting the sky and covering the earth (*putiangaidi*). I had no time to think. I was not the type of person who wanted to plan the future carefully; at least I was not such a type at that time.

You are not the first person to ask me such a question. The first day I arrived in the States, I was asked how I felt at the moment that I was boarding the plane. Other than lying, I had nothing to say. At the time, I lied with stories such as "I was worried that I would not be able to return to China." Now I have to admit that those were lies. Actually my brain went blank [when I boarded the plane to leave China].

"When I left China and later returned, I became emotional at the border."

That was different. You had a quiet environment to think for yourself. I didn't have that. There were always people around me both inside and outside prison. When I was taken out of prison, they [the authorities] allowed me to meet my parents briefly and then I was taken to the airport. I was like on a fast-moving machine and I didn't have even a minute to take a break.

For the first three or four months after I got to the States, whenever I was alone, I wanted to sleep. If I were like you and alone by myself, I probably would have had thoughts and feelings such as you did, but I didn't have that kind of environment. Journalists came like a tide (*xiang chaoshui yiyang*) with waves of questions. I didn't have any time to think for myself.

"A Man in a Strange Land"

"Can you share your experience after coming to the United States?"

The stress was incredible. My English was terrible. All of a sudden I was at Harvard, such a famous university. At first I couldn't understand a single word in class. That was just scary. It was like all of a sudden you completely forgot what had happened to you the day before—you would feel frightened and wonder what you could do. I had always believed that there is a way out no matter how bad things are, but not in that situation. I couldn't bring an interpreter with me to class, right? That was just dreadful.

Two things that supported me at that time were my friends and my faith. When I had questions I turned to friends for advice and help. For example, I had no idea how to open a bank account, so my friends helped me. My convictions were also important to me. The most important thing I learned from my prison experience is that there is nothing in this world that cannot be overcome. No matter how difficult things are they will eventually turn out okay after you endure the sufferings.

For example, once when I was kept in the No. 2 Prison, the room was very small—a single bed could barely fit in. I said to myself how will I ever be able to survive this? I stayed there for four months. I can't remember how I made it through. But after experiences like that, you learn that things will eventually be all right after suffering. So whenever I had difficulties, such as not understanding any English in class, even though I had no idea what I could do, I knew that as long as I was still alive, I would overcome and survive. I have faith in that.

"You describe yourself as 'a man in a strange land' (yixiangren) in your social media. How do you see your identity in the West?"

My identity is clear enough—I am Chinese and I would like to return to China. The things that I am concerned about are all in China, so China is my future. As you can see, I rarely try to merge with the mainstream in the U.S. With my background, if I were to want to be like Li Lu, Harry Wu, or Shen Tong and mingle with mainstream society, I am sure I could do that as well. But that isn't my goal, so I rarely network in Washington DC. This is *intentional*. Subconsciously, I don't consider the mainstream society as my mainstream. For me, mainstream means foreign, even though I live in this country.

Wang Dan rarely used English during our conversations but he did use the English word "intentional" here. He has been active in advocating the rights of Chinese dissidents to return home. He has urged the Chinese government to allow the generations of political exiles, including himself, to return to China:

China should stop creating stateless people. China should allow them to go home, at least to die there. Fallen leaves must return to their roots, as the Chinese saying goes...Canceling passports, refusing to extend passports, refusing to issue new passports, and barring citizens from returning home will create stateless people, and that is exactly what the United Nations is concerned about...China has signed two UN treaties on human rights, so China should respect international human rights codes.[31]

In a speech he delivered at the National Press Club in Washington on November 29, 2007, Wang Dan discussed the issue of returning home in connection to the 2008 Beijing Olympics:

We are very happy to see that the Olympics Games are going to be held in China next year. And therefore, we hope that these Olympics Games is [sic] going to give the Chinese government an opportunity to become more liberal and open and also to allow the exiles to return home. And we hope that this is an issue that the entire world will pay attention to.[32]

"What if you cannot return to China?"

Even if I can't go back, I will still consider myself an outsider [in the U.S.]. I will not change in order to merge with the mainstream. I have confidence that a country like the U.S. will be tolerant to outsiders like me, and it will accept such a multi-existence, so I will not lose my living space (*shengcun kongjian*) even if I am not part of the mainstream.

"Why do you want to hold on to a country that has forsaken you?"

I do not see it this way. I was born in China and I grew up in China. My soul and my blood are related to that piece of land. The reason I would like to go back is that China is where I am supposed to be. It has nothing to do with whether or not they want me back. I can't give you any other good reasons why I would like to go back. I think it is subconscious and it is in my bones. It is true though that if I were to stay in the U.S., I could have a good life.

But I can't rule out the possibility that I may change my mind in the future. Human beings tend to change. I could never understand why Professor Yu Ying-shih never wanted to go back to China. He was born in mainland China and educated in Taiwan and the U.S. With his experience, background, and reputation, he would have been highly respected if he had returned, but he chose to stay [in the United States]. He simply didn't want to go back. Another example is Lin Yusheng, another scholar. He returned to Taiwan for one year then he came back [to the United States]. I can't understand why they don't want to go back because they all can go back if they want, and they would be held in high esteem if they were to go back. But they chose not to. So I may change my mind as well in the future. But for the time being, I still would like to return to China.

As mentioned in earlier chapters, Princeton professor Yu Ying-shih is a leading scholar of Chinese culture. One mark of his distinction is that in 2006, he was awarded the John W. Kluge Prize for lifetime achievement in the humanities, an honor equivalent to the Nobel Prize. In response to Wang Dan's question about why a preeminent scholar of Chinese culture would not want to return to China, Professor Yu cited Confucius's refusal to visit the state of Qin (during the Spring and Autumn period of Chinese history) because it was a tyranny. He hasn't been to China since 1989 for the very same reason.

"You were often stopped by U.S. immigration at airports because you don't have a valid passport. So you are stateless. How did you feel in those moments? Did you feel rejected?"

Yes. It happened because I am not a U.S. citizen and I am not part of the mainstream. It made me feel that this is not my home. It is *their* home, not *our* home. I live among *them*, not among *us*. But so what? I can put up with being questioned by the immigration officials. If they were to enter our world in China, they would be questioned as well. I can think rationally about this and I can put up with such frustrations. It does not bother me that much. However, such experiences reinforced my feelings about the distance between *them* and *us*. I mean, I live among *them*, not among *us*. If I return to China, I will again be living among *us*. Again, this is a subconscious feeling. I know if I stay in the United States, I probably will have a better life with more freedom, or at least I will be more respected. If I return to China, I will face persecution, but then I will be able to live among *us*.

"But if you were to go back to China now, you would have limited freedom."

I don't think I would like to go back to China now in view of the current social and political situation. That China is also *them*, not us. It is a nondemocratic society with no freedom. Everybody has to tell lies. I can't accept that and I would be uncomfortable living there. Of course I would be able to put up with it because from living there I am already used to it. But before I didn't have such clear ideas about the society as I do now. I was ignorant then so I didn't feel the pain. But now that I understand what is going on, it would be very difficult. Now that I have a clearer mind, I don't want to go back.

So for me, both worlds (the United States and China) are *them* (the other). People always say that it must be painful to be an exile. I disagree. I don't think such people understand the exiles. I think I am happy to be an exile because I don't have to return to China to suffer. I feel happy from the bottom of my heart.

"So wherever you go, you are always living among them (or the other) not among us?"

If you compare the two different *them*—China and the United States—I would prefer the United States *them* because the United States will not force me to do things that I don't want to do, whereas the China *them* would force me to do things against my will. Since I don't have other choices, I have to pick the one that will present the least harm to me. I don't want to return to China if things don't change.

Within a few minutes, Wang Dan had expressed contradictory thoughts about his identity even though he had claimed to be "clear"about it. First he said he would like to return to China, and then he said he would like to remain in exile. Both Danxuan and Shen Tong revealed such contradictory feelings as well. The difference is that no matter how contradictory it sounds, Danxuan continues to think about going home, and Shen Tong has chosen to live a new life as an American. Wang Dan did not lean in either direction—he didn't feel like living among "us" either in China or in the United States. Probably that is why he said he is happy to live a life in exile even while he is fighting for his right to return home.

"If you were not Wang Dan, not a public figure, do you think you would still carry on the cause like this? What kind of force drives you to continue?"

I think there are two parts of me. First, idealism: I think I am a born idealist. For example, if I see an old woman begging on the street, I feel sorry for her. I understand that it is not my fault that she is begging on the street but I still feel sorry for her. I still become angry if I see unjust things. It is true that I probably shouldn't be so idealistic now that I am no longer that young. Second, calculations: it is because of all that I have been through that I am the Wang Dan that I am today. I have accumulated resources and credits. If I stop doing what I have been doing, others couldn't take over because they are not me. I wish I didn't need to carry on like this but I also don't want to waste the resources. Also, finally, I would feel guilty if I didn't do anything for the lost lives—so many people were killed. You know my worldview is to be happy. I am not saying I am very happy when I am working for the democratic cause, but I will not be happy and I will feel guilty if I don't continue. So I do it for myself—to make myself happy.

"Do you feel any conflicts when you plan your career path while continuing the democracy work? In Danxuan's case, companies did not want to hire him because they didn't want to offend the Chinese government."

Yes, there have been conflicts. For example, I would like to be a songwriter in Taiwan. I have lots of friends in that field. I am sure I could make a good living as a songwriter. However, people would have concerns about using me because they don't want to offend the mainland market.

"In my interview with Shen Tong, he talked about the identity crisis related to the conflicts in the overseas democracy community. When he tried to be part of the community, he got hurt. Now he has chosen to stay in the business world, but he still feels lost. What are your thoughts about this?"

I think for people who became involved in June 4 to the extent that Shen Tong and I did, it is not possible to erase the scars on our identity. I can fully understand Shen Tong's feelings toward his identity even though he is doing business now. Actually I see the same identity crisis with Kaixi. I think I am luckier than them because I don't have any talent or interest in business. My major is in the social sciences and it is related to social movements.

Besides, I think our identity is related to how we position ourselves. I view the democracy cause as a process of accumulating failed experiences. Most people became discouraged or decided to give up [the cause] because they wanted to succeed, which is understandable. But I have my own personal views about this. For me, the democracy cause, or say the opposition movement, is doomed to failure again and again. It is not possible to succeed. It is the fate of the opposition to lose. If you are part of an opposition movement, you always lose because once you succeed, you will no longer be in the opposition—you will have already taken over power. So before you come to power, as long as you are still the opposition, failure is a just a matter of course (*lisuodangran*). We need to learn from the experience of failure so we will be able to succeed one day. This is how I see myself different from the others. I believe that the democracy cause means failure. We have to carry on because we have the moral support.

"So in this sense, you think the dream of 1989 is still alive, right? Danxuan doesn't like the term 'dream,' but for me, it is a metaphor for the ideals of 1989."

I too don't fully agree with the term "dream." I think we are no longer at an age to dream. Instead, we have clear goals toward which we are working. If I say that in 1989 we didn't have any clear ideas, I should say that today I have concrete ideas about what I want to do. It is based on practical calculations that I have decided to carry on, otherwise all of our efforts during those years would go down the drain. This is the reality we are facing, but of course there are also idealistic elements in the actual world. We are no longer the children of Tiananmen. In 1989 we talked about our dreams and ideals, but now we need a better balance.

If we were to remain the children of 1989 who only have dreams and ideals, we would have to give up the cause because over and over again we would face failure. But at our age, we need to find a way to balance our ideals and our interests—to have a balance between living happy lives and working for a better future for our country. If we can do that, we can say that we have achieved our goals.

"How has your experience of living in the West all these years influenced your understanding of democracy?"

I learned that democracy is a state of mind (*jingshen zhuangtai*). As Shen Tong put it, be yourself. The essence of democracy is cultural and spiritual. This is the most significant change in my thinking about democracy. In the past, I understood democracy as something political so I emphasized political institutions, organizations, operations, social movements, and demonstrations. But now I have shifted my focus away from the means to the intellectual dimensions (*jingshen cengmian*). Previously, our goal was to change the political system, but now it is more about cultivating the moral, intellectual, spiritual, mental, and cultural aspects of the society.

If our goal is merely to change the political system, then the means to reach this goal could be a violent revolution or the establishment of a new political party. However, in the long run, we need to change various aspects of the society, so we need to do things such as voicing different opinions and setting up NGOs. I knew nothing about these things in 1989 but now these are what I would like to do.

I think June 4 was a good learning experience for me. It taught me how to choose my life path, so I am grateful for the experience. After my experiences of imprisonment and the ongoing work for the cause, I have come to value democracy even more. These experiences helped me to understand the essence and core of democracy, as well as my youthful ideals. If it had not been for all those experiences, I would not have understood as much as I had when I was young—it would become meaningless and a waste of time. Now I have a clearer idea about what I was fighting for when I was young. So I do not have any regrets.

Second, my experiences made me realize how valuable freedom is, so I will fight hard for my personal freedom. I have been stating this in my public speeches: if some day my personal interests come into conflict with the collective interests or the national interests, I will take care of my personal interests first. Of course it is my goal to establish a good balance between national interests and personal interests. If I can't make such a balance, I will choose my personal interests. To be able to make such a choice is the greatest lesson I learned from June 4—this is real freedom. I have come to realize that individual freedom is the most important. If I can't even protect my own interests, what can I possibly do for my country? We will not be able to bring about positive changes in our society until we ourselves live in happiness and dignity. If someday I can't do anything for China, I will choose to be myself.

Both Wang Dan and Danxuan emphasized that they had learned from their experiences the importance of personal freedom. As Danxuan put it, democracy is not a "big slogan" but a way of life. However, they were still anxious to return to China despite the difficult situation which would await them. I have the feeling that theoretically and rationally they understand things well, but their prior political socialization in China made it difficult for them to make life decisions for themselves. Again, they are torn between living an ordinary life and fighting for the unfinished cause.

"With all the infighting in the democracy community, do you feel hurt?"

I don't care what others say about me. I do these things for myself. I don't care about others' comments. That is the reality. How can we change the reality? I don't think one past event will ever be able to keep a group of people together forever. With so many people involved in 1989, how many are now left still fighting for the cause? My major was history. Can you give me one example in history when one historical event kept a group of people together for their entire lives? After so many years, it is just normal that people are no longer close.

Wang Dan was avoiding my question about the infighting, of which he was well aware.

"Do you miss your parents?"

Of course, but what else can you do? They can come to visit me and we talk over the phone as well. That helps. And of course I still hope that I will be able to go home someday, and be able to be with them after I return to China.

Wang Dan's mother, Wang Lingyun, recalls in her published memoir Suiyue Cangcang [During Those Dark Years] *that the police came to their home and lied to her and said they would like to take her to the police station to ask some questions.*[33] *They promised Wang Dan's father that they would bring her back home soon "in the same car" in which they were taking her away. However, she was taken directly to a prison cell. Because of the conditions in the prison, her left leg developed serious problems and she could no longer walk normally.*

Wang Dan had no idea that his mother had been imprisoned—the authorities did not tell him because they knew he was close to his mother and they were afraid that he would react strongly. Nor did his family tell him because they didn't want him to worry. It was only from a friend who was in the same prison that Wang Dan found out what had happened to his mother.

The authorities were so unscrupulous (*shangxinbingkuang*). Ever since my mother graduated from *Beida*, she had always been a hard worker for decades doing research on the history of the Party at the National Museum of the Chinese Revolution. She had been a Communist Party member for ten years. During the 1989 movement, she never once posted a big-character poster; she never participated in any demonstrations; she never said anything "counter-revolutionary." All that she did was to be a mother, and worry about her son, waiting for me outside Tiananmen Square days and nights. She didn't have many opportunities to see me, but still she was arrested, merely because she is my mother. That something like this could happen in the eighties—it is so unfortunate for the nation.[34]

"Do you feel guilty for not being able to return to China to visit your parents?"

Of course. That has become one of the greatest feelings of guilt in my life. I wish I could make it up to them, but there is nothing I can do. Whenever I discuss with my parents over the phone whether they should come to visit me, I struggle a lot. On the one hand, I am anxious to see them; on the other hand, I know it would be a long and tiring trip. It should be me who goes home to see them. When I call home and my Mom tells me that she doesn't want to come because the trip is too tiring, I get upset. I know she very much wants to see me but still she says that she doesn't want to come. This tells me how difficult the trip is for her.

I know I am not a hero, I feel so helpless. What else can you do if you can't go home? However, I am not going to give up because of this. I think we always need to pay a price for the things we do. Parents are all the same—they are always worried. Sometimes I try to comfort myself in a selfish way: I think that parents should be prepared for anything—either good or bad—that will happen to their children before they decide to become parents, and they should endure whatever might happen later.

"What's your expectation for a home?"

So you are trying to get into my private life and my privacy. I refuse to talk to you about this.

"I am not inquiring about your personal life. I just want to know how you understand home. You talk about an intellectual home a lot in your writings. What about the relationship between home and nation? You are denied the right to return home because of your ideals for a better nation in 1989; meanwhile you don't feel at home with the mainstream in the country that has accepted you and where you now reside."

I think *home* means two people being together. That's home. We have entered the twenty-first century. Home and country now have broader meanings. We can always have an intellectual home inside ourselves. No one could take that away from me even when I was deprived of my freedom in prison. They could humiliate me but they couldn't crush me. I think we always have happiness in our heart and no one can take that away from us. That is the strength of the human spirit.

When I was about to ask Wang Dan to elaborate on his answer, Danxuan walked into the room to see if we were ready for the group discussion. Wang Dan seemed relieved. He spoke in a loud voice as if he was making a formal announcement:

Now let's start our group discussion—the origin of totalitarian democracy.

*   *   *

When I went to Beijing, I visited Wang Dan's parents. Their home phone was tapped so I didn't call beforehand. Some security guards downstairs asked for my ID, I pretended to remain calm while playing out in my mind how I should react. Wang Dan's mother was surprised and excited to see me show up at their door. I gave her a big hug, which is uncommon in Chinese culture, and she held my hands and led me into the apartment as she spoke: "It is great you can come back to the country. Have you visited your home? Your parents must be very happy." She invited me to stay for dinner and started preparing the meal in the kitchen. Wang Dan's nephew was staying with them at the time. The young boy looked exactly like Wang Dan. He was doing his homework. I wondered if the image of the young boy doing his homework ever reminded Wang Dan's parents of their own son who used to spend a lot of time reading those revolutionary stories at home. It was a dinner with a full table of dishes. It was a poignant moment watching the parents sitting at the dining table, without their son, not knowing when he could return home, or if he would ever be allowed to. Wang Dan's mother told me that whenever she saw other Chinese students who lived overseas visiting their homes, she wished that he could return home too:

"I still cherish the memory of how he left home with his school bag on his bicycle. He left all of a sudden and never had a chance to come back. We are still waiting for him to come home."

Of all my impressions of Wang Dan, one image stays in my mind. One time he and I were walking on the campus of the University of Toronto before we participated in a Tiananmen anniversary event there. He stopped outside the Sidney Smith building when he saw a couple of birds flying toward him. He fed them a piece of bread that he was holding in his hand. At that moment, I saw no politics, no moral obligations, and no June 4. In front of me was a human being, a child who longs to be like those birds and when he gets tired, he wants to be able to fly home.

CHAPTER 6

Romance and Revolution: Group Discussions

I held two group discussions in New York City with the three participants—one with Shen Tong and Danxuan, and the other with Wang Dan and Danxuan. The group discussions were extensions of and reflections on the individual interviews that I had conducted. In this sense, the participants not only contributed to their own individual biographical profiles, but also to the discussion of broad themes that informed the entire process. Both Wang Dan and Danxuan seemed to be more relaxed and comfortable in the group discussions than during individual interviews—they were more engaged and motivated to contribute their thoughts in a group setting. I didn't see this difference in Shen Tong—he was as expressive during the meeting as he had been in the interview. I have identified each speaker in front the direct quotes so that readers will not be confused: DX for Danxuan, ST for Shen Tong, WD for Wang Dan, and RH, of course, for myself. In the discussions, they all referred to me as "Xiaoqing," my Chinese name.

* * *

A Home for the Homeless: A Discussion with Shen Tong and Danxuan

Danxuan, Shen Tong, and I started the discussion with Danxuan bringing up the topic of home, showing a painting he had just bought on a street of Manhattan.

> **DX**: I bought it [the painting] because the scenery looks similar to the pond that was close to our home when I was a child. I was living in a small town with my mother at the time. The scenery also looks like the pond near my high school when I was in Guangzhou. When I saw the painting, I immediately

wanted to buy it. We talked about home during our interview. I think home is something concrete. For me, home is connected to memory. Home is the town where I stayed with my mother in Hunan, and home is also Guangzhou where I attended high school. The painting reminded me a lot of my memories of home. I think home includes not only rational choices, but also emotional attachments.

A Homeless Mind

RH: Danxuan mentioned in our interview that he only kept two suitcases when he first came to the States because he thought he would return to China the next day.

ST: In those days, I would not purchase things that I couldn't fit in a car either.

DX: When I got my student visa to the United States, my sister called me from the States and I told her that I didn't want to leave China. She said that if you didn't like it here, you could always go back. I wanted to come to the States only to continue my studies. I had thought that I would return to China once I finished my degree. However, things didn't go smoothly for me, I believe that had a lot to do with my state of mind (*xintai*). I was always getting ready to leave.

RH: Exiled students were treated differently abroad depending on when they left China and where they came from. Those who came right after Tiananmen received much more public support than those who came later; and those who came from Beijing were taken care of better than those who came from other provinces. In fact, the repression in other provinces was more severe because there was less public monitoring and media attention.

ST: Ridiculous things happened in those days right after 1989. Because of public interest in the event, some people who hadn't been very much involved in the movement became the focus of public attention and consequently they benefited from it, whereas some who actually played important roles didn't get noticed. That was a strange phenomenon. Whether you came out early or late, everyone had a story and everyone's story was different. Wang Dan came out late but he still got a lot of public attention.

RH: Wang Dan's case is not typical though—he was too prominent for people to forget, no matter when he left China.

ST: I think the willingness to learn English made a huge difference [in the settlement process]. But the center and home of the exiles, whether you were exiled by the government or you exiled on your own, lay elsewhere, both intellectually and psychologically. "Living somewhere else," as Milan Kundera puts it. It was a homeless mind. We lived in a place that we could not merge into.

After I was arrested when I returned to China in 1992, an American journalist wrote an article that said: "I asked myself why a young and bright Chinese student who could do well in this country [the U.S.] would give up everything and return to China to be a martyr," something like that. He didn't answer that question directly but he said maybe that was the difference between Americans and revolutionaries. Actually I didn't see myself as a revolutionary, but it is true that for about ten years, I was always getting ready to return to China. It wasn't because I didn't like the United States. I came here when I was in my early twenties and I have no problem with the language. That was one of the reasons that I picked liberal arts, which I thought provided the most flexible lifestyle, and also why I spent so much time on it during my graduate studies. I didn't have a career path for myself. I made a living mainly through writing. I used a pen name to publish in journals in China. Everything I did on that track was related to China and I always had the illusion of returning home.

DX: How did you change? What made you change?

ST: It has all been recent changes, very recent.

Shen Tong went into further detail about his experience of infighting in the dissident community. He shared his disappointment, and talked about the damage to his reputation.

To Be Professional or To Be Pure

ST: Professionally it discredited all the potential political influence I had. Probably it wasn't as bad as I imagined—it was just because I was sad…or maybe I could have avoided it, but it was very hard. I knew I should carry on, but…This is the major reason that I felt unsettled all these years…There is a difference between instrumental rationality and formative rationality. If you think your ultimate goal is right, you need to use every effective method to reach that goal. Of course I don't mean that we should take any means at all (*buzeshouduan*), but we can't pay excessive attention to purity (*jiepi*) when engaging in the operation of social movements. I don't mean that we should do dirty things, but we have no right to be aloof from politics and worldly considerations (*qinggao*) either—we could do that in 1989 because it was pure idealism. Now there is more than just pure ideals—we need to be professional.

As overseas dissidents, we should study for a degree or develop our own career paths. We need to be professional especially when we are facing difficult circumstances—when we are in tough situations. I feel badly that I quit. I have always enjoyed working with the media. The media work I used to do was related to the democratic cause, but not now.

DX: You just pointed out something important—it is important to have a basis for cooperation. Either we have rules and regulations or we form a group bond of brotherhood. Of course, neither can be completely pure. I think there is a lack of professionalism in Chinese culture. It always relies on morality or emotions to judge and defeat people. It is always easy to criticize others by taking the moral high ground (*daode zhigaodian*). However, it is important to be professional in our operation.

ST: I understand everyone makes calculations and I don't see that as a problem. Everyone works toward the best for their own interests. Positive competition is reasonable and appropriate. The problem is that when we are in the same boat, there is no point in making the boat sink. That's not wise.

The Lost Home: Between Family and Ideals

DX: Could you share with me your experiences and thoughts when you made personal and career decisions? It seems that you were clear about the path you wanted to take.

ST: Not in regard to June 4, though. It is just that I have a family life now. This is the single most important thing for me. As I mentioned to Xiaoqing earlier, I had nightmares almost every night for many years after June 4. I had many opportunities to release my feelings so I didn't need to talk to a psychiatrist—I talked to people all the time. But when I slept, unconsciously, I couldn't get rid of the nightmares. But ever since Yanyan was born, the nightmares have never come back. I haven't had one in the past six months. Never! Not once!

DX: Amazing! I still have nightmares from time to time. During the time when I was imprisoned, I had many nightmares about being chased and running for my life.

ST: For me, it was all about death—very graphic. After my father passed away, I dreamed of him intensely for a year or two. My nightmares stopped six months ago. This changed everything. Now I have a family life. This family doesn't have to be here, but I would like them to be in a comfortable city, and I can do things I would like to do, which is basically impossible in China.

DX: The time when I most wanted to have a home was when I was in jail. I was sick for a long time—I had a fever for almost two months and it didn't go away. In those days I really wanted to have a family life—I wanted to spend time with my parents—to go out for a walk with them after dinner. I remember there was a popular song at that time called "I Want to Have a Home."

ST: I didn't think of having a home until things happened naturally. I didn't have a plan. I don't mean that I didn't plan to have a home, but not so intensely and with so much detail. I simply never imagined it.

I think idealists are selfish. According to common sense, I am not a good son—I couldn't go back to China, and my mother and my family suffered a lot because of me. I understand that such suffering is common among families in the dissident community. However, it is definitely inhuman and abnormal for family members to be harmed like that—my parents had to withstand the pressure from their work units, the inconveniences added to their daily life, and the change in lifestyle and friends—my family lost almost all of their intellectual friends after June 4. The change of mind was more serious and obvious among intellectuals than among the general public after the crackdown.

When I decided to do something to "liberate" the world—maybe I shouldn't put it so big; say, when I decided to do something for China, China in an abstract sense—my immediate family members were seriously hurt. During all those years, it would not have been difficult for me to change the situation if I had wanted to. For example, if I had had a career in the U.S. and I worked hard, I am sure that I could have done well. I could have given my family many more things and made them happier. It is all related to concrete things, say, they could have had money for travel [to the United States] to see me more often. When I decided to sacrifice for my ideals and for the cause of democracy, my immediate family members suffered more than I did and they had no choice about it—I could make a choice about what I wanted to do but they couldn't choose not to be my family members. Regardless of what other people say, we all suffered a lot. Some have said that we shouldn't have left China after June 4, etc., but I think that is nonsense. I think I have been selfish in the process of pursuing my ideals.

RH: I felt the same kind of guilt toward my mother. I had been living an unstable life as a new immigrant and never had a real sense of home abroad. If it had not been for June 4, I would not be doing what I am doing now. My mother gave me everything she could—love and support—but I didn't have much to give her in return.

I think our struggle has a lot to do with the education we received about home and country. When Xu Wenli[1] left China, people challenged him saying that he used to say that he would stay in prison until the CCP collapsed, but he had already left China. He responded that he started to realize that democracy should first of all be a way of living. He said he had been in prison for sixteen years—his daughter had lived a life without a father and his wife without a husband. He said that he hadn't been democratic to his family. What he said left a deep impression on me. Of course I understand that we don't actually have many choices when we live in such historical contexts. I did make major life decisions for myself, but there actually was no choice about the decision to go into exile and to continue to work for the cause.

ST: I think people should be able to make personal choices. I remember last year at the June 4 anniversary, news came that Chai Ling had started to do business in China. Both Kaixi and Wang Dan commented that we should not criticize her because she had already done a lot of things for the cause. She should have the right to choose a more private life.

RH: I was actually with Wang Dan and Kaixi when they responded to the media regarding the news that Chai Ling was doing business in China. I remember Kaixi said something like "as the group of '89 students, we should support one another."

ST: I think it is also important for idealists to create a balance. When we talk about common sense, there are problems as well. I mean, in a group, there should always be someone who will stand up and sacrifice for something bigger. But where is the balance?

There has been gossip in the news about Wang Dan's sexual orientation. I know some people are critical of that. But come on, doesn't he also deserve a life? The kid has not had a life since 1989. He is a quiet guy and I can imagine how difficult it is for him. I am not happy either about the attacks from the dissident community, but at least I would openly talk about it.

DX: We are actually touching on the topic of cultural values. Who should sacrifice and who has the right to sacrifice others? Human lives are to be respected in the American value system. However, after September 11, we faced a question: Do we have the right to take others' lives for the purpose of protecting our home and our country? I think there are dark hidden sides of human nature in Eastern culture. For example, we were told that in the name of a great cause, anything can be sacrificed. But actually, those who told us to sacrifice were not that unselfish. They had their own agendas. That's why a lot of people in pro-democracy circles became disappointed and were left heartbroken. Democratic countries recognize the dark side of human beings, so they stress the importance of checks and balances of power. That's why a system of balances is established. Personally, I think it is not right to exaggerate about either side. As human beings we all have shortcomings and our abilities are limited. So I fully agree it is important to find a balance.

ST: But I don't know where the balance is. I am now satisfied that I can take better care of my family. I can't say I am happier, but I am less depressed. So something good must have happened. As we discussed earlier, I am not happy with the fact that what I find meaningful to do right now has little to do with the ideals I used to value. I don't know...Maybe it is just inertia—like the skyline became awkward without the Twin towers. Of course this has a lot to do with my disappointment with the exile community and my personal expectations.

RH: As we talk about home here, I think there are two different meanings of home. Before 1989, home was more about home in China with our parents—we were children of our parents. But after 1989, we struggled abroad without a home attached to a home country. We all know that many of our friends in exile didn't have a chance to see their parents when they died, and many failed to establish a real home for themselves in exile.

ST: I think home means a home with one's parents, as Danxuan put it just now. Home is also related to one's basic senses like sight and taste. When I returned to China, I tried various snacks on the street but I found that none of them tasted the same way as they did when I ate them as a kid. From this you can tell that even for concrete things like snacks, my memory will betray me. They simply tasted different although I was eating the same food. This can be a big topic.

Values versus Power

DX: For me, before the year 2001, I always considered my home to be home in China. I never considered that there was a possibility of setting up a home in the United States. Never! But after September 11, for a period of time in 2001, I seriously considered applying for U.S. citizenship.

ST: Why?

DX: Intellectually (*jingshenshang*), I identified with the core values of U.S. society, such as respect for human lives and individual freedom.

ST: For me, the impact was just the opposite, but for the same reason. I don't have any problems as a New Yorker; however, as an American, I am faced with an identity challenge. Being American is always problematic because it is a country of immigrants. It is a personal choice whether or not to become an American. To some extent I had no choice about this because I didn't have a passport. I had been stateless for a long time. I couldn't travel widely without a passport. Citizenship is a political concept and this country has a problematic government. So September 11 had a big impact on me. It was the opposite [than the impact on Danxuan]. I don't want to be an American today!

The post–September 11 setting…Let me put it this way. It is related to 1989. It is related in the way that I talked about the relationship between birth and death—I mean Yanyan's birth and the end of my nightmares about death. Two versions of the historical narratives of 1989 appeared in the nineties, written and controlled by two groups, respectively, the Chinese government and the Western mainstream media. I think both versions of the narratives are problematic. Of course I understand the fact that, strictly speaking, any narrative will have some distance from the truth—it is far from truly presenting the historical facts.

I wrote a novel before September 11 with six major characters. Actually these six characters were all about myself: I should admit that it is a self-centered piece of fiction. The novel starts with news about Wang Weilin—the tank man standing in front of columns of tanks. Of the six characters, one is persecuted after June 4, one is exiled, one is killed, one chooses to join the

Communist Party, and one is self-exiled. The novel tells stories about the different possible paths taken by the '89 cohort. Strictly speaking, no individual has complete control over the path they would like to take—of course they can make some personal decisions but they can't change the historical context. All the post–September 11 narratives, including the Iraq War, are packaged by the news media.

DX: Sorry for interrupting: when did you get your U.S. citizenship?

ST: In 2000. That's why my identity was later challenged. Why did I choose to become an American?

DX: So you were talking about your thoughts and feelings after the Iraq War, but when I said I wanted to become an American just now, I was talking about my immediate reaction to September 11.

ST: I see.

DX: I was at work when September 11 happened. I was working for Radio Free Asia in DC. We started working at six o'clock in the morning to prepare for the daily news. We had a small TV on the desk and one of my colleagues first noticed that a plane had hit the Twin Towers. Because the TV screen was very small, at first we thought that a private plane had accidentally hit the towers. Then all of a sudden we saw another plane hit the tower. I knew this wasn't a re-play because smoke was coming out of the other tower that had just been hit. My colleagues and I were preparing the news as a team and gradually we started to realize how serious it was. Soon after that we heard that the Pentagon was attacked as well.

Before September 11, in my mind the U.S. was the symbol of the defender of freedom. I identified with the values of the country. So America is like my intellectual home. At the same time, I felt more attached to my family, friends, and language back in China—the United States didn't play any role in that part. However, the attack on the Twin Towers all of a sudden drew me closer to the U.S.

ST: This was how I felt when I first moved to New York. I think New York is a home for the homeless.

DX: I think the values of freedom, tolerance, and of a pluralistic society are all reasons why the United States is strong. But the policy of unilateralism after September 11 actually negated, and deviates from, the core values of the United States. That foreign policy emphasizes the importance of protecting the homeland and therefore it doesn't care about having dialogues with others. The U.S. was strong in the international community not only because of its power, but also because of its values. This was the reason that America was strong and forever young, but the Bush government changed that situation.

ST: Now I get your point. Our reactions were reflecting different layers of the impact. I wasn't in the U.S. when September 11 happened. I was in Taipei. I watched the news there and CNN reported that 93 percent of Americans supported the war. At that time, I was thinking that if that were true, I would rather not be an American. That was my immediate reaction. Fortunately, when I came back here, I found out that most of my friends in New York didn't think in that way.

No Direction Home

ST: I have traveled extensively outside the U.S. over the years. I experienced three stages of identity development as a new immigrant. The first stage was the time when I first landed at Kennedy airport in New York in 1989. I didn't feel that I was an exile at that time. I knew I was in a foreign country (*yixiang*), but I also felt that I was home (*daojia*). There are two reasons for this. The first reason is the same that you gave just now—I felt that the United States was my intellectual home (*jingshen jiayuan*). I identified with its values—that is, in a serious sense. Besides, U.S. popular culture provided another sense of home for me—my familiarity with the pop culture. You know, Kentucky Fried Chicken was the ideal place for dating in Beijing. It was a pricey place, not fast-food.

The second stage was more conscious. When I was in high school, I wondered why the word "I" was capitalized in English. There are two layers to this perspective. First, I felt I was liberated in the States. I felt free. Besides, I felt that at last I had a chance to be away from home—it was something that I had thought of doing for a long time, to leave home (*lijiachuzou*). Of course there were still feelings of exile. But it was more about being away from home. I don't mean that I had found a home, but it was a feeling of being on the road. Like Bob Dylan—his home was on the road. He has a song called "No Direction Home," which is similar to the homeless mind I talked about earlier.

So to sum up, when I first came to New York, I knew it wasn't my home, but I felt at home. Second, we could do lots of things here. I remember someone once said that June 4 was like a rape that we could never avenge. But we could do lots of things abroad during those days. I know Danxuan was in prison at that time. Before 1993, there had been a lot of support for the democracy cause in Europe and North America. It was a very effective healing process for me. Because of the political and social systems and the cultural environment in the West, we could do things that were not possible in Asia. During that period of time, I would defend the United States whenever I was abroad, even though I could be critical of it when I was inside the country. Then came the third stage. I couldn't agree with the country's policies on things such as international affairs and its unilateralism in the allocation of international resources. After September 11, I think I was fortunate to be living in New York. Otherwise I can't imagine myself as an American today.

I think New York is a home for the homeless. During the third stage of my identity development, I felt I would forever be a foreigner. In 1998 and 1999, I started to realize that even if I could return to China, I would not be able to adapt to the environment there. So I tried to let go (*fangxia*) although in the bottom of my heart, I could not accept it. I decided that I would be a foreigner wherever I went. This wasn't only something intellectual and abstract—it was something real in daily life. For example, my friends were living in different cities; I didn't have much furniture; everything I had was travel-light—instead of having big suitcases, I had small suitcases. I wore the same suit for formal occasions for nine years. New York City is an ideal place for me. It is a real multi-cultural city. You don't have to think about differences between being mainstream and being marginal.

RH: The word "sacrifice" hit me when I saw the planes hit the Twin Towers on September 11, reminding me of the essence of the political indoctrination that we had been exposed to in China. We were always told to sacrifice for the nation and the people. We were taught that even individual happiness should be sacrificed. Our generation grew up with the notions of home and home country associated with one another. We learned a lot of isms that were not related to the social reality and that didn't prepare us to handle daily life. When I first returned to China after I immigrated to Canada, I felt the line at customs was my position in this world. I chose to leave China but I would like to return to China. It might seem that I had made some important choices for myself but actually those were not exactly the choices I would have liked to have chosen.

ST: The irony is, these seem to be our own choices but these are the only choices that we could afford to make given the particular historical circumstances.

DX: I think there are individual differences in our understanding of home, which is related to our values. I mean, it depends on what you most value— your family, your language, places you feel familiar with, or your identity associated with certain values. When we struggled over whether or not we should apply for U.S. citizenship, we were struggling to decide what we most valued. When we make up our mind to gain something, we know that at the same time we are also going to lose something. Shen Tong put it clearly just now. The U.S. after the Iraq War was very different from the U.S. after World War II. The U.S. used to be the symbol of the free world. But it changed a lot after the Iraq War. I think this was a big shock for Americans, especially for immigrants.

Now I still consider China to be my home. The main reason for this is that I believe that if I, as a Chinese person, can identify with these values [of freedom and democracy and so forth] I will someday be able to convince my fellow countrypersons to identify with these values as well. When this day comes, China will be a different China.

Under the Shadow of History: 6/4 and 9/11

ST: I started to have a well-defined identity crisis after September 11. I felt I was more a New Yorker than an American. I was very familiar with the Twin Towers. Every time I returned to the city, especially if I came back through Newark airport, I still couldn't get used to the skyline without the Twin Towers. When I applied for U.S. citizenship, it was more for the sake of convenience. As mentioned earlier, there was also a period of time before I got my U.S. citizenship when I identified with respect and pride the political values of the U.S. Similarly, I feel that I am more Beijingese than Chinese—the alleys, *Beida*, and the places I biked for outings, all made up parts of my life.

Now let's get back to our discussion about June 4. I don't know how to put it—it is too complicated. Sometimes I suspect that I am anti-intellectual (*fanzhi*). When I see what has been happening in recent years in China, such as the reactions to the bombing of the Chinese embassy in Belgrade,[2] the anti-Japanese and anti-American demonstrations, and when I look at *Beida*—the so-called symbol of independent thinking—and think about those scientists who supported Hitler during World War II, I start to think that in an era of dramatic social changes, intellectuals tend to lack common sense. *Beida* has been involved in different kinds of things, both good and bad. We should ask, when we talk about June 4, to what extent are we able to put things in perspective? I think we need to keep some distance if we would like to put things in perspective. Who am I? Am I Chinese or American? Am I a New Yorker or a Beijingese? What exactly happened during the historical event that I regarded as ideal and pure and that has had such a huge impact on my personal life? The event left me with six identities—I had no choice. If I had been imprisoned like Danxuan, or if I had chosen to become cynical and join the CCP, or if I had started to do business...

We talked about common sense just now and I described myself as anti-intellectual. I think many of the problems in my life, including the struggles, actually have a lot to do with the influence of the fairly superficial intellectual environment in which I grew up, such as the education we had when we were kids—that part was imposed on us—and the pursuit of freedom and democracy when I was in university—particularly my participation in several student movements in the eighties. I guess I wasn't very enthusiastic at first but my participation re-enforced my pursuit, especially after June 4. In recent years, I have discovered that it is really difficult to undo those concepts, values, and ideas in my mind. This is especially difficult after witnessing events such as September 11 and the Iraq War. I used to associate the U.S. with freedom, democracy, and pop culture. However, now I need to unpack, if not de-construct, the baggage I have been carrying.

I think the process would be less difficult for those people who are comparatively less intellectual. For example, my mother is a medical doctor but she is not an intellectual; or my wife—she is a PhD but she is not an intellectual in the sense we have discussed—with clear values and judgments, not just knowledge. When I look at nonintellectuals like them, I don't think they have such difficulties and struggles because they rely more on common sense.

DX: May I call this the myth of the rational? I agree that intellectuals tend to have such problems.

Cynicism and Nationalism in the Post-Tiananmen Era

ST: When I saw the Chinese university students demonstrating after the bombing of the Chinese embassy in Belgrade, it was such a sharp contrast compared with the demonstrations of university students in 1989. This time the demonstrations were anti-U.S. and pro-Chinese government. That had a big impact on me. It had been nine years since I had seen similar scenes—university students taking to the streets. The Taiwan issue is another example. If you went to *Beida*, everybody would shout that we should start a war with Taiwan. However, if you ask a worker on the street in Beijing, he would tell you that "we are still developing our economy, why should we spend money on war? Taiwan is doing fine." My point is: sometimes we don't need lots of knowledge—we can simply use our common sense.

RH: The rising nationalism has a lot to do with the values the younger generations have been exposed to during their experiences and education in the post-Tiananmen era.

DX: Shen Tong, why do you think intellectuals would become anti-intellectual?

ST: You are a member of the IFCSS.[3] You should know this better than I do. In the past fifteen years, people have changed from being willing to carry out hunger strikes and not being afraid of dying for their ideals—even though, to be cynical, the ideals were not very clear at that time. Pro-democracy dissidents, as well as liberals both inside and outside of China, are being marginalized and despised—fortunately not all of them, but most of them. This is a serious issue.

RH: Do you think the dissident groups need to reflect as well? We too are disappointed with the dissident community, aren't we?

ST: We are talking about two things here—disappointment about the dissident groups and disappointment about the ideas of freedom and democracy, social reform, and justice. We were a generation of idealists, no matter how unclear those ideals were. Our appeal (*haozhaoli*) to the society in those days came from populism—from people's demands (*suqiu*) for less corruption. Now the younger generation is cynical. Starting from the late nineties, the intellectual class in China has become totally cynical. No matter how the dissident groups behave, people are just cynical.

RH: I used to have a friend who was deeply involved in 1989 but he no longer cares about the cause. He was sent back to his hometown after the military crackdown. It took him a long time to struggle all the way back onto the academic track. So he is being very careful nowadays.

ST: Do you think he regrets what he did during June 4?

RH: I don't know.

ST: I think some people can go that far, [regretting what they did in 1989]. There are different reactions—some treat June 4 as something in the past. It is like an old picture kept at the bottom of your suitcase. You leave it there and you don't want to touch it again; some think that the event is no longer relevant; and some even say that there would not have been such great economic development without the crackdown.

RH: I think people's reactions have a lot to do with the purge after June 4.

ST: What about those who were not persecuted and punished? They were willing to die in 1989! Also, for overseas Chinese students, I didn't like the idea of the June 4 Protection Act.[4] At that time, I thought that once those students and scholars all got their U.S. green cards, the flag of democracy would fall. Of course I didn't realize it would be as serious [as it has now become]. I just thought that these people would become new immigrants after they got their green cards. In ten or twenty years, they would start to behave like most immigrants— criticizing the problems of the U.S. and fighting in the name of culture. However, I couldn't say those things at that time. If you look at the changes in these people, how can you explain them? They didn't pay any price, but they actually benefited from 1989.

RH: Just last week a journalist asked Danxuan a related question. She said that the IFCSS had lobbied the U.S. government to grant 80,000 June 4 green cards to Chinese students and scholars. However, why did very few people attend the candlelight vigil on the anniversary of June 4 this year?

DX: I think June 4 is like a graduation—different students have different experiences afterward. I think everyone has the right to choose his or her own lifestyle. However, as the Chinese saying goes: when you drink water, think of its source (*yinshuisiyuan*). We all understand how difficult it is as overseas Chinese students to get permanent residence status. It takes a lot of time and effort. As a result of the June 4 crackdown, 80,000 Chinese students and scholars received their June 4 green cards overnight. In this sense, I think June 4 should be remembered by these people.

You talked about a bottom line and anti-intellectualism. I think people sometimes become confused by simple things. As Kuide puts it in his article: let's get back to common sense: call a crime a "crime."[5] It turns out that a crime is no longer considered a crime. The overseas Chinese students and scholars benefited from the June 4 green card, but most of them don't care about June 4 anymore. In recent years, I think a lot about the bottom line and religion.

Danxuan was referring to Chen Kuide, an exiled intellectual. Kuide's article titled "Murder Is Murder" was a response to the Beijing regime's justifications for the military crackdown in 1989. He asserts that ordering its own army to fire on its own unarmed people was a crime, nothing else.

A Dream Renamed, Redefined, and Revived

RH: How do you think we can keep our dream of 1989 alive?

ST: How can you be sure that the dream is still alive?

RH: Because you told me just now that you are not happy if what you are doing professionally is not what you want to do for your ideals. It shows that you still value that part of your life.

ST: Maybe the unhappiness is my mourning for a dream that no longer exists. It is a question. We somehow assume that June 4 is very important—it is larger than life and therefore it is forever alive. But is it really? Is this true?

I think whether or not the dream is alive is in your heart, right?

DX: What is your definition of the dream? Is the definition the same as that in 1989? Are we talking about the dream in the same way that we did in 1989? In 1989 we understood the dream as the ideals of freedom, democracy, and a better China. It was very abstract. But now the dream is more concrete. One of the former 1989 students once told me that after all that he experienced in 1989, he started to value family as the most important.

RH: I don't have a fixed definition of the dream. The dream is developing, is being re-defined and revived. It is an unfolding story. It is an ongoing process, not an ending. And we are trying to keep it alive.

At this point, Shen Tong's daughter, Yanyan, woke up from her nap. Shen Tong held her in his arms and she looked at us with her big eyes.

"How is your father going to struggle to keep the dream alive?" Shen Tong asked Yanyan.

Yanyan started to smile, and so did we. Her smiling face ended our conversation with a sense of hope for the future.

Life in Prison and Imprisoned Life:
Discussion with Wang Dan and Danxuan

"What is the difference between an individual interview and a group discussion?" Wang Dan started the group discussion by raising this question and then following with his own answer: "The individual interview is one person crying alone while the group discussion is two people crying together."

"And the third person will watch us cry," Danxuan added. Wang Dan, Danxuan, and I have had many interactions over the years, so we were familiar with the ways we joke as well as the ways we disagree. I had already become used to the two of them downplaying the heaviness of their experiences. I started to think that maybe this is how they survived their hardship in life.

WD: I suggest that you turn your study into a documentary.
RH: I wish I had the resources to do that.
WD: When we have money we should support projects like yours.
DX: I didn't like her using the word "dream."
WD: I agree. Dream is not an accurate term.
RH: Shen Tong had no problem with the word.
WD: Shen Tong has a more romantic personality.
DX: I agree.

From my perspective, they all had romantic personalities.

The Fact That They Can Choose to Give Up Is Democracy

We continued to discuss the phenomenon that some former student leaders in 1989 had chosen to give up on the cause.

WD: I am aware of the fact that people involved in 1989 have chosen different life paths, with some still continuing the cause, and others having given
it up. I have been asked many times "how come those students gave up the
cause while you still carry on alone?" I tell them that, first, I am not the only
one who is still carrying on. I am just one of the most well-known ones.
Second, I tell them that even if other student leaders choose not to continue
the cause, so what? It is their right to decide whether to give up or to stay—if
you don't respect their choices, you are against democracy. I think this is a big
lesson I learned from June 4. After all these years of experience, if I still don't
understand this, then our fellow students died in vain in 1989. So I will stand
up and argue with anyone who challenges why some student leaders are no
longer fighting for the cause. I think the fact that they can choose to give up
is democracy. If they can't even choose their personal life paths, what kind of
democracy is that?
RH: Over 80,000 students and scholars received their green cards to stay in
the U.S. as a result of June 4. But only a few of them show up June 4 for the
anniversary activities each year. People simply disappeared after they got their
green cards.
DX: After a historical event, it is just like after graduation from school: everyone
can choose what they want to do afterwards. This is just natural. Of course the
historical event did have a great impact on us. That is for sure. For example,

the experience of imprisonment has had an impact on us psychologically, and might have changed our values and worldviews. But I think personal choice should be respected. For those who received the June 4 green cards, it is their right to choose what they would like to do.

I once wrote an open letter on the twelfth anniversary of June 4 [as president of IFCSS]. I pointed out in the letter that everyone has a right to pursue individual happiness. We cannot challenge that (*wukehoufei*). And I don't think they should be criticized because they no longer cared about June 4 after they got their green cards. However, as mentioned in our discussion with Shen Tong, I think as human beings, we should think of the source when we drink the water. As Chinese students abroad, we all understand how difficult it is to get permanent residence status in the U.S. It takes a lot of time and effort. In this sense, I think June 4 should be remembered.

Identity Is a Choice

RH: You were the president of the IFCSS but you yourself refused to apply for U.S. citizenship.

DX: We already discussed this in our interview. I wasn't involved in the process of lobbying for the June 4 green card. Of course that is part of the history of the IFCSS. I did consider applying for U.S. citizenship right after September 11. I identify with the key values of the mainstream society in the U.S. and I feel I am closer to those values. However, I was born in China and I grew up in China. Do you remember the painting I bought on the day that we had the group discussion with Shen Tong? The reason I bought the painting is that the pond in the picture is similar to the pond that was close to my home when I was a kid. It reminded me of all sorts of memories of life in China. So when we talk about identity and values, it doesn't only involve rational elements, but also our emotional attachments to people and experiences. When the Twin Towers were hit, I felt that the values I upheld were being attacked as well. So I had an impulse to become an American citizen to guard those values that I believed in. However, I disagreed with the government's policy, especially the unilateral policy after September 11.

RH: Wang Dan mentioned in his interview that life in the U.S. was about *them* not *us*; but even if he returns to China, it is still *them* and not *us* because of the government in power. So is it the same situation for you? I mean, can you identify as an American here in the States?

DX: I think identity is a choice. If you choose to take American citizenship, you will gain something; meanwhile you will also lose something, and vice versa. So it is a matter of choice—what kind of life you choose to live.

RH: You and Wang Dan had very different experiences after you came to the U.S. For Wang Dan, the difficulties he encountered in exile were more about difficulties in school, such as language problems, while you had to work very hard to survive financially.

WD: I never denied the fact that I was luckier than others. But I think different people had different experiences under particular conditions.

DX: When I was arrested, I was cross-examined by the police and they tried every method to get me to give information about other student leaders. They would say things like "look at those student leaders who ran away—they are having fun abroad, but you are suffering here." I told them that we as student leaders play different roles for the revolution—some need to get out of China to preserve the seeds of fire (*huozhong*), while some need to stay in prison. Of course that was just my answer for them. I think there are always uncertainties in life, or we call them fate or destiny.

Whatever Happens, It Is Better Than Being Kept in Jail

RH: The other day I was at a subway station and I heard a Chinese musician playing a song of our generation. It reminded me so much of my youth and the past. I can't imagine how life would have been different for me if it had not been for 1989. I can't remember the name of the song but it goes like this...

I started to sing the song.

"The Story of Time!" (Guangyin de gushi) Wang Dan and Danxuan said the name of the song almost simultaneously. And they then joined me in singing. That was one of the most touching moments I had during the research process. No matter how different we were in terms of personalities and ideas, we drew closer simply because of a popular song of our generation before 1989.

DX: I think it is important that we have different sources for our human spirits. If one source doesn't work, we should have another one. However, I have the impression that June 4 is your only spiritual source. So once you saw problems, such as the infighting, you were badly hurt and disappointed. I told you many times that June 4 is earthly, which means things will change. We need something spiritual, such as having a belief.

RH: But Wang Dan doesn't have a belief.

WD: Who said I don't have a belief? Belief doesn't necessarily need to be something concrete like Buddhism or Catholicism or Christianity. To be happy and peaceful is my belief. I think as human beings we all need happiness and peace, not just people who have religious beliefs. Religions are intended to help people to achieve happiness and peace.

As I told you earlier, after my personal experience of lots of things all these years, I started to realize that most of the heroic stories that touched me when

I was younger must have been made up. My experience is supposed to be dramatic—a young man being confined to Qincheng Prison overnight. However, I didn't feel anything special. I don't have much to say. It wasn't very heroic. I became angry when I was supposed to be angry and I felt tired when I was tired. That's it—so nothing dramatic. I learned from my experience that life is not dramatic. If you have lived through life you will know that life is not dramatic.

I don't know how others feel about life. For me, after experiencing imprisonment, separation from family, and so forth, now every day is a gift. So I am happy—no matter what happens, it is better than being kept in jail. After being deprived of freedom, I learned to value freedom. That's why I always say that I am grateful for my past. Every time I am not happy or I am angry with someone, I would subconsciously adjust myself—things can't be worse than they were when I was in prison.

DX: Being imprisoned is quite an experience, of course, but I don't encourage people to go to prison. I heard that some people intentionally put themselves in prison in order to train their perseverance. I think that was more for entertainment. When I was first set free, people asked me how I felt about being imprisoned. I would tell them that there were gains and losses. What I lost was time, but being confined forced me to think a lot—that was the only thing I was able to do—they could imprison your body but they couldn't imprison your mind. So I thought a lot—that was a by-product of imprisonment.

June 4 Should Not Be the Only Meaningful Thing in Our Lives

WD: I think what Danxuan said just now is very important. It is true that we shouldn't forget June 4 and for sure we will never forget it. However, June 4 shouldn't be the only thing we remember in our lives. We should explore other aspects of life that can be just as meaningful as June 4. June 4 should not be the only meaningful thing in our lives—this is something that we should try to do as members of the '89 generation. If someone decides to go into business, that is fine. That means he or she is exploring other aspects of life. As long as you don't take the side of the government to oppose the ideals of June 4, that's fine. I don't think everyone needs to stick to June 4. We should have a diverse group.

RH: I've been trying hard to adjust to this since June 4. For many years after 1989, I had a sense of guilt. It was like when Christians think about the crucifixion of Jesus. In those years, I felt that so many people had been killed, and so many others were still in prison. So I punished myself by not allowing myself to sing or dance, something I enjoyed a lot in the past. I didn't even take vacations. For a period of time, I felt that June 4 was my religion.

WD: If you ask me about my expectation for the '89 generation, I would write an article titled "If there is a song..." No matter how many years have passed; no matter how far away we are from one another; no matter what we are doing, if there is such a song as "The Wound of History" that we still become emotional about when we hear it, that is enough.

For me, every time I hear the song, I am still touched, or it can change my mood. I think this is enough for members of our generation. For other things, such as whether or not one is still supporting the cause, it doesn't matter that much. But if someone has no feelings when he or she hears this song, I think that something is wrong.

"The Wound of History" is a song written by Taiwanese singers to commemorate Tiananmen.

DX: As I stated in the open letter about the June 4 green card holders, I said that for the June 4 victims and their family members, the meaning of the loss of life lies in the hope for a better life for the next generation. In my favorite movie *Saving Private Ryan*, before the commander dies he tells Ryan that he hopes Ryan will live a good life. Actually, at the beginning of the movie, when Ryan brings his family to visit the grave of the commander and stands in front of the grave and he says something like: I have lived a good life. Of course I can't speak on behalf of the victims about their understanding of life, but that is how I understand freedom and democracy. We should live a full, happy, and meaningful life to make the sacrifice of those who were killed worthwhile. I don't think the victims would like to see us unhappy.

RH: Wang Dan, when you talked about songs, do you still remember there was a disagreement about the songs we should sing on the fifteenth anniversary? We meant to sing "Blood-stained Glory" (*Xueran de fengcai*),[6] but some didn't like the idea because they considered it to be a CCP song and they suggested that we sing "The Wound of History." Eventually we still decided to sing "Blood-stained Glory" because that was what we sang during the movement in 1989. I think our decision was related to our memory and experience associated with the song. "The Wound of History" didn't come out until after June 4.

WD: That's why I said that as long as we share the same emotions (*qinggan*) when we hear a song that is enough. I think the biggest difference between the generations of earlier dissident movements and our '89 generation is that the former mainly target the CCP, while our focus is the China of tomorrow. So I will not link everything to the CCP, but I will consider whether it is good for the future of China.

The tradition of Chinese power transitions has always been one empire replacing another. I think the ultimate goal of democracy should not be power. Even if democracy is achieved, one cannot stay in power forever—that is the meaning of democracy. So what are you going to do when you are no longer in power? Look at the former presidents of the U.S. They are willing to return to normal lives. We discussed before that in China, historically losing power could mean losing one's life and freedom. Chinese history has proved this again and again, so no one wants to and can afford to lose power.

DX: I think that has a lot to do with the values that have been instilled. For example, before Zhang Zhixin was executed, her throat was cut. Why? Those who carried out the order to execute her didn't need to cut her throat, but why did they do it? Why did this happen in China? If we look at Russia, when the revolutionaries were exiled to Siberia, people could send them flowers and their families could accompany them to live in exile. That would have been impossible in China. Another story I read about in a book was that, when the prison warden saw that two prisoners couldn't communicate because they were separated by walls in between, he ordered that the walls be torn down. In contrast, in China, they would try to keep the prisoners as far apart as possible if they saw that you two prisoners were trying to communicate with each other.

Zhang Zhixin, a member of the Communist Party, criticized the cult of Mao and the ultra-left during the Cultural Revolution. She was imprisoned in 1969 and finally executed in 1975. Prior to her execution, the prison guards slit her throat to prevent her from denouncing the regime before her death.

WD: I think the key point of those stories is in the system. For example, the person who cut Zhang's throat knew that if he did that he would not face punishment. The political atmosphere at that time allowed things like that to happen. So the system can turn human beings into animals.

* * *

Between Home and Homeland

I have chosen quotes from Wang Dan and Danxuan as subtitles for the group discussions: "The fact that they can choose to give up is democracy," "Identity is a choice," "Whatever happens, it is better than being kept in jail," and "June 4 should not be the only meaningful thing in our lives." Judging by these quotes, neither Wang Dan nor Danxuan has a problem putting the past behind him and starting a new life in exile. Each believes that he should live a full, happy, and meaningful life despite all that has happened to him. However, the fact that the meaning of life for them lies in fighting for their lost dreams in China makes a new ordinary life complicated, if not impossible.

Shen Tong indicates that in different contexts he feels "unsettled" and "homeless," that he has "no direction home." In reality, he has become an entrepreneur and he is no longer involved in the democracy movement. In other words, even though Wang Dan and Danxuan stated that they had no qualms about starting a new life, in reality they had experienced many problems attempting to do so. Shen Tong expressed that he struggled with his decisions yet has been living a comparatively normal life in North America. Although Shen Tong has been criticized by some people, I somehow feel that his words and actions are more consistent than those of Wang Dan or Danxuan. Shen Tong wants to provide a better life for his family, so he has made decisions that, to use his own words, have more "common sense" and less "idealism." Danxuan too would like to live a happy life, but his activism makes it impossible. Wang Dan doesn't feel that he is living among "*us*," regardless of where he is. Exile was not just forced upon him; he had also decided that a life in exile is the best choice for him at the time.

Years ago I had a conversation with Danxuan years ago around the time of the Chinese New Year. "Do you miss home?" I asked him.

"No, not at all," he replied defiantly.

That wasn't the answer that I was expecting.

"Why? Don't you miss home? Don't you want to go home and visit your family?"

"I've told you already," Danxuan responded impatiently. "No, I don't want to go home, and I don't want to talk about this anymore."

Our conversation ended unpleasantly. I didn't know what I had done wrong. Later I came to realize that that was one of the most stupid questions I had asked. The two suitcases that Danxuan kept for all those years constituted an authentic and honest answer to my question—of course he wanted to go home. If someone like me, who had the option whether or not to visit China, was still homesick around the time of the Chinese New Year, I can only imagine his feelings of dislocation and loss. He had no choice in the matter. For an exile banished from home by a dominant and all-powerful state, "homesick" is a term that is both too superficial and too luxurious to even utter.

Conclusion

CHAPTER 7

Citizenship in Exile

Several years ago, during a talk I gave on civic education and youth values at the Harvard Graduate School of Education, a Chinese graduate student asked me, "What made your generation believe that if you did something like that in 1989, you wouldn't be punished? We learned from day one what the result would be if we ever try to challenge the government. How could you be so naïve as to think otherwise?"

More recently, a young Chinese professional who had received her graduate education in the United States told me that the 1989 protestors' motives must have been selfish: "I don't believe those students took to the streets for ideals. Chinese people only care about their day-to-day interests. It is impossible for them to protest for abstract and vague things like democracy."

These questions from the younger generation of Chinese perhaps can best be answered by a single image from 1989: unarmed young students holding hands and singing "The Internationale" while facing Communist machine guns. The crackdown crushed not only human lives, but also people's trust in the government and their hopes for a more open and just society. June 4, as a watershed in history, marks the transition of Chinese society from a time of idealism to a period of prolonged and endemic cynicism, producing a generation that cannot even imagine a society whose youth would be willing to make sacrifices on behalf of their ideals.

The popularity of "The Internationale" during the Tiananmen movement has been used by critics as evidence that the 1989 protesters were confused about their demands and incompetent with respect to their tactics. How could the students use a song promoted by the Communist Party for generations when they were protesting against that same Party? In 2011, there was a news report about a play performed by my students at a Tiananmen symposium at Harvard, which ended with the students singing together the Chinese song called "Nothing to My Name." Dai Qing, a well-known Chinese critic and former political prisoner, noted that those young Harvard students, "whose souls have never been twisted by power," were not singing "The Internationale" like the students in Tiananmen Square on June 4.[1] She implied that the Harvard students knew better.

"Nothing to My Name" was written in 1986 by Cui Jian, who is considered to be the godfather of Chinese rock and roll. It tells the story of a young man pleading with his girlfriend to accept his love even though he is poor: "I have asked endlessly, / when will you go with me? / But you always laugh at me, for having nothing to my name." The song captures the changing political mood among China's increasingly activist youth in the 1980s. It conveys their feelings of disillusionment and dispossession but at the same time also their hopes: "I want to give you my dreams, / and my freedom, / but you always laugh at me..." This is precisely the attitude that electrified the Tiananmen movement. "Nothing to My Name" rocked China before the Tiananmen movement erupted and Cui Jian became an idol of the Tiananmen Generation. As he himself puts it:

> Back then, people were used to hearing the old revolutionary songs and nothing else, so when they heard me singing about what I wanted as an individual they picked up on it...When they sang the song, it was as if they were expressing what they felt.

On May 20, 1989, Cui Jian went to Tiananmen Square and sang "Nothing to My Name" to support the students. The song is now considered the "unofficial anthem" of the Tiananmen protests.[2] But if we are to designate the "anthems" of the Tiananmen movement, there should actually be two instead of one: both "The Internationale" and "Nothing to My Name." In fact, it was the former that was sung much more often during the protests in 1989.

As I have participated with the exiled students in Tiananmen memorial activities over the years, we've often faced the dilemma of which songs we should sing. We did not have many options, as the only songs that we had learned about freedom and justice when we were growing up were revolutionary songs like "The Internationale" and "Blood-stained Glory." On one occasion, as mentioned in Wang Dan's interview, dissidents of an earlier generation interrupted us when we started to sing "Blood-stained Glory." On the one hand, those revolutionary songs were sung again and again in 1989, and they carry powerful memories and emotions. On the other hand, they have always been part of the repertory of Communist propaganda.

Those moments of contradiction are symptomatic of the Tiananmen Generation: born toward the end of Mao's Cultural Revolution and growing up at the beginning of Deng's reform era, they were under the influence of both the Communist ideology as promoted in the revolutionary stories and also of the new individualistic ideas that abounded in the political writings of the time and the emerging literary genres such as Misty Poetry and Scar Literature. The contradictions in my generation's thinking and behavior, as reflected in the tension between singing "The Internationale" and singing "Nothing to My Name," are not individual flaws but rather the result of the conflicting values characterized by a period of opening, searching, and uncertainty after the totalitarian Mao era. These contradictions demonstrate precisely why young people today, like their generational predecessors, actually need the fulfillment of the demands of the 1989 student protesters—free access to information and free speech—in order to become informed, responsible, and active citizens.

Political Socialization, Youth Values, and Power

Individual thinking is closely associated with the social conditions into which the individual is born and brought up, and it is influenced by the institutional structure of a society.[3] Thus, any acquired identities may not be fixed, but they are powerful determinants of "the horizon within which one is capable of taking a stand."[4] In return, people's perceptions and behavior maintain and transform the institutional structure in which they live.

Individual thinking is also shaped by political socialization, a process of identity formation by which junior members of a group or institution are taught its values, attitudes, and behaviors of the society. As a result of political socialization, the citizen "acquires a complex set of beliefs, feelings, and information which help him comprehend, evaluate, and relate to the political world around him."[5] In modern democracies, schools typically offer opportunities for young people to acquire civic knowledge and values and to become more actively engaged in politics. Political socialization under Communist regimes tends to take a more didactic approach, stressing the importance of order and submission to the party leadership.[6] Despite the persistence of early orientation, *de-socialization* and *re-socialization*—unlearning and relearning—do occur in contexts of what is known as a "reality shocks." Individuals come to learn, "at the cost of considerable psychological pain that their conceptions and expectations of the world do not conform to reality, and that there are numerous inaccuracies in this respect in terms of the earlier socialization that was provided for them."[7] In authoritarian contexts, it may be difficult for citizens to acquire the informational basis that is a prerequisite for a critique of political orthodoxy.

Since the establishment of the People's Republic of China, political socialization has been tightly controlled by the Chinese Communist Party through the state-run education and media. When the regime uses its jails, censorship, and indoctrination to dominate the flow of information and to manipulate public opinion, an informed citizenry and critical thinking, both considered core ingredients and prerequisites for democratic citizenship, are not possible. Any deviation from the official core messages is banned and those who risk speaking with a different voice may be subject to silencing. Youths of a particular generation thus tend to be exposed to a consistent program of indoctrination that reflects the political concerns of the regime at that time. Individual memories are shaped to conceal truth and to suit political agendas, and historical memories are transformed into pernicious national myths for instrumental purposes.[8]

The consistency in values within a given generation and the divides in values between and across generations have given rise to the concept of "generational thinking." For example, student protesters in the late 1980s tend to be ignorant of the activism of the previous generations (even the Democracy Wall Movement of the late 1970s). Chinese of the post-Tiananmen Generation know little about the struggles of the late 1980s. While students of the 1980s were highly critical of their own government and pushed for political reforms, students of the post-89 generation tended to make no distinction between the regime and the nation and defended the Beijing government as if they were defending China and the Chinese people. It is in this context that the experiences of domestic political socialization of the three Tiananmen student exiles profiled in this volume took place.

The Exile Syndrome

Unlike the Red Guard Generation[9] that had few resources to turn to in their struggle to find a way out of the mental prison of Maoism during the Cultural Revolution, the first generation of China's reform era was exposed to a variety of ideas and enjoyed considerably more freedom, despite the constant official political indoctrination. In her 1985 book *Children of Mao*, Anita Chan concludes that while the Red Guard generation continued to be a "troubled generation," she was optimistic about the younger generation because "the particular climate that encouraged the development of the authoritarian 'social character' no longer prevails. The 1980s are not the 1960s; and the children of Deng are not the children of Mao."[10] The spontaneous mass movement of 1989 seemed to identify the post-Mao generation with democratic ideals, thus giving it the name "the Tiananmen Generation". But such simple labels do not fully capture the conflicting identities of many of the members of this generation, including the three exiles who participated in this study.

Living in the shadows of historical amnesia and a distorted nationalism in post-'89 China, the three participants are torn between home and homeland, between a longing for an ordinary life and sacrificing for an unfinished cause. I use the term "the exile syndrome" to describe their dilemmas and struggles, which are related to the conflicting core values between the Communist doctrines to which they were exposed during their political socialization experiences in China and their desocialization and resocialization experiences in exile.

Between "Ordinary Life" and "Good Life"

The notion of an "ordinary life," as defined by the philosopher Charles Taylor in contrast to the traditional Aristotelian notion of an ethical "good life," stresses the importance of "those aspects of human life concerned with production and reproduction, that is, labour, the making of the things needed for life, and our life as sexual beings, including marriage and the family."[11]

While the Tiananmen Generation was growing up, the concept of a "good life" in China was defined by Maoist ideology, which preached that personal needs and desires should be held in check and the group or the collective was more important, indeed higher, than an ordinary life. Although student participants in the movement valued their ordinary lives and were unwilling to sacrifice for the sake of the Party, "they *were* prepared to sacrifice for the sake of the *country.*"[12] These conflicting values continued to play out during their lives in exile. Living in a democratic society, each could choose to embark on a new life, to focus on a new career, and to establish a new home. However, when Wang Dan and Danxuan chose to continue their activism, they both knew that they would have to face the consequences of not being allowed to return home. When Shen Tong decided to do business with China, he knew that he would have to give up his fight on behalf of the democratic cause. Although he made this choice to focus on his family and his professional life, he explicitly expressed many times that he was not happy with his decision. Thus, none of the three was able to achieve both political expression and an ordinary life.

I use two terms to describe such a contradiction: *adults in childhood* and *children in adulthood.* When the exiles were children, they were taught to sacrifice and to be patriotic, as if they were adults. The term "revolution" was romantic, heroic, and noble, and romantic stories were always associated with revolutionary themes and loyalty to groups. Family life was secondary: the priority was to give way to the socialist revolution and to make China strong. However, as adults, especially when they were exposed to different values in real life and in exile, the exiles came to realize that romance was not confined to revolutionary ideals—romance can also be living a normal life and taking responsibility for those you love. Even though de-socialization and re-socialization occurred while they were in exile, the value orientations that were developed during their formative years in China continued to have a strong impact. The changing concepts of romance and revolution and the changing connection between them in different social and political contexts are the root of the exiles' conflicted identities. As Craig Calhoun puts it:

> Our daily lives are full of examples of caution, but our narratives of revolution and popular struggle contain far more tales of bravery rather than of prudent common sense. As a movement takes participants beyond the range of usual

experience, they are thrown back more and more on such heroic images in their struggle to find acceptable guidelines for action...

They [the Tiananmen students] held themselves to such high standards of courage and struggle that failing to accept the danger would have meant a collapse of personal identity. That so many rose to the challenge of their own ideals was crucial to giving the events of 1989 their enduring significance.[13]

The Betrayal of Loyalty

All three exiles said that they had had no intention of overthrowing the government in 1989. Instead, they were following the long-standing tradition of Confucian dissent to help the rulers improve. To use Wang Dan's words, they took to the streets out of love, not out of hatred. *Youhuanyishi*, or a "worrying mentality," was pervasive among Chinese intellectuals in the eighties: "Those who work to improve society, whether they succeed or not, represent the courageous ideal of the Chinese intellectual in its purest form."[14] Shen Tong's changed perspective, from a student leader opposing the hunger strike in 1989 to believing that 1989 might have had a different ending had he and his colleagues sought a real revolution, further suggests that the students in 1989 had no intention of attempting to overthrow the regime.

In this sense, the exiled students were "patriots" betrayed by the Beijing regime: they did what they had been taught—to sacrifice for the good of the country—but, ironically, they were punished by the very system that had instilled in them these values and they were abandoned by the country for which they had sacrificed. And this is not the only betrayal. The exiles' hope for justice has been confounded by rising tensions between them and the younger generation. Growing up with their collective memory and values that were influenced by distorted histories and the state's intensification of patriotic education, those who came of age in the decades after 1989, who also see themselves as patriots, consider the exiled students of the 1989 generation to be national traitors.

Life for the exiles likely would be easier if they were willing to give up political activism. Student leaders who chose to compromise with the CCP and stay away from politics have been allowed to return home, and some have become professionally successful. But the implications of such decisions are profound. Sociologists have widely discussed how social movements transform the identities of the participants and affect subsequent activism. Participants in social movements tend to become more committed activists.[15] Their sustained commitment to political activism can "trigger a process of alteration that can affect many aspects of the participants' lives" and "the consequences of this process may be lifelong or at least long term."[16] In the case of the three exiled students in this study, the more committed they are, the farther they will be kept away from their homeland, and the more conflicted their identities will become. It is exactly because of their continuous activism and their unrequited love for their native country that they are marginalized and demonized by the state and its followers. Thus the betrayal of loyalty does not only apply to the exiled students' experiences in 1989. It has also been an ongoing reality.

Trauma and Infighting

Surviving with the scars of imprisonment, memories of a massacre, and the ongoing betrayal of their loyalty, the exiles live their lives in a post-traumatic state, but usually without receiving counseling or professional support. Student exile Danxuan, in an article co-authored with fellow IFCSS member Xue Tianhan, points out that "many survivors of the tragedy, family members of the dead, and participants of the demonstrations suffered also from symptoms of post-traumatic stress disorder, depression, and anxiety":

> The Chinese government has thus far denied all requests for a fair investigation of the tragedy and for compensation to the families. Survivors and families continue to live in injustice and this situation is likely to affect their health. In the 13 years since the atrocity, there have been barely any apparent efforts to assess the health consequences of the Tiananmen tragedy and to provide treatment and care for the victims.[17]

Although the term "post-traumatic stress disorder"(PTSD) was not brought up directly in individual interviews and group discussions—in fact, we had never even heard of such a term in China—I have observed signs and behavior of PTSD among almost every single exiled dissident whom I have encountered over the years, in both their personal and public lives. The splits, infighting, and interpersonal bitterness within the community of exiled dissidents arise partially from their domestic political socialization experiences in China that focused on struggles against nature and the people, rather than conflict resolution and leadership. They are also partially due to the traumas of their own experiences. Although political socialization is never finalized, early orientations are foundational and serve as the lenses through which individuals interpret political events and experiences later in life. The range of beliefs, information, and attitudes adopted in later life are limited by early political education. Betrayed by the state that once claimed it would protect them, once in exile, some have turned upon one another, as the victims of abuse become the abusers themselves.

Memory, Citizenship, and Social Changes

Despite the repeated repression of advocacy for political reforms in China, the last decade has witnessed growing resistance and the rise of citizenship movements in Chinese society. Historian Merle Goldman argues that although the new developments do not necessarily imply movement toward democracy, they are indeed prerequisites for the establishment of a democratic political system:

> Though they were suppressed, those who attempted to act as citizens in China in the 1980s and 1990s, whether they advocated liberal democracy or organized pressure from below to move the government toward political change, have had a profound influence.... the transition from comrade to citizen in the People's Republic of China has begun.[18]

Yet, without essential elements such as free speech and a free press, the development of the forces of a nascent civil society in China will continue to face many obstacles. In his essay "Bellicose and Thuggish: On the Roots of Chinese 'Patriotism,'" Nobel Peace Prize Laureate Liu Xiaobo[19] argues that a dictatorial monopoly over the dissemination of information is key to the development of what he calls "bellicose expansionist patriotism" in post-Tiananmen China. It is time to break the vicious cycle, to recover memory and history that would allow individuals to reenter the public sphere psychologically and politically, and to create healthy contexts of political socialization for the younger generation: "There can be citizenship without democracy, but there cannot be democracy without citizen participation."[20]

Citizens understand their responsibilities for a country's future by debating the moral meaning of history. Whereas memory can be manipulated and voices can be silenced by those in power, repression of memory and history is accompanied by political, social, and psychological distortions. The moment the government ordered its army to fire on its people in the name of national pride and economic development, it sent the message that any principle can be compromised to "become rich" and to accomplish "the rise of China." This mentality has become the root of major social and political problems in post-Tiananmen China. Deng Xiaoping's clear signals to the Chinese people in the 1990s—make money any way you like but forget about all unapproved politics, religion, and related matters—grew out of the crisis of 1989. Deng's policies over the years have led to a booming economy, higher average living standards, and a more prominent place for China in the world, but have also engendered enormous wealth inequality, massive corruption, growing environmental problems, profound popular cynicism, an erosion of public trust, massive expenditures on "stability maintenance," and new signs of belligerence on the international stage.

If something like the Tiananmen movement ever occurs again, it will not emerge from trust and passions like those of 1989; more likely it will explode from a mix of anger, frustration, and grievances. Sadly and ironically, "The

Internationale" has become even more relevant in today's China, twenty-five years after Tiananmen:

> There has never been a Savior,
> No saviour from on high delivers
> No faith have we in prince and peer
> Our own right hand the chains must shiver
> Chains of hatred, greed, and fear
> E'er the thieves will out with their booty
> And give to all a happier lot....
>
> So comrades, come rally
> And the last fight let us face
> The Internationale unites the human race.[21]

Many of the rights activists in China today, both those who are imprisoned and those who are quietly working on NGO projects, are veterans of the Tiananmen movement. They were not high-profile leaders in Tiananmen Square, but those extraordinary days in the spring of 1989 have changed their life trajectories profoundly.

Tiananmen may remind us of repression, but it also symbolizes people's power and the eternal human struggle for freedom and human rights. As the desire for freedom is deeply humane, and human beings' longing for basic rights is universal, history will witness the Tiananmen spirit, as the power of the powerless, again and again.

The Beginning of an End

The year 2014 marks the twenty-fifth anniversary of the Tiananmen Massacre. In the long course of history, twenty-five years is but the blink of an eye; for an individual, a quarter of a century takes us from birth through childhood and on into our adult years. It encompasses all the years of our youth. Life unfolds as history evolves.

When I first began my research, Danxuan had not even started graduate school. He put most of his time and energy into political activism and insisted that he would never apply for American citizenship. The day he was denied entry at the Chinese border, I was attending a conference in Canada on political change in China. When human rights issues were raised, a Canadian scholar teaching in Beijing argued that China had its special conditions and human rights were not a priority. I called Danxuan's mother to express support, but she sounded desperate: "He should just apply for American citizenship. I am too old to go through another round of fear."

On one occasion Danxuan came to speak at my Tiananmen seminar. He told my freshman students that when he walked into Harvard Yard, he was touched by the scene of the blue sky, sunshine, green grass, youth, and hope. He wished he could relive his college life. Unusual for him, he answered my students' questions without much reservation. In my final class for that semester, when I asked the students to name an unforgettable moment, many of them chose Danxuan's description of his life in prison, which he had never told me in detail in all the years I had known him. "I will not take freedom for granted anymore," one student said.

Danxuan is now an American citizen and has a stable job. He started a family and has become a father. When Shen Tong first heard about Danxuan's citizenship, he expressed disbelief: "I thought it was carved in stone that Danxuan would not become an American citizen!" I was not sure whether he felt relieved that he had the company of one more fellow dissident, or whether he felt sad that even Danxuan had come to face reality. Or both.

Shen Tong, who had just become a new father when I interviewed him, is now a father of three children. Financially secure and stable in his personal life, he is gradually returning to activism after years of absence. He has come to speak to my students every semester with or without pay, as he is able to afford it. Once a student asked him what he would advise young people in China about political activism. He responded that if he were asked in public, he would say that historical progress requires sacrifice; but if the person who asked the question was a personal friend, he would ask him or her to think twice. "Being idealistic can mean being selfish to your family," he said. "I chose to be idealistic and I was prepared to pay the price; but my family did not make that decision. They did not get to choose to be my family members, and they had to pay the price for my personal decision."

Wang Dan has been teaching in Taiwan for several years since receiving his PhD in history from Harvard. He has officially requested to have his Chinese passport renewed and expressed his eagerness to return to China, but the Chinese authorities have ignored him. During a question and answer session at a public forum in which we were both participating in 2009, he was asked if he ever regretted his participation in 1989. He replied that he rarely regretted what he had done, except in one situation: whenever he sees that his aging parents have to travel all the way to the United States to visit him, he thinks that perhaps he should not have become involved in 1989.

When Wang Dan visited Cambridge, he gathered some "friends of the Tiananmen Generation," as he calls us, to have dinner together. I knew most of the people and was familiar with their experiences of escape, imprisonment, and exile. I had thought I would be immune to any strong emotions, but I was wrong. We were introduced to a middle-aged man who had just left China and arrived in the United States. They said he had gotten a temporary job repairing houses. He barely spoke the whole night, but when people started to talk about 1989, he became emotional and recited the pledge that the students had taken together in Tiananmen Square on June 4: "Heads may be cut off and blood may flow, but the people's Square must not be lost . . ."[1] Later I learned that he had been imprisoned right after the crackdown and had been persecuted all the years since. "It took just a song, a poem, or a pledge, for the Tiananmen Generation to connect," Wang Dan said in the car after we left dinner. One thing that never changes is that Wang Dan can still talk like a child from time to time. After all the intense activities around the twentieth anniversary, he said to Danxuan and me: "I am so tired. I am getting old. I can't do this anymore." But each year, he makes a public statement expressing his determination to carry on however long it takes.

Liane, whose story is told in the prologue, quit writing her newspaper column in order to spend more time with her family and daughter. Still, each year, wherever she is, she flies either to Hong Kong or Toronto to organize memorial activities in the two cities that always have the biggest crowds for June 4 events: "Rowena, how can history be twisted like that? How can they do this? I was there. I saw it with my own eyes. How can all those politicians and businessmen speak as if nothing ever happened? What happened to this world and the people?"

Like Danxuan, who to everyone's surprise applied for American citizenship, Ma moved back to China with his family for several years. Ma's young son, who grew up in Canada and loves little animals and outdoor activities, asked me a week before they left Canada, "Auntie Xiaoqing, can you convince my parents not to go back to China? I want to stay in Canada." I thought of talking to Ma and his wife, but decided not to. I knew that if only they had a choice, they would not have chosen to go back. They stayed in China a few years but recently moved back to Canada again, as their children would like to go to college in the United States. Their children's lives remind me of my childhood: moving from one place to another with my parents for reasons that I never understood.

I left China in 1998 with nothing but two suitcases and my memories of June 4. As I now revise this book manuscript, it is fifteen years later. My old friends and former classmates in China have gotten married, settled down, and have had children. One thing that hasn't changed is that my grandmother is still waiting for me to come home to visit her. She is in her late eighties, living in a senior residence home. The house in which I stayed with her during my childhood has been sold—it had been in poor condition and Grandmother couldn't afford to repair it. When I first heard that news I blamed myself for not being able to keep the house—if I had continued my career in the business world in China, or if I hadn't decided to pursue a doctoral degree, I would have been able to afford whatever repairs were needed. The house was my root, my home. I started to understand why San Gupo, my grandfather's sister, had wanted to stay in her old dark house, where she felt she belonged. But I don't even know where I belong. And the thought that I belong nowhere scares me.

Grandmother lost most of her memory after a stroke last year. Before that, I called her almost every week to talk to her. She liked to talk about the past, repeating the same stories because she didn't remember that she had just told them. One of her most often repeated stories was about Grandfather being forced to confess. From time to time she would ask nervously: "Is it OK to talk about this now? Nobody is listening, right?"

Another of Grandmother's favorite stories was of me sitting quietly next to the door of the nursery center: "I was so worried that there was something wrong with you because you didn't move or talk."

When I visited Grandmother in the summer of 2009, she was lying in a hospital bed with broken bones. She had fallen just a few days earlier. Her caretaker told me that Grandmother had been so bored, particularly because she hadn't heard from me for a while, that she tried to walk around and then fell. I blamed myself for this—Grandmother might not have fallen if she had known that I was actually on my way back to China to see her. I didn't tell her about my trip beforehand because I had no idea if I would be denied entry at the border, like those I had been studying. For a long period of time, I was obsessed with the thought that my research was the reason for Grandmother's suffering. "You have finished school, haven't you? Are you going to get married, soon?" Grandmother asked me while I was changing her diaper. "Yes, I have, and I will."

Before the trip, I had played out in my mind many times with the idea of taking Grandmother to her favorite restaurants and taking her to visit the neighborhood where we shared our memories. But I was told that she would never be able to get out of bed again. I visited the neighborhood by myself. "She would have been much happier if Grandfather had survived the Cultural Revolution," I thought to myself as I was standing in front of our old house, which had been turned into a storage facility for a nearby store. Grandmother has become the reason that I wanted to stay away from my research topic, and at the same time, she is the reason that I carry on.

In an essay on memory and ethics, Sinologist Perry Link, who has been banned from visiting China, writes that those who remember the Tiananmen Massacre like yesterday were at once upon a time mainstream, but

> today they stand as a lonely few, while the mainstream has flowed elsewhere. But their loss in number of companions is not the only loss that we need to consider. Much larger and more worrisome, is what the mainstream itself has lost.[2]

When I was forced to remove my black armband in 1989, I thought that would be the end of it. Bodies had been crushed, lives destroyed, voices silenced. They had guns, jails, and propaganda machines. We had nothing. Yet somehow it was on that June 4 that the seeds of democracy were planted in my heart, and the longing for freedom and human rights nourished. So it was not an ending after all, but another beginning.

Notes

Foreword

1. Mario Vargas Llosa, "Anti-Authoritarianism in the Age of the Internet," January 4, 2014. Retrieved on March 10, 2014, from http://www.newrepublic.com/article /116095/internet-dissidents-cuba-china-russia-profiled-new-book.

Prologue   Surviving 1989

1. The oath was led by student leader Chai Ling. Students in the Square first took the same oath on May 24, led by Chai Ling. Eddie Cheng, *Standoff at Tiananmen* (Berkeley: Sensys Corp., 2009), pp. 217, 258.
2. Minzhu Han, ed., *Cries for Democracy: Writings and Speeches from the 1989 Chinese Democracy Movement* (Princeton, NJ: Princeton University Press, 1990), p. 362.
3. Wu Renhua, *Liusi shijianzhong de jieyan budui* [The Martial Law Troops during the June 4 Incident] (Alhambra, CA: Zhenxiang Publishers, 2009).
4. Timothy Brook, *Quelling the People: The Military Suppression of the Beijing Democracy Movement* (Stanford, CA: Stanford University Press, 1998), pp. 4–5.
5. Liane thought the young boy was the younger brother of the teenage boy but she was not sure.
6. The Hong Kong Federation of Students was the biggest student organization in Hong Kong.
7. At first, I assumed that the doctor spoke to Liane in English because people in Hong Kong speak Cantonese, a dialect different from Mandarin, the official language in China. But Liane explained to me that the doctor actually spoke to her in Mandarin, speaking English only when she told Liane to leave the country. Liane thought the doctor was speaking English so other people would not understand that she was telling Liane to escape in order to bear witness to the massacre. Quotation marks are not used here because Liane is uncertain of the exact words of the doctor.
8. John Schidlovsky, "Waiting for Their Turn to Die: The Battle for Tiananmen Square," *Toronto Star*, June 5, 1989, p. A14.
9. Li Lanju, "Hafo guiyu: Zhongguo liuxuesheng ying Jiang naoju" [Chinese Students Welcoming Jiang at Harvard], *Jiushi niandai* [The Nineties] (December 1997). Retrieved on January 3, 2014, from http://www.angelfire.com/hi/hayashi/text2.html. *The Nineties* was a Chinese-language monthly published in Hong Kong.
10. I have decided not to use Tony's Chinese name for safety reasons.

11. My interview with Tony was published in June 2002 in *Beijing Spring*, a Chinese-language magazine based in New York and run by exiled Chinese intellectuals. Direct quotes here have been translated into English from the original Chinese. Feng Qing, "Yaxiya de gu er" [The Orphan of Asia], *Beijing zhichun* [Beijing Spring], *110* (June 2002), 68–74.

12. The "bloody crackdown" here refers to the "white terror" under the Nationalist Party (KMT). This was a dominant theme in children's storybooks and school textbooks controlled by the Chinese Communist Party (CCP) after the Nationalist Party fled to Taiwan and the CCP seized power. Participants in this study often referred to the propaganda in textbooks about the atrocities committed by the Nationalist Party, while the evils of the Communist Party were never mentioned.

13. The song *Orphan of Asia (Yaxiya de guer)* was written by Lo Ta-yu, a popular Taiwanese singer-songwriter and a major cultural icon in Taiwan and China in the eighties. The song was inspired by a novel of the same name written by Wu Chuo-Liu, published in 1946, during the period when Taiwan was abandoned by Japan and not recognized by China. Many student participants in the 1989 movement identified with the narratives of abandonment and betrayal in this song. Right after the massacre in 1989, the song was repeatedly played on the campuses of Peking University and People's University.

14. I have changed his name and omitted certain details to protect his privacy.

15. Milan Kundera, *The Book of Laughter and Forgetting* (New York: Harper Perennial, 1978).

I June 4: History and Memory in Exile

1. Tao Ye, "Qianglie kangyi Zhongguo zhengfu boluo wo zuowei Zhongguo gong-min de rujing quan" [Protest against the Chinese Government for Depriving my Rights to Return Home as a Chinese Citizen], October 19, 2006. Retrieved on January 3, 2014, from http://www.epochtimes.com/gb/6/10/19/n1491857.htm.

2. Ardra L. Cole and J. Gary Knowles, *Lives in Context: The Art of Life History Research* (Walnut Creek, CA: AltaMira Press, 2001); Carola Conle, "Why Narrative? Which Narrative? Struggling with Time and Place in Life and Research," *Curriculum Inquiry* 29(1) (1999), 7–32; Corrine Glesne and Alan Peshkin, *Becoming Qualitative Researchers: An Introduction* (White Plains, NY: Longman, 1992); J. Amos Hatch and Richard Wisniewski, eds., *Life History and Narrative* (London: Falmer Press, 1995).

3. Shen Tong left China with legal documents, but he told me that he would not have been able to leave without the help of many people whom he chose not to name.

4. Sen Lee, "Ten Years after the Tiananmen Square Crackdown: An Interview with Shen Tong," *Global Beat Issue Brief*, No. 53 (June 1, 1999). Retrieved on June 3, 2013, from http://www.bu.edu/globalbeat/pubs/ib53.html.

5. A campaign to oppose what the Chinese Communist Party considers to be insidious Western efforts to subvert its power by promoting "peaceful evolution."

6. Bao Pu, Renee Chiang, and Adi Ignatius, eds., *Prisoner of the State: The Secret Journal of Premier Zhao Ziyang* (New York: Simon & Schuster, 2009), p. 5.

7. Guobin Yang, "Emotional Events and the Transformation of Collective Action: The Chinese Student Movement," in Helena Flam and Debra King, eds., *Emotions and Social Movements* (London: Routledge, 2005), pp. 79–98.

8. "It Is Necessary to Take a Clear-Cut Stand against Turmoil," *People's Daily*, April 26, 1989, front page.

9. "Hunger Strikers' Statement," in Minzhu Han, ed., *Cries for Democracy: Writings and Speeches from the 1989 Chinese Democracy Movement* (Princeton, NJ: Princeton University Press, 1990), p. 201.

10. Timothy Brook, *Quelling the People: The Military Suppression of the Beijing Democracy Movement* (Stanford, CA: Stanford University Press, 1998), p. 37.

11. George Black and Robin Munro, *Black Hands of Beijing: Lives of Defiance in China's Democracy Movement* (New York: John Wiley, 1993).

12. Orville Schell, *Mandate of Heaven: The Legacy of Tiananmen Square and the Next Generation of China's Leaders* (New York: Simon & Schuster, 1994), p. 216.

13. Chinese Human Rights Defenders, "Qianglie yaoqiu yizhi shifang 'liusi' shijiu zhounianhou renzai yuzhong fuyingde Beijing shimin" [We Strongly Demand the Immediate Release of Beijing Citizens Who Are Still Serving Prison Sentences 19 Years Following the June 4 Incident], June 2, 2008. Retrieved on June 3, 2013, from http://groups.google.com/group/weiquanwang_CHRD/tree/browse_frm/month /2008–06/40eeb7de0aa8dc78?rnum=1&_done=%2Fgroup%2Fweiquanwang _CHRD%2Fbrowse_frm%2Fmonth%2F2008–06%3F.

14. Craig Calhoun, *Neither Gods nor Emperors: Students and the Struggle for Democracy in China* (Berkeley: University of California Press, 1994), p. 5.

15. Asia Watch, "Punishment Season: Human Rights in China after Martial Law," in George Hicks, ed., *The Broken Mirror: China after Tiananmen* (Essex: Longman Current Affairs, 1990), p. 383.

16. Radio Beijing is now called China Radio International.

17. "Listen to this Haunting Broadcast Made by Radio Beijing on June 4, 1989," *Shanghailist*, June 4, 2013. Retrieved on June 3, 2013, from http://shanghaiist .com/2013/06/04/radio_beijing_english_language_broadcast_june_3_1989 _tiananmen_square_massacre.php

18. According to Zhang Weiguo, director of the Beijing Office of the *World Economic Herald*, the registration of the newspaper was revoked in April 1990. The four detained members of the editorial board were: Chen Lebo, Ruan Jiangning, Xu Xiaohui, and Zhang Weiguo.

19. "Rumors and the Truth," *Beijing Review* 32(37) (September 11–17, 1989), 20.

20. "People Comment on the Riot in Beijing," *Beijing Review* 32(28) (July 10–16, 1989), 21, 25.

21. "Hunger Strike Shakes the Nation," *Beijing Review* 32(22) (May 29–June 4, 1989), cover story.

22. An Zhiguo, "Notes from the Editors: On the Events in Beijing," *Beijing Review* 32(26) (June 26–July 2, 1989), 4.

23. *Guangming Daily*, November 17, 1989.

24. Zhong Bu, ed., *Xinshiqi zui ke'ai de ren: Beijing jieyan budui yingxiong lu* [The Most Beloved Men in the New Era: List of Heroes of the Beijing Martial Law Enforcement Troops] (Beijing: Guangming Daily Press, 1989).

25. "The Gate of Heavenly Peace," Long Bow Group Film, 1995. Retrieved on January 3, 2014, from http://www.tsquare.tv/film/transcript_end.php.

26. "Chinese Charter 08 Signatories Awarded Homo Homini: Speeches by Vaclav Havel, Xu Youyu, and Cui Weiping," Prague, March 13, 2009. Retrieved on June 11, 2013, from http://old.initiativesforchina.org/2009/03/13/chinese-charter-08-signatories -awarded-homo-homini-speeches-by-vaclav-havel-xu-youyu-and-cui-weiping/.

27. Ding Zilin, *Xunfang liusi shounanzhe* [In Search of the Victims of June 4] (Hong Kong: Open Press, 2005), p. 84.

28. Rowena Xiaoqing He, "Still Seeking Justice for the Tiananmen Massacre," *Washington Post*, June 4, 2012. Retrieved on January 3, 2014, from http://www.washingtonpost.com/opinions/still-seeking-justice-for-the-tiananmen-massacre/2012/06/04/gJQAd1weDV_story.html.

29. WikiLeaks is an international online organization that publishes secret information, news leaks, and classified media from anonymous sources.

30. "Tiananmen Massacre a Myth," *China Daily*, July 14, 2011. Retrieved on June 3, 2013, from http://www.chinadaily.com.cn/opinion/2011–07/14/content_12898720.htm.

31. Liu Xiaobo, "Listen Carefully to the Voices of the Tiananmen Mothers," in Perry Link, Tienchi Martin-Liao, and Liu Xia, eds., *No Enemies, No Hatred: Selected Essays and Poems* (Cambridge, MA: Harvard University Press, 2012), p. 6.

32. The two maps were created in 2009. Retrieved on January 30, 2014, from http://chrdnet.com/2012/06/june-3–4-2009–20th-anniversary-of-tiananmen-square-massacre-maps-victims-name-lists/ (in English), and http://www.tiananmenmother.org/the%20truth%20and%20victims/The%20list%20of%20the%20victims/the%20death%20location%20of%20the%20victims.jpg (in Chinese).

33. "Hope Fades as Despair Draws Near: Essay by the Tiananmen Mothers on the 24th Anniversary of the June Fourth Tragedy," *Human Rights in China*, May 31, 2013. Retrieved on June 6, 2013, from http://www.hrichina.org/content/6709.

34. "Testimonies of Families of June 4 Victims," 2010. Retrieved on January 3, 2014, from http://www.youtube.com/watch?v=XjaoFS2NnTo.

35. Jeffrey F. Meyer, "Moral Education in the People's Republic of China," *Moral Education Forum* 15(2) (1990), 3–26; Ronald Price, "Moral-Political Education and Modernization," in Ruth Hayhoe, ed., *Education and Modernization: The Chinese Experience* (Oxford: Pergamon Press, 2002), pp. 211–237; Stanley Rosen, "The Effect of Post-4 June Re-education Campaigns on Chinese Students," *The China Quarterly*, No. 134 (1993), 310–334.

36. For example, Chinese Communist Party Central Committee, "Aiguozhuyi jiaoyu shishi gangyao" [Outline on the Implementation of Patriotic Education], in Guo Qijia and Lei Xian, eds., *Zhonghua renmin gongheguo jiaoyu fa quanshu* [Complete Education Laws of the People's Republic of China] (Beijing: Beijing Broadcasting Institute Press, 1995), pp. 117–122; State Education Commission, *Zhongxue deyu gangyao* [Secondary Education Moral Education Guidelines] (Shanghai: Shanghai Education Press, 1995); State Education Commission, *Xiaoxue deyu gangyao* [Primary Moral Education Guidelines] (Shanghai: Shanghai Education Press, 1993).

37. Christopher R. Hughes, *Chinese Nationalism in the Global Era* (London: Routledge, 2006).

38. Edward Vickers, "The Opportunity of China? Education, Patriotic Values and the Chinese State," in Marie Lall and Edward Vickers, eds., *Education as a Political Tool in Asia* (New York: Routledge, 2009), pp. 69–70.

39. Gregory P. Fairbrother, "Patriotic Education in a Chinese Middle School," in W. O. Lee et al., eds., *Citizenship Education in Asia and the Pacific: Concepts and Issues* (Norwell, MA: Kluwer Academic, 2004), p.161.

40. Wang, Zheng, *Never Forget National Humiliation: Historical Memory in Chinese Politics and Foreign Relations* (New York: Columbia University Press, 2012).

41. Monica Waterhouse, "A Pedagogy of Mourning: Tarrying with/in Tragedy, Terror, and Tension," *Transnational Curriculum Inquiry* 5(2) (2008), 19.

42. "Grace Wang: Caught in the Middle, Called a Traitor," *Digital Times*, April 20, 2008. Retrieved on January 6, 2014, from http://chinadigitaltimes.net/2008/04/grace-wang-caught-in-the-middle-called-a-traitor/.

43. Gong Yue, "Xiagan yidan xie chunqiu: Ji huanying 'huangque xingdong' muhou yingxiong chendaizheng zuotanhui" [Forum on the Unsung Heroes of "Operation Yellowbird," *Beijing zhichun* [Beijing Spring], No. 170 (July 2007), 75–78.

44. Gavin Hewitt, "The Great Escape From China; How 'Operation Yellow Bird' Saved Scores of Dissidents from Beijing's Secret Police," *Washington Post*, June 2, 1991, D1. Retrieved on February 6, 2014, from http://www.highbeam.com/doc/1P2–1067967.html.

45. Chai, Ling, *A Heart for Freedom* (Carol Stream, IL: Tyndale House, 2011), p. 241.

46. Andrew J. Nathan, "The Dissenting Life," *The New Republic*, January 14, 2002, 37–41.

47. Geremie R. Barmé, *In the Red: On Contemporary Chinese Culture* (New York: Columbia University Press, 1999), pp. 44–45.

48. Denise Chong, *Egg On Mao: The Story of an Ordinary Man Who Defaced an Icon and Unmasked a Dictatorship* (Berkeley, CA: Counterpoint, 2009).

49. Jim Yardley, "Man Freed after Years in Jail for Mao Insult," *The New York Times*, February 23, 2006.

50. Fang shared his experiences with my students when I invited him to speak to my class.

51. "Independent Federation of Chinese Students and Scholars," *Sourcewatch*, July 30, 2008. Retrieved on February 12, 2014, from http://www.sourcewatch.org/index.php?title=Independent_Federation_of_Chinese_Students_and_Scholars#First_Term_1989.8_.7E_1990.8

52. Ge Xun, "21 Hours in Bejing," *Seeing Red in China*, February 2012. Retrieved on June 3, 2013, from http://seeingredinchina.com/2012/02/08/ge-xun-21-hours-in-beijing/. Translated by Yaxuan Cao.

53. Richard Madsen, *China and the American Dream: A Moral Inquiry* (Berkeley: University of California Press, 1995).

54. J. D. Brewer, "Sensitivity as a Problem in Field Research: A Study of Routine Policing in Northern Ireland," in Claire M. Renzetti and Raymond M. Lee, eds., *Researching Sensitive Topics* (Newbury Park, CA: Sage Publications, 1993), pp. 123–145.

55. Sandra J. Curran and Daniel Cook, "Research in Post-Tiananmen China," in Renzetti and Lee, eds., *Researching Sensitive Topics*, pp. 71–81.

56. Han, ed., *Cries for Democracy*, p. xxi.

57. Li Xiaojun, *The Long March to the Fourth of June*, trans. E. J. Griffiths (London: Duckworth, 1989), p. xiii.

58. Yajie Sun, "Children of Tiananmen," unpublished masters' thesis, University of Toronto, 1993, p. 2.

59. Link is emeritus professor at Princeton University, and currently holds the Chancellorial Chair for Innovative Teaching at the University of California, Riverside.

60. Edward Friedman, "Studying China is Dangerous," keynote speech delivered at the 49th annual conference of the American Association for Chinese Studies, University of Richmond, October 5–7, 2007.

61. Gao Wenqian, speech delivered at a candlelight vigil commemorating the Tiananmen Massacre, 2009.

62. Gwendolyn Etter-Lewis, *My Soul Is My Own: Oral Narratives of African American Women in the Professions* (New York: Routledge, 1993), p. xii.

63. Bernhard Giesen, *Triumph and Trauma* (London: Paradigm, 2004), p. 2.

64. Charles Taylor, *Sources of the Self: The Making of the Modern Identity* (Cambridge, MA: Harvard University Press, 1989), p. 211.

65. William F. Pinar, "Whole, Bright, Deep with Understanding: Issues in Qualitative Research and Autobiographical Method," *Journal of Curriculum Studies 13*(3) (1981), 184.

66. Carola Conle, "Resonance in Preservice Teacher Inquiry," *American Educational Research Journal 33*(2) (1996), 52.

67. Ivor F. Goodson, ed., *Studying Teachers' Lives* (London: Routledge, 1992), p. 6.

68. Cole and Knowles, eds., *Lives in Context*, p. 80.

69. D. J. Clandinin and F. M. Connelly, "Personal Experience Method," in Norman K. Denzin and Yvonna S. Lincoln, eds., *Handbook of Qualitative Research* (Thousand Oaks, CA: Sage Publications, 1994), p. 4.

70. C. T. Patrick Diamond and Carol A. Mullen, *The Postmodern Educator: Arts-Based Inquiries and Teacher Development* (New York: Peter Lang, 1999).

71. William Pinar, *What Is Curriculum Theory?* (Mahwah, NJ: Lawrence Erlbaum, 2004).

72. Glesne and Peshkin, *Becoming Qualitative Researchers*, p. 104.

73. Patricia Hampls, "Memory and Imagination," in James McConkey, ed., *The Anatomy of Memory: An Anthology* (Oxford: Oxford University Press, 1996), p. 209.

74. Carola Conle, "Learning Culture and Embracing Contraries: Narrative Inquiry Through Stories of Acculturation," unpublished doctoral thesis, University of Toronto, 1993, p. vii.

75. Cole and Knowles, eds., *Lives in Context*, p. 126.

76. Karl D. Hostetler, "What Is 'Good' Education Research?" *Educational Researcher 34*(6) (2005), 21.

2　Seeds of Fire

1. This section *If We Want Light, We Must Conquer Darkness* mainly covers the period between the late 1960s to the early 1990s. The section is not arranged in a strict chronological sequence as the stories presented here are based on family stories told and retold, remembered as images and feelings rather than strictly documented history. Still for my family and me they are emblematic and have the ring of truth. I intentionally kept this in its original format, with specific information

regarding places and times omitted. The city where my parents grew up and went to school was Guangzhou in Guangdong province. My mother was assigned to work in an area called Hebianchang, meaning "riverside factory"; my father was assigned to work in an area called Lishi. The closest city near Hebianchang and Lishi is Shaoguan in the northern part of the province. Our family first lived in Hebianchang where my mother worked; my father and I moved to Lishi after my mother was allowed to leave the area and join an opera troupe in Shiqiao town of Panyu County near Guangzhou. My father and I joined my mother in Shiqiao toward the end of the Cultural Revolution.

2. Barefoot doctors (*chijiao yisheng*) were farmers who received minimal basic medical and paramedical training and served as medical workers in rural villages during the Cultural Revolution.

3. The prison is called Shaoguan Prison. My father told me the prison was called No. 2 Prison of Guangdong province when we lived in the area. Based on the online bus route, the prison is two bus stops away from where we used to live.

4. San Gupo lived in Zhongshan city, in Guangdong.

5. Grandfather died in 1967, the second year of the Cultural Revolution.

6. The land reform campaign (1947–1952) was launched in rural China. Land and other property was forcibly taken from landlords and redistributed among peasants. The land reform campaign increased the Communist Party's popularity among Chinese peasants, "but, as a consequence, it is unlikely that fewer than 1.5 to 2 million people were killed" between 1947 and 1952. Frank Dikötter, *The Tragedy of Liberation: A History of the Chinese Revolution, 1945–57* (London: Bloomsbury, 2013), p. 83.

7. Father attended Sun Yat-sen University of Medical Science located in Guangzhou, Guangdong province. The school originally was from Boji Medical College established in 1886.

8. The rhyme was written in Cantonese, the local dialect that our family speaks.

9. Poet Bei Dao had lived in exile since 1989 but he was allowed to return to China a few years ago.

10. The street is called Beijing Road, where major bookstores in the city are located.

11. The park is called Yuexiu Park. The museum I visited is inside Zhenhai Tower. It was built in 1380 by Zhu Liangzu, a vassal in the Ming dynasty. Two red sandstone lions standing in front of the tower were carved during the Ming dynasty. The tower was first called Wanghai Tower, meaning a tower watching the sea. The locals call it Five-Story Tower as it has five stories. The tower has served as the Guangzhou Museum since 1956.

12. I cannot remember when this incident occurred. I think it was before I attended elementary school, which would have been before 1979. The reason I say this is because my grandmother was more willing to take me to the museum when I was not tall enough to require an admission ticket. When I got taller, she couldn't afford to take me there as often as I wanted.

13. I participated in the student demonstrations in Guangzhou, not in Beijing. Although the world's image of the Tiananmen movement is in Tiananmen Square, Beijing, the movement engulfed cities and towns throughout the entire country.

14. "Carry on Till Tomorrow" (Tom Evans/Pete Ham), from Badfinger's "Magic Christian Music" (1970, Apple Records).

15. Canadian Airlines operated until 2001.
16. This poem was written by Gu Cheng. Gu Cheng, "Wo shi yige renxing de haizi" [I Am a Willful Child], March 1981. Retrieved on January 8, 2014, from http://site.douban.com/106701/widget/notes/91769/note/100561992/.

3   On the Road: Yi Danxuan

1. This is a quote from my interview with Danxuan.
2. Orville Schell, *Mandate of Heaven: The Legacy of Tiananmen Square and the Next Generation of China's Leaders* (New York: Simon & Schuster, 1994), p. 216.
3. Wang Dan, *Wang Dan huiyilu: Cong liusi dao liuwang* [Wang Dan Memoir: From June 4 to Exile] (Taibei: Shibao wenhua chuban, 2012), pp. 106–108. My translation.
4. Shen, Tong, with Marianne Yen, *Almost a Revolution*, 2nd ed. (Ann Arbor: University of Michigan Press, 1998), p. 334.
5. Jonathan Unger, ed., *The Pro-democracy Protests in China: Reports from the Provinces* (Armonk, NY: M.E. Sharpe, 1991).
6. The household registration system was a system of residency permits in China. A household registration record officially identified a person's residence. People who worked outside their authorized area of residence did not qualify for grain rations, employer-provided housing, or health care. There were also controls over education, employment, and marriage.
7. *Spartacus* is a novel about a slave rebellion by Howard Fast, who was an American Communist writer at the time of publication. After Soviet leader Nikita Khrushchev's "secret speech" denouncing Stalin in 1956, Fast renounced his Communist beliefs.
8. As noted in the introduction to this volume, Hu Yaobang was the former Communist Party General Secretary who had been forced to resign from his position because of his refusal to take tough measures against the pro-democracy student protesters of 1986–1987. His sudden death on April 15, 1989, touched off the nationwide movement. Danxuan's recollection indicates that Hu's death touched off student activism not only in Beijing, the center of the movement, but also in Guangzhou.
9. Minzhu Han, ed., *Democracy: Writings and Speeches from the 1989 Chinese Democracy Movement* (Princeton, NJ: Princeton University Press, 1990), pp. xix–xx.
10. Martial Law was implemented in Beijing, not in any other city, but Beijing was considered the epicenter of the political climate in the whole country.
11. Macau is a city located south of Guangdong province and west of Hong Kong. It had been under Portuguese control for 442 years before it reverted to full Chinese sovereignty on December 20, 1999, two years after the handover of Hong Kong to China.
12. Wang Dan, *Wang Dan huiyilu*, pp. 233–234. My translation.
13. Wang Dan, *Wang Dan yu zhong huiyilu* [Prison Memoirs] (Taibei: Xin xin wenhua shiye gufen youxian gongsi, 1997), p.107.

14. *Laogai* is a Chinese system of prison factories, detention centers, and re-education camps. The system was first created by Mao in the early 1950s, modeled after the Soviet *gulag*. In November 2013, China formally dismantled this penal system.

4 No Direction Home: Shen Tong

1. Bao Pu, Renee Chiang, and Adi Ignatius, eds., *Prisoner of the State: The Secret Journal of Premier Zhao Ziyang* (New York: Simon & Schuster, 2009), p. 43.
2. Vivian Wu, "Demolition of Democracy Wall Criticised," *South China Morning Post*, November 3, 2007. Retrieved on February 3, 2014, from http://www.scmp.com/article/614196/demolition-democracy-wall-criticised
3. "Free Democracy Advocates, 74 from Senate Urge Beijing," *The New York Times*, October 11, 1992. Retrieved on August 4, 2008, from http://query.nytimes.com/gst/fullpage.html?res=9E0CE7D81730F932A25753C1A964958260.
4. "Statement by Shen Tong," *World Affairs 154*(4) (1992), 136.
5. Sen Lee, "Ten Years After the Tiananmen Square Crackdown—An Interview with Shen Tong," *Global Beat Issue Brief 53* (June 1, 1999). Retrieved on August 4, 2008, from http://www.bu.edu/globalbeat/pubs/ib53.html.
6. R. M. Murphy, "A Tiananmen Rebel Turns Capitalist: After Fleeing to the U.S., an Entrepreneur Returns to Do Business with His Former Oppressors," *Fortune Small Business*, April 17, 2007. Retrieved on August 4, 2008, from http://money.cnn.com/magazines/fsb/fsb_archive/2007/04/01/8403869/index.htm.
7. Geremie R. Barmé, *In the Red: On Contemporary Chinese Culture* (New York: Columbia University Press, 1999), pp. 42–45; Ian Buruma, *Bad Elements: Chinese Rebels from Los Angeles to Beijing* (New York: Random House, 2001).
8. Shen Tong, with Marianne Yen, *Almost a Revolution*, 2nd ed. (Ann Arbor: University of Michigan Press, 1998), p. 3.
9. Judy Polumbaum, "Review of *Almost a Revolution*," *Journal of Asian Studies 50*(2) (April 1991), 400–401.
10. Wang Dan, *Wang Dan yu zhong huiyilu* [Prison Memoirs] (Taibei: Xin xinwen wenhua shiye gufen youxian gongsi, 1997), p. 022. My translation.
11. Guobin Yang, "Emotional Events and the Transformation of Collective Action: The Chinese Student Movement," in Helena Flam and Debra King, eds., *Emotions and Social Movements* (London: Routledge, 2005), p. 84.
12. Roger Garside, *Coming Alive: China after Mao* (New York: New American Library, 1981), p. 114.
13. The Qingming Festival, also known as "Tomb Sweeping Day," is the time that Chinese mourn the dead.
14. *Hutongs* are narrow streets or alleys, most commonly associated with Beijing, where the *hutongs* are alleys formed by the lines of the *siheyuan*, traditional courtyard residences. Many neighborhoods were formed by joining one *siheyuan* to another to form a *hutong*, and then by joining one *hutong* to another. The word *hutong* is also used to refer to such neighborhoods. The number of Beijing *hutongs* has dropped significantly as they are being demolished to make way for new roads and buildings.

15. Neighborhood committees are the most basic social organizational unit in mainland China under control of the Communist Party. They exist on every street or small alley.
16. Havel writes about what happens to man's soul in a society where people learn to survive by sustaining and promoting a Communist lie. He also details how the lie is institutionalized. Václav Havel et al., *The Power of the Powerless: Citizens against the State in Central-Eastern Europe* (Armonk, NY: M. E. Sharpe, 1985).
17. *Zhongnanhai*, which is translated as "Central and Southern Lakes," is also known as the Sea Palaces. For outsiders and the Western media, it is the equivalent of "China's Kremlin." Since the founding of the People's Republic in 1949, *Zhongnanhai* has been home to the highest-ranking members of the Communist Party. Offices of the Central Committee of the Communist Party, the State Council, the Central People's Government, and the Military Commission of the Party Central Committee are all located here.
18. *Shangfang* refers to China's system of petitioning.
19. Shen Tong, with Marianne Yen, *Almost a Revolution*, 2nd ed., p. 83.
20. Ibid., p. 49.
21. TVB is a major television station in Hong Kong.
22. Majiang, also known as "mah-jong" in Cantonese, is a Chinese game played by four people sitting around a table.
23. Dakun was one of Shen Tong's best friends in China, as introduced in his book *Almost a Revolution.*
24. Chai Ling, also an exiled student leader, was the general commander in Tiananmen Square.
25. Yang, "Emotional Events and the Transformation of Collective Action," p. 86.
26. Shen Tong, with Marianne Yen, *Almost a Revolution*, 2nd ed., p. 191.
27. Dingxin Zhao, *The Power of Tiananmen: State–Society Relations and the 1989 Beijing Student Movement* (Chicago: University of Chicago Press, 2001), p. 163.
28. Li, Lu, *Moving the Mountain: My Life in China from the Cultural Revolution to Tiananmen Square* (London: Macmillan, 1990) is an autobiography written by another Tiananmen student leader.
29. Both Li Lu and Chai Ling cut their ties with the exile community and became successful in business. Like Shen Tong, in recent years Chai Ling has resumed her activism.
30. Shen Tong is referring to other student leaders' disagreement with his comments about the late General Secretary Zhao Ziyang.
31. Shen Tong, with Marianne Yen, *Almost a Revolution*, 2nd ed., p. xxii.
32. Ibid., p. 316.
33. Ibid., p. 339.
34. Ibid., p. 336.

5   Living Somewhere Else: Wang Dan

1. Hannah Beech, "The Exile and the Entrepreneur," *Time*, June 7, 2004. Retrieved on February 6, 2014, from http://content.time.com/time/world/article /0,8599,2047348,00.html.

2. Wang Dan, *Wang Dan yu zhong huiyilu* [Prison Memoirs] (Taibei: Xin xinwen wenhua shiye gufen youxian gongsi, 1997), p. 243. My translation.

3. Wang Lingyun, *Suiyue cangcang* [During Those Dark Years] (Hong Kong: Mingbao chubanshe youxian gongsi, 1999). My translation.

4. Wang Dan, *Yu zhong huiyilu*, p. 114. My translation.

5. Beech, "The Exile and the Entrepreneur."

6. Phil Ponce, "Online News Hour: Wang Dan," April 27, 1998. Retrieved on February 6, 2014, from http://www.pbs.org/newshour/search-results/?q=ponce%20wang %20dan%20news%20hour#gsc.tab=0&gsc.q=ponce%20wang%20dan%20 news%20hour&gsc.page=1.

7. Ya Yi, *Liuwangzhe fangtanlu* [Interviews with Exiles] (Hong Kong: Xiafeier chuban youxian gongsi, 2005). My translation.

8. Edward A. Gargan, "For a Dissident, Too Much Fame and Freedom," *The New York Times*, April 28, 1998. Retrieved on August 4, 2008, from http://query.nytimes. com/gst/fullpage.html?res=9C01EFDA1F3FF93BA15757C0A96E958260.

9. Beech, "The Exile and the Entrepreneur."

10. Wang Dan, *Wang Dan huiyilu: Cong liusi dao liuwang* [Wang Dan Memoir: From June 4 to Exile] (Taibei: Shibao wenhua chuban, 2012), p. 052. My translation.

11. Ibid., p. 39. My translation.

12. Another campaign against "spiritual pollution" was launched in late 1983.

13. The Criticize Lin and Criticize Confucius Campaign, which was launched in 1974, targeted Lin Biao, Mao's chosen successor who had died in a mysterious plane crash in September 1971 following an alleged coup attempt. The attack on Confucius was Mao's attempt to discredit Premier Zhou Enlai, then Mao's second-in-command.

14. *Wuxia* literally means "martial heroes." It is a distinct quasi-fantasy subgenre of the martial arts genre in literature, television, and cinema. *Wuxia* has figured prominently in the popular culture of Chinese-speaking areas from ancient times to the present. The *Wuxia* genre is a blend of the philosophy of *xia* (an ethical person, knight-errant) and China's long history of *Wushu* (martial arts). A male martial artist who follows the code of *xia* is called a swordsman, a *xiake*.

15. Wang Dan told me in our interview that this occurred when he was in Grade Four, but in his memoir, he writes that it was Grade Five when he was twelve years old.

16. The Gang of Four (*sirenbang*) was a group of radical Communist Party leaders, led by Mao's wife Jiang Qing. The group was arrested and removed from their positions in 1976 following the death of Mao. They were officially blamed for the events of the Cultural Revolution.

17. Jianying Zha, "Enemy of the State: The Complicated Life of an Idealist," *The New Yorker*, April 23, 2007. Retrieved on June 7, 2013, from http://www.newyorker. com/reporting/2007/04/23/070423fa_fact_zha.

18. Wang Dan, *Wang Dan huiyilu*, p. 63. My translation.

19. This official expression is difficult to translate. It conveys the meaning of "wanting to be revolutionary," or "wanting to follow the Party closely," or simply "wanting to be 'good.'"

20. Zoya Kosmodemyanskaya was a Russian female partisan. She carried out acts of sabotage behind enemy lines but was captured and tortured in 1941. She revealed no information and was executed by hanging. She was left hanging there as a warning to the Russians and her body was mutilated by German soldiers. Zoya's brother Shura was killed in combat near the end of World War II. He also received posthumous recognition as a Hero of the Soviet Union. Their story was published in 1953.

21. Jonathan Unger, ed., *The Pro-democracy Protests in China: Reports from the Provinces* (Armonk, NY: M. E. Sharpe, 1991), p. 15.

22. "League" here refers to the Communist Youth League. It is a Chinese organization run by the Communist Party for youth between the ages of fourteen and twenty-eight. The Communist Youth League is also responsible for guiding the activities of the Young Pioneers (for children under the age of fourteen).

23. *Beijing Spring* is a dissident and human rights magazine based in New York. Wang Dan is currently a member of the editorial board. But when the above-described interview took place, Wang Dan did not have anything to do with the magazine.

24. Ya Yi, *Liuwangzhe fangtanlu*, p. 72. Translated from Chinese.

25. Fang Lizhi was a professor of astrophysics and former vice chancellor of the University of Science and Technology in Hefei, Anhui province. He was described as a "black hand" behind the 1989 movement as many of his writings had inspired the students. He was expelled from the Party in 1987 and he died in exile in 2012.

26. *The Railroad Guerrillas* is a 1956 movie. It presents a story about Chinese guerrilla forces battling Japanese and Nationalist collaborators. The movie is said to be based on historical events that took place in Shandong province during World War II.

27. *Tunnel Warfare* was shot in 1965. It tells the story of how village peasants, on the plain of central Hebei province, outwit the Japanese army during World War II by striking at them from a huge network of tunnels.

28. Li Xiangyang is a major character in the movie *Guerrillas on the Plain*. The movie was shot in 1955. In the film legendary Li Xiangyang leads a guerrilla band against the Japanese invaders.

29. Geremie Barmé, *In the Red: On Contemporary Chinese Culture* (New York: Columbia University Press, 1999), p. 42.

30. Craig J. Calhoun, *Neither Gods nor Emperors: Students and the Struggle for Democracy in China* (Berkeley: University of California Press, 1994), p.165.

31. Deutsche Presse-Agentur News, "Tiananmen Protest Leader Wang Dan Asks to Return to China," October 3, 2007. Retrieved on February 6, 2014, from http://www.digitaljournal.com/article/236410.

32. "Wang Dan Discusses China at DC's National Press Club on November 29, 2007," *China Support Network*, December 1, 2007. Retrieved on August 4, 2008, from http://chinademocracy.blogspot.com/2007/12/statement-from-wang-dan.html.

33. Wang Lingyun, *Suiyue cangcang*. My translation.

34. Wang Dan, *Yu zhong huiyilu*, p. 106. My translation.

6 Romance and Revolution: Group Discussions

1. Xu Wenli is a dissident who served sixteen years in prison in China for his activities during the 1978–79 Democracy Wall Movement. He was exiled to the United

States in 2002 and is currently a senior fellow at Brown University. In a speech delivered at Brown University's commencement in May 2003, Xu said democracy is not just a political system, but "a way of living, essential as bread, air and water." Retrieved on February 7, 2014, from http://www.humanrightsfirst.org/our-work /refugee-protection/success-stories/xu-wenli-china/.

2. Most Chinese students believed that the bombing of the Chinese embassy in Belgrade in 1999 was a deliberate action by the United States. For four days, thousands of students shouted anti-U.S. slogans, burned American flags, threw bricks, and besieged the American embassy in Beijing.

3. Shen Tong is referring to the Independent Federation of Chinese Students and Scholars (IFCSS), one of the largest organizations formed by overseas Chinese students after the Tiananmen crackdown. Danxuan had served two terms as president for IFCSS.

4. In the wake of Tiananmen, the IFCSS lobbied the U.S. Congress to pass the "Chinese Students Protection Act" in 1992. As a result, some 80,000 Chinese in the United States were granted "June 4 green cards."

5. Chen Kuide was editor-in-chief of *Observe China*, a Chinese Web site that published works by liberal intellectuals in China. The site was banned in China. Chen's piece mentioned here was published on June 3, 2005, entitled "Ba sharen kanzuo sharen" [Murder is Murder]. Retrieved on December 30, 2013, from http://www .tiananmenmother.org/Forum/forum080601002.htm.

6. "Blood-stained Glory" [*Xueran de fengcai*] is a Chinese song written in 1987 in memory of those who died during the 1979 Sino-Vietnam War. It was sung by students throughout the 1989 movement.

7 Citizenship in Exile

1. Dai Qing, "The Twenty-Second Anniversary of June 4," *Radio Free Asia*, June 2, 2011. Retrieved on June 13, 2014, from http://www.rfa.org/cantonese/commentaries/daiqing-06022011121308.html

2. Max Fisher, "This is the Song of Tiananmen: 'Blindfold My Eyes and Cover the Sky,'" *Washington Post*, June 4, 2013. Retrieved on February 7, 2014, from http:// www.washingtonpost.com/blogs/worldviews/wp/2013/06/04/this-is-the-song -of-tiananmen-blindfold-my-eyes-and-cover-the-sky/.

3. John Dewey, *Experience and Education* (New York: Macmillan, 1958, c.1938).

4. Charles Taylor, *Sources of the Self: The Making of the Modern Identity* (Cambridge, MA: Harvard University Press, 1989), p. 27

5. Richard E. Dawson and Kenneth Prewitt, *Political Socialization: An Analytic Study* (Boston: Little, Brown and Company, 1969), p. 17.

6. Cheng Yinghong, "You xuanze he bei caozong de ai he hen" [Selective and Manipulated Love and Hatred] *Dongxiang* [The Trend], No. 238 (2005), 34–35.

7. Gordon J. DiRenzo, "Socialization for Citizenship in Modern Democratic Society," in Orit Ichilov, ed., *Political Socialization, Citizenship Education, and Democracy* (New York: Teachers College Press, 1990), p. 37.

8. He, Yinan, "Remembering and Forgetting the War: Elite Mythmaking, Mass Reaction and Sino-Japanese Relations, 1950–2006," *History and Memory* 19(2) (Fall/Winter 2007), 43–74.

9. The Red Guard generation was born about 1949 and was in middle school (junior and senior high) in 1966 when the Cultural Revolution started.
10. Anita Chan, *Children of Mao: Personality Development and Political Activism in the Red Guard Generation* (Seattle: University of Washington Press, 1985), pp. 224–225.
11. Taylor, *Sources of the Self*, p. 211.
12. Craig J. Calhoun, *Neither Gods nor Emperors: Students and the Struggle for Democracy in China* (Berkeley: University of California Press, 1994), p. 255.
13. Ibid., pp. 268–268, 270.
14. Perry Link, *Evening Chats in Beijing: Probing China's Predicament* (New York: Norton, 1992), p. 249.
15. Paul Lichterman, *The Search for Political Community: American Activists Reinventing Commitment* (New York: Cambridge University Press, 1996).
16. Doug McAdam, "The Biographical Consequences of Activism," *American Sociological Review 54*(5) (1989), 750.
17. Danxuan Yi and Tianhan Xue, "Have We Forgotten the Victims of the Tiananmen Tragedy?" *The Lancet 360* (9344) (November 9, 2002), 1518; Yi Danxuan, "Quanmei zilian zhuxi zhi 'Zhongguo xuesheng baohu fa'an' shou huizhe de gong-kai xin" [An Open Letter to the Beneficiaries of the "Chinese Students Protection Act"], *Independent Federation of Overseas Chinese Students and Scholars*, June 2, 2001. Retrieved on January 9, 2014, from http://ifcss.org/home/?m=200106.
18. Merle Goldman, *From Comrade to Citizen: The Struggle for Political Rights in China* (Cambridge, MA: Harvard University Press, 2005), p. 234.
19. Liu Xiaobo, "Bellicose and Thuggish: The Roots of Chinese 'Patriotism' at the Dawn of the Twenty-First Century," in Perry Link, Tienchi Martin-Liao, and Liu Xia, eds., *No Enemies, No Hatred: Selected Essays and Poems* (Cambridge, MA: Harvard University Press, 2012), p. 74.
20. Goldman, *From Comrade to Citizen*, p. 233.
21. "The Internationale." Retrieved on February 7, 2014, from http://www.marxists.org/history/ussr/sounds/lyrics/international.htm.

Epilogue   The Beginning of an End

1. "I am Chai Ling...I am Still Alive" (excerpts), in Minzhu Han, ed., *Cries for Democracy: Writings and Speeches from the 1989 Chinese Democracy Movement* (Princeton, NJ: Princeton University Press, 1990), p. 362.
2. Perry Link, "June Fourth: Memory and Ethics," *China Perspectives*, No. 2 (2009), 16.

Bibliography

An, Zhiguo (1989). "Notes from the Editors: On the Events in Beijing." *Beijing Review* 32 (26) (June 26–July 2), 4–5.

Asia Watch (1990). "Punishment Season: Human Rights in China after Martial Law," in George Hicks, ed., *The Broken Mirror: China after Tiananmen*. Essex: Longman Current Affairs, pp. 369–389.

Bao Pu, Renee Chiang, and Adi Ignatius, eds. (2000). *Prisoner of the State: The Secret Journal of Premier Zhao Ziyang*. New York: Simon & Schuster.

Barmé, Geremie R. (1999). *In the Red: On Contemporary Chinese Culture*. New York: Columbia University Press.

Beech, Hannah (2004). "The Exile and the Entrepreneur." *Time*, June 7. Retrieved on February 6, 2014, from http://content.time.com/time/world/article/0,8599,2047348,00.html

Black, George and Robin Munro (1993). *Black Hands of Beijing: Lives of Defiance in China's Democracy Movement*. New York: John Wiley.

Brewer, J. D. (1993). "Sensitivity as a Problem in Field Research: A Study of Routine Policing in Northern Ireland," in Claire M. Renzetti and Raymond M. Lee, eds., *Researching Sensitive Topics*. Newbury Park, CA: Sage Publications, pp. 123–145.

Brook, Timothy (1998). *Quelling the People: The Military Suppression of the Beijing Democracy Movement*. Stanford, CA: Stanford University Press.

Buruma, Ian (2001). *Bad Elements: Chinese Rebels from Los Angeles to Beijing*. New York: Random House.

Calhoun, Craig J. (1994). *Neither Gods nor Emperors: Students and the Struggle for Democracy in China*. Berkeley: University of California Press.

"Carry on Till Tomorrow" (Tom Evans/Pete Ham), from Badfinger's "Magic Christian Music" (1970, Apple Records).

Chai, Ling (2011). *A Heart for Freedom*. Carol Stream, IL: Tyndale House.

Chan, Anita (1985). *Children of Mao: Personality Development and Political Activism in the Red Guard Generation*. Seattle: University of Washington Press.

Chen Kuide (2005). "Ba sharen kanzuo sharen" [Murder is Murder], June 3. Retrieved on December 30, 2013, from http://www.tiananmenmother.org/Forum/forum 080601002.htm

Cheng, Eddie (2009). *Standoff at Tiananmen*. Berkeley, CA: Sensys Corp.

Cheng, Yinghong (2005). "You xuanze he bei caozong de ai he hen" [Selective and Manipulated Love and Hatred]. *Dongxiang* [The Trend], No. 238 (2005), 34–35.

"Chinese Charter 08 Signatories Awarded Homo Homini: Speeches by Vaclav Havel, Xu Youyu, and Cui Weiping" (2009). Prague, March 13. Retrieved on June 11, 2013, from http://old.initiativesforchina.org/2009/03/13/chinese-charter-08-signatories-awarded-homo-homini-speaches-by-vaclav-havel-xu-youyu-and-cui-weiping/

Chinese Communist Party Central Committee (1995). "Aiguozhuyi jiaoyu shishi gang-yao" [Outline on the Implementation of Patriotic Education], in Guo Qijia and Lei Xian, eds., Zhonghua renmin gongheguo jiaoyu fa quanshu [Complete Education Laws of the People's Republic of China]. Beijing: Beijing Broadcasting Institute Press, pp. 117–122.

Chinese Human Rights Defenders (2008). "Qianglie yaoqiu lizhi shifang 'liusi' shijiu zhounianhou renzai yuzhong fuxingde Beijing shimin" [We Strongly Demand the Immediate Release of Beijing Citizens Who are Still Serving Prison Sentences 19 Years Following the June 4 Incident], June 2. Retrieved on June 3, 2013, from http://groups.google.com/group/weiquanwang_CHRD/tree/browse_frm/month/2008–06/40eeb7de0aa8dc78?rnum=1&_done=%2Fgroup%2Fweiquanwang_CHRD%2Fbrowse_frm%2Fmonth%2F2008–06%3F

Chong, Denise (2009). Egg On Mao: The Story of an Ordinary Man Who Defaced an Icon and Unmasked a Dictatorship. Berkeley: Counterpoint.

Clandinin, D. Jean and F. Michael Connelly (1994). "Personal Experience Method," in Norman K. Denzin and Yvonna S. Lincoln, eds., Handbook of Qualitative Research. Thousand Oaks, CA: Sage Publications, pp. 413–427.

Cole, Ardra L. and J. Gary Knowles (2001). Lives in Context: The Art of Life History Research. Walnut Creek, CA: AltaMira Press.

Conle, Carola (1993). "Learning Culture and Embracing Contraries: Narrative Inquiry Through Stories of Acculturation," unpublished doctoral thesis, University of Toronto.

Conle, Carola (1996). "Resonance in Preservice Teacher Inquiry." American Educational Research Journal 33(2), 297–325.

Curran, Sandra J. and Daniel Cook (1993). "Doing Research in Post-Tiananmen China," in Claire M. Renzetti and Raymond M. Lee, eds., Researching Sensitive Topics. Newbury Park, CA: Sage Publications, pp. 71–81.

Dai, Qing (2011). "The Twenty-second Anniversary of June 4." Radio Free Asia, June 2. Retrieved on June 13, 2014, from http://www.rfa.org/cantonese/commentaries/daiqing-06022011121308.html

Dawson, Richard E. and Kenneth Prewitt (1969). Political Socialization: An Analytic Study. Boston: Little, Brown and Company.

Deutsche Presse-Agentur News (2007). "Tiananmen Protest Leader Wang Dan Asks to Return to China," October 3. Retrieved on February 6, 2014, from http://www.digitaljournal.com/article/236410

Dewey, John (1958 [1938]). Experience and Education. New York: Macmillan.

Diamond, C.T. Patrick and Carol A. Mullen (1999). The Postmodern Educator: Arts-based Inquiries and Teacher Development. New York: Peter Lang.

Dikötter, Frank (2013). The Tragedy of Liberation: A History of the Chinese Revolution, 1945–57. London: Bloomsbury.

Ding Zilin (2005). Xunfang liusi shounanzhe [In Search of the Victims of June 4]. Hong Kong: Open Press.

DiRenzo, Gordon J. (1990). "Socialization for Citizenship in Modern Democratic Society," in Orit Ichilov, ed., Political Socialization, Citizenship Education, and Democracy. New York: Teachers College Press, pp. 25–46.

Etter-Lewis, Gwendolyn (1993). My Soul is My Own: Oral Narratives of African American Women in the Professions. New York: Routledge.

Fairbrother, Gregory P. (2004). "Patriotic Education in a Chinese Middle School," in W.O. Lee et al., eds., *Citizenship Education in Asia and the Pacific: Concepts and Issues*. Norwell, MA: Kluwer Academic, pp. 215–238.

Feng Qing (2002). "Yaxiya de guer" [The Orphan of Asia]. *Beijing zhichun* [Beijing Spring], No. 110 (June), 68–74.

Fisher, Max (2013). "This is the Song of Tiananmen; 'Blindfold My Eyes and Cover the Sky.'" *Washington Post*, June 4. Retrieved on February 6, 2014, from http://www.washingtonpost.com/blogs/worldviews/wp/2013/06/04/this-is-the-song-of-tiananmen-blindfold-my-eyes-and-cover-the-sky/

"Free Democracy Advocates, 74 from Senate Urge Beijing" (1992). *The New York Times*, October 11. Retrieved on August 4, 2008, from http://query.nytimes.com/gst/fullpage.html?res=9E0CE7D81730F932A25753C1A964958260

Friedman, Edward (2007). "Studying China Is Dangerous." Keynote Speech Delivered at the 49th Annual Conference of the American Association for Chinese Studies, University of Richmond, October 5–7.

Gargan, Edward A. (1998). "For a Dissident, Too Much Fame and Freedom." *The New York Times*, April 28. Retrieved on August 4, 2008, from http://query.nytimes.com/gst/fullpage.html?res=9C01EFDA1F3FF93BA15757C0A96E958260

Garside, Roger (1981). *Coming Alive: China After Mao*. New York: New American Library.

"The Gate of Heavenly Peace" (1995). Long Bow Group Film. Retrieved on January 3, 2014, from http://www.tsquare.tv/film/transcript_end.php

Ge, Xun (2012). "21 Hours in Bejing," *Seeing Red in China*, February 2012. February. Retrieved on June 3, 2013, from http://seeingredinchina.com/2012/02/08/ge-xun-21-hours-in-beijing/

Giesen, Bernhard (2004). *Triumph and Trauma*. London: Paradigm.

Glesne, Corrine and Alan Peshkin (1992). *Becoming Qualitative Researchers: An Introduction*. White Plains, NY: Longman.

Goldman, Merle (2005). *From Comrade to Citizen: The Struggle for Political Rights in China*. Cambridge, MA: Harvard University Press.

Gong Yue (2007). "Xiagan yidan xie chunqiu: Ji huanying 'huangque xingdong' muhou yingxiong chendaizheng zuotanhui" [Forum on the Unsung Heroes of "Operation Yellowbird"]. *Beijing zhichun* [Beijing Spring], No. 170 (July), 75–78

Goodson, Ivor F., ed. (1992). *Studying Teachers' Lives*. London: Routledge.

"Grace Wang: Caught in the Middle, Called a Traitor" (2008). *Digital Times*, April 20. Retrieved on January 6, 2014, from http://chinadigitaltimes.net/2008/04/grace-wang-caught-in-the-middle-called-a-traitor/.

Gu Cheng (1981). "Wo shi yige renxing de haizi" [I am a Willful Child], March. Retrieved on January 8, 2014, from http://site.douban.com/106701/widget/notes/91769/note/100561992/

Hampl, Patricia (1996). "Memory and Imagination," in James McConkey, ed., *The Anatomy of Memory: An Anthology*. Oxford: Oxford University Press, pp. 201–211.

Han, Minzhu, ed. (1990). *Cries for Democracy: Writings and Speeches from the 1989 Chinese Democracy Movement*. Princeton, NJ: Princeton University Press.

Hatch, J. Amos and Richard Wisniewski, eds. (1995). *Life History and Narrative*. London: Falmer Press.

Havel, Václav et al. (1985). *The Power of the Powerless: Citizens Against the State in Central-Eastern Europe*. Armonk, NY: M. E. Sharpe.

He, Rowena Xiaoqing (2012). "Still Seeking Justice for the Tiananmen Massacre." *Washington Post*, June 4. Retrieved on January 3, 2014, from http://www.washing tonpost.com/opinions/still-seeking-justice-for-the-tiananmen-massacre/2012/06/04 /gJQAd1weDV_story.html.

He, Yinan (2007). "Remembering and Forgetting the War: Elite Mythmaking, Mass Reaction and Sino-Japanese Relations, 1950–2006." *History and Memory* 19(2) (Fall/ Winter), 43–74.

Hewitt, Gavin (1991). "The Great Escape from China: How 'Operation Yellow Bird' Saved Scores of Dissidents from Beijing's Secret Police." *Washington Post*, June 2, D1. Retrieved on February 6, 2014, from http://www.highbeam.com/doc/1P2–1067967. html

"Hope Fades as Despair Draws Near: Essay by the Tiananmen Mothers on the 24th Anniversary of the June Fourth Tragedy" (2013). *Human Rights in China*, May 31. Retrieved on June 6, 2013, from http://www.hrichina.org/content/6709.

Hostetler, Karl D. (2005). "What Is 'Good' Education Research?" *Educational Researcher* 34(6), 16–21.

Hughes, Christopher R. (2006). *Chinese Nationalism in the Global Era*. London: Routledge.

"Hunger Strike Shakes the Nation (1989). *Beijing Review* 32(22) (May 29–June 4), cover story.

"Independent Federation of Chinese Students and Scholars." (2008) *Sourcewatch*, July 30. Retrieved on February 12, 2014, from http://www.sourcewatch.org/index .php?title=Independent_Federation_of_Chinese_Students_and_Scholars#First_Term _1989.8_.7E_1990.8

"The Internationale." Retrieved on February 7, 2014, from http://www.marxists.org /history/ussr/sounds/lyrics/international.htm.

"It Is Necessary to Take a Clear-cut Stand against Turmoil" (1989). *People's Daily*, April 26, front page.

Kundera, Milan (1978). *The Book of Laughter and Forgetting*. New York: Harper Perennial.

Lee, Sen (1999). "Ten Years after the Tiananmen Square Crackdown: An Interview with Shen Tong." *Global Beat Issue Brief*, No. 53 (June 1). Retrieved on August 4, 2008, from http://www.bu.edu/globalbeat/pubs/ib53.html

Li Lanju (1997). "Hafo guiyu: Zhongguo liuxuesheng ying Jiang naoju" [Chinese Students Welcoming Jiang at Harvard]. *Jiushi niandai* [The Nineties] (December). Retrieved on January 3, 2014, from http://www.angelfire.com/hi/hayashi/text2.html

Li, Lu (1990). *Moving the Mountain: My Life in China from the Cultural Revolution to Tiananmen Square*. London: Macmillan.

Li, Xiaojun (1989). *The Long March to the Fourth of June*, trans. E. J. Griffiths. London: Duckworth.

Lichterman, Paul (1996). *The Search for Political Community: American Activists Reinventing Commitment*. New York: Cambridge University Press.

Link, Perry (1992). *Evening Chats in Beijing: Probing China's Predicament*. New York: Norton.

Link, Perry (2009). "June Fourth: Memory and Ethics." *China Perspectives*, No. 2, 4–16.

"Listen to this Haunting Broadcast Made by Radio Beijing on June 4, 1989" (2013). *Shanghailist*, June 4. Retrieved on June 3, 2013, from http://shanghaiist

.com/2013/06/04/radio_beijing_english_language_broadcast_june_3_1989_tianan men_square_massacre.php.

Liu, Xiaobo (2012). "Listen Carefully to the Voices of the Tiananmen Mothers," in Perry Link, Tienchi Martin-Liao, and Liu Xia, eds., *No Enemies, No Hatred: Selected Essays and Poems.* Cambridge, MA: Harvard University Press, pp. 3–13.

Madsen, Richard (1995). *China and the American Dream: A Moral Inquiry.* Berkeley: University of California Press.

Maps of the Tiananmen Massacre (2009). Retrieved on June 3, 2013, from http://chrdnet .com/2012/06/june-3–4-2009–20th-anniversary-of-tiananmen-square-massacre -maps-victims-name-lists/ (in English); http://www.tiananmenmother.org/the%20 truth%20and%20victims/The%20list%20of%20the%20victims/the%20death %20location%20of%20the%20victims.jpg (in Chinese).

McAdam, Doug (1989). "The Biographical Consequences of Activism." *American Sociological Review* 54 (5), 744–760.

Meyer, Jeffrey F. (1990). "Moral Education in the People's Republic of China." *Moral Education Forum* 15 (2), 3–26.

Murphy, Richard McGill (2007). "A Tiananmen Rebel Turns Capitalist: After Fleeing to the U.S., an Entrepreneur Returns to do Business with his Former Oppressors." *Fortune Small Business*, April 17. Retrieved on August 4, 2008, from http://money. cnn.com/magazines/fsb/fsb_archive/2007/04/01/8403869/index.htm

Nathan, Andrew J. (2002). "The Dissenting Life." *The New Republic*, January 14, 37–41.

"People Comment on the Riot in Beijing" (1989). *Beijing Review* 32 (28) (July 10–16), 21–22.

Pinar, William F. (1981). "Whole, Bright, Deep with Understanding: Issues in Qualitative Research and Autobiographical Method." *Journal of Curriculum Studies* 13(3), 173–188.

Pinar, William (2004). *What is Curriculum Theory?* Mahwah, NJ: Lawrence Erlbaum.

Polumbaum, Judy (1991). "Review of the book *Almost a Revolution.*" *Journal of Asian Studies* 50 (2) (April), 400–401.

Ponce, Phil (1998). "Online Focus: Wang Dan." *PBS NewsHour*, April 27. Retrieved on February 6, 2014, from http://www.pbs.org/newshour/search-results/?q=ponce%20 wang%20dan%20news%20hour#gsc.tab=0&gsc.q=ponce%20wang%20dan%20 news%20hour&gsc.page=1

Price, Ronald (2002). "Moral-Political Education and Modernization," in Ruth Hayhoe, ed., *Education and Modernization: The Chinese Experience.* Oxford: Pergamon Press, pp. 211–237.

Rosen, Stanley (1993). "The Effect of Post-4 June Re-education Campaigns on Chinese Students." *The China Quarterly*, No. 134, 310–334.

"Rumors and the Truth" (1989). *Beijing Review* 32 (37) (September 11–17), 20–26.

Schell, Orville (1994). *Mandate of Heaven: The Legacy of Tiananmen Square and the Next Generation of China's Leaders.* New York: Simon & Schuster.

Schidlovsky, John (1989). "Waiting for Their Turn to Die: The Battle for Tiananmen Square." *Toronto Star*, June 5, A14.

Shen, Tong, with Marianne Yen (1998). *Almost a Revolution*, 2nd ed. Ann Arbor: University of Michigan Press.

State Education Commission (1993). *Xiaoxue deyu gangyao* [Primary Moral Education Guidelines]. Shanghai: Shanghai Education Press.

State Education Commission (1995). *Zhongxue deyu gangyao* [Secondary Education Moral Education Guidelines]. Shanghai: Shanghai Education Press.

"Statement by Shen Tong" (1992). *World Affairs* 154 (4), 136.

Sun, Yajie (1993). "Children of Tiananmen," unpublished masters' thesis. University of Toronto.

Tao Ya (2006). "Qianglie kangyi Zhongguo zhengfu boluo wo zuowei Zhongguo gongmin de rujing quan" [Protest Against the Chinese Government for Depriving my Rights to Return Home as a Chinese Citizen], October 19. Retrieved on January 3, 2014, from http://www.epochtimes.com/gb/6/10/19/n1491857.htm

Taylor, Charles (1989). *Sources of the Self: The Making of the Modern Identity*. Cambridge, MA: Harvard University Press.

"Testimonies of Families of June 4 Victims" (2010). Retrieved on January 3, 2014, from http://www.youtube.com/watch?v=XjaoFS2NnTo.

"Tiananmen Massacre a Myth" (2011). *China Daily*, July 14. Retrieved on June 3, 2013, from http://www.chinadaily.com.cn/opinion/2011–07/14/content_12898720.htm

Unger, Jonathan, ed. (1991). *The Pro-democracy Protests in China: Reports from the Provinces*. Armonk, NY: M. E. Sharpe.

Vickers, Edward (2009). "The Opportunity of China? Education, Patriotic Values and the Chinese State," in Marie Lall and Edward Vickers, eds., *Education as a Political Tool in Asia*. New York: Routledge, pp. 53–82.

Wang Dan (1997). *Yu zhong huiyilu* [Prison Memoirs]. Taibei: Xin xin wenhua shiye gufen youxian gongsi.

"Wang Dan Discusses China at DC's National Press Club on November 29, 2007" (2007). *China Support Network*, December 1. Retrieved on August 4, 2008, from http://chinademocracy.blogspot.com/2007/12/statement-from-wang-dan.html

Wang Dan (2012). *Wang Dan huiyilu: Cong liusi dao liuwang* [Wang Dan Memoir: From June 4 to Exile]. Taibei: Shibao wenhua chuban.

Wang Lingyun (1999). *Suiyue cangcang* [During Those Dark Years]. Hong Kong: Mingbao chubanshe youxian gongsi.

Wang, Zheng (2012). *Never Forget National Humiliation: Historical Memory in Chinese Politics and Foreign Relations*. New York: Columbia University Press.

Waterhouse, Monica (2008). "A Pedagogy of Mourning: Tarrying with/in Tragedy, Terror, and Tension." *Transnational Curriculum Inquiry* 5(2), 16–32.

Wu Renhua (2009). *Liusi shijianzhong de jieyan budui* [The Martial Law Troops During the June 4 Incident]. Alhambra, CA: Zhenxiang chubanshe.

Wu, Vivian (2012). "Demolition of Democracy Wall Criticised." *South China Morning Post*, November 3. Retrieved on February 3, 2014, from http://www.scmp.com/article/614196/demolition-democracy-wall-criticised

Ya Yi (2005). *Liuwangzhe fangtanlu* [Interviews with Exiles]. Hong Kong: Xiafeier chuban youxian gongsi.

Yang, Guobin (2005). "Emotional Events and the Transformation of Collective Action: The Chinese Student Movement," in Helena Flam and Debra King, eds., *Emotions and Social Movements*. London: Routledge, pp. 79–98.

Yardley, Jim (2006). "Man Freed After Years in Jail for Mao Insult." *The New York Times*, February 23. Retrieved on January 3, 2014, from http://query.nytimes.com/gst/full page.html?res=F10A16FA355A0C708EDDAB0894DE404482

Yi Danxuan (2001). "Quanmei zilian zhuxi zhi 'Zhongguo xuesheng baohu fa'an' shou huizhe de gongkai xin" [An Open Letter to the Beneficiaries of the "Chinese

Students Protection Act"], *Independent Federation of Overseas Chinese Students and Scholars*, June 2, 2001. Retrieved on January 9, 2014, from http://ifcss.org/home/?m=200106.

Yi, Danxuan and Tianhan Xue (2002). "Have We Forgotten the Victims of the Tiananmen Tragedy?" *The Lancet* 360 (9344) (November 9), 1518.

Zha, Jianying (2007). "Enemy of the State: The Complicated Life of an Idealist." *The New Yorker*, April 23. Retrieved on June 7, 2013, from http://www.newyorker.com /reporting/2007/04/23/070423fa_fact_zha

Zhao, Dingxin (2001). *The Power of Tiananmen: State–Society Relations and the 1989 Beijing Student Movement.* Chicago: University of Chicago Press.

Zhao, Suisheng (1998). "A State-led Nationalism: The Patriotic Education Campaign in Post-Tiananmen China." *Communist and Post-Communist Studies* 31(3), 287–302.

Zhong Bu, ed. (1989). *Xinshiqi zui ke'ai de ren: Beijing jieyan budui yingxiong lu* [The Most Beloved Men in the New Era: List of Heroes of the Beijing Martial Law Enforcement Troops]. Beijing: Guangming Daily Press.

Index